A Vine Transplanted

*Dubuque Franciscans in Latin America
1965-2015*

Pat Farrell, OSF

A Vine Transplanted

Dubuque Franciscans in Latin America

1965-2015

By Pat Farrell, OSF

"The Day will Come" Pablo Neruda poem. P. 38.
Neruda, Pablo. *Canto General*. Translated by Jack Schmitt. © 1991 by the Fundación Pablo Neruda and the Regents of the University of California. Published by the University of California Press. P. 148. Used with permission.

Scripture quotations, as noted, are from
The New Revised Standard Version Bible, copyright © 1989 the Division of Christian Education of the National Council of the Churches of Christ in the United States of America. Used by permission. All rights reserved.

The Holy Bible, New International Version®, NIV® Copyright © 1973, 1978, 1984, 2011 by Biblica, Inc.® Used by permission. All rights reserved worldwide.

Cover design by Kelli Buchenau

Every effort has been made to provide complete information about all copyright holders and to acknowledge sources properly. We regret any errors or oversights.

For information about this book or to learn more about the ministry of the Sisters of St. Francis of Dubuque, IA, check our website: www.osfdbq.org, call: 563-583-9786, E-mail: communications@osfdbq.org, or write: Mount St. Francis Center- 3390 Windsor Ave. -Dubuque, IA 52001-1311

ISBN: 10: 1974138321   EAN-13: 978-1974138326

Contents

Acknowledgements

It takes a whole community to capture and record its own story. I am grateful to many people who helped make possible the writing of this history of the Dubuque Franciscans in Latin America. The congregational Leadership Teams of both 2008-2014 and 2014-2020 have offered immense encouragement and provided the time, space and the means for me to go apart and write. I am also grateful to Jean Beringer, OSF, for her help with the archives of the Sisters of St. Francis of Dubuque, Iowa, and for the personnel of the archives of the Maryknoll Sisters in Ossing, New York. Pat Sievers was always ready to lend technical and moral support, with grace and efficiency. I am grateful to Mary Sawyer for the extensive time she spent interviewing Sisters Anna Marie Manternach, OSF, and Amelia Thole, OSF, recording those conversations, and for her consistent interest, support, and encouragement. I am also thankful for Margaret Wick, OSF, and her eagle eye, graciously lent for editing purposes. EXCEL in Okolona, Mississippi provided a lovely space in their volunteer house, and I am grateful to Liz Brown, CSJ, and Nancy Schreck, OSF, for their hospitality. I am particularly indebted to Nancy for keeping me on task and for her friendship which has sustained me.

As the text of this book moves toward publication, further acknowledgments are in order. Kate Katoski, OSF, has worked extensively to format the book and work on the index. Maureen Leach, OSF, and her team have been doggedly attentive to correcting details, creating a picture index, and finalizing the formatting. Truly, it "takes a village" to complete a project like this. Sister Maureen Leach's team included: John Roby on photos, Luis Navarro on layout and technical issues, Colleen Leach Theobald, indexing details, Sally Mitchell, OSF, and Carolyn Atkins proofreading, Jessica Russo and numerous sisters with locating and identifying photos along with Maxine Lavell, OSF, as archivist. Thank you one and all!

And most importantly, I am grateful to the women whose story is told in these pages and whose feedback helped me to tell it as accurately as I could.

Dubuque Franciscan Sisters who have Served in Latin America

Chile

Anna Marie Manternach (Mary Albert)
Amelia Thole (Ida)
Peg Moran (Shaun)
Elaine Gehling (Bibiana)
Rosa Lyons
Darleen Chmielewski
Jean Hurley
Carol Hawkins
Nancy Meyerhofer
Pat Farrell

Guatemala

Darleen Chmielewski
Maureen Leach

El Salvador

Kay Koppes
Pat Farrell
Carol Besch
Nancy Meyerhofer

Mexico

Carol Ann Berte

Honduras

Nancy Meyerhofer
Brenda Whetstone
Erika Calderon
Carol Hawkins
Pat Farrell
Mary Beth Goldsmith

Dubuque Franciscan Associates in Latin America

Guatemala

Olga Aurora Barrenos Acabal

Mario Adolfo Dominguez

Andy and Magdaly Estrada

Yesenia Estrada Figueroa (2016)

Lurvelina Rodas

Brigida Lozano Vargas

Julio Romualdo Sasche Vasquez

El Salvador

Sonia and Miguel Guerra

Jose Orlando and Cruz Maria   Menjivar

Honduras

Suyapa Diaz

María Irene (Nena) Diaz

John Donaghy

Betty Grissom

Doris Menjivar

Juana María (Juanita) Reyes

Introduction

For more than fifty years Dubuque Franciscans have lived and worked in Latin America. As a congregation we have been shaped and enriched by that experience, with a clear sense that we share in the lives and ministries of our sisters wherever they are. Those who have served in Latin America have been irreversibly transformed by the peoples with whom they shared life in Chile, Guatemala, El Salvador, Mexico and Honduras. Their story is our story. It needs to be told, to be heard, to be remembered. The following text is not intended to be an exhaustive narrative of their lives and ministries in those countries. Each person's individual experience merits an entire book. However, I present here a skeletal chronicle of some very rich community history, in the hope that others will add to it over time. As a participant myself in much of the story, I claim no objectivity and little perspective. What I offer is a mixture of memoir and recent historical narrative which incorporates the feedback of those whose stories are reflected in these pages.

The fifty-year time frame of this account (1965-2015) spans a period of massive and tumultuous change in Church, Society, and Religious Life. Moreover, most of the countries and contexts in which our sisters have served were filled with violence and chaos of one sort or another: dictatorship, war, coups, gang violence. Universally, these countries were and continue to be plagued by the structural violence of impoverishment and domination. The challenges have been manifold. The courage, commitment, faith and ingenuity of these women have been equally as varied and abundant. I dedicate these pages to them, particularly to Kay Koppes and Peg Moran who at the time of this writing have already gone before us into eternal life.

Pat Farrell, OSF

Gracias, Lempira, Honduras

January 2015

Transplant

By Julia Esquivel,
Guatemalan poet

Strong woman of Moab,
answer, I pray, my question:
What irresistible force
impelled you to uproot yourself
from your land and from your people
to transplant yourself
and bear fruit in the land of Naomi?

Only a profound excavation
into the depths of yourself
could wrench from your soul
the impossible decision:
"Wherever you go
I will go,
wherever you live, I will live;
your people will be my people,
and your God, my God,."

To wrest yourself
from your kinsfolk,
from familiar soil,
to put down the roots of your being
in another land and another God.

Essential transplant,
perhaps sensing without being able to explain,
that you were the mother of the shoot of Jesse.

Fertile uprootedness, from whose womb
sprang forth that trunk
where there is neither Jew nor Gentile,

atheist or believer,
man or woman,
Indian or mestizo…

Woman of uprootedness
who digs deep
and uproots decisively.

Transplanted vine
that becomes fertile
and bears fruit and sprouts
in Him who was
crushed by suffering
to become generous wine
and whose descendents are without number.
Woman of uprootedness
and of transplanting.

Our grandmother,
our bones,

Strong woman of Moab.[1]

Chile (25 years of congregational presence, 1965-1990)

The Seed

Pope John XXIII left an indelible mark on the world Church in convening the Second Vatican Council. A less publicized but nonetheless very significant impact was his request to the dioceses and religious congregations of the developed world to support the Latin American Church. Concern for Latin America had been in the air for some time and a number of influences preceded John XXIII's invitation. Key structural pieces were newly in place. CELAM (*Consejo Episcopal Latinoamericano*---Latin American Bishops' Conference) was officially established November 2, 1955. The U.S. Episcopal Committee for Latin America had set up the Latin American Bureau. The Vatican had been encouraging the establishment of national conferences of religious around the world. For women religious in the U.S., the same newly minted national organizations that facilitated the rapid and thorough response to Vatican II (The Conference of Major Superiors of Women, later called the Leadership Conference of Women Religious, LCWR, and the Sister Formation Conference) helped reinforce the mobilization of sisters for Latin America.

The Sisters of St. Francis of Dubuque first heard rumblings of the anticipated call when Mother Ruth Mary attended the Major Superiors Conference in Chicago in 1960. Then in 1961 Msgr. Agostino Casaroli, representing the Pontifical Commission for Latin America at the Second National Congress of Religious, communicated the Papal plan for Latin America:

> *Each of the communities represented here today can already see the part it could play therein, either to begin its apostolate in Latin America or to enlarge and intensify those works that several have already undertaken there….. Interpreting the mind of the Pontifical Commission, I offer you an ideal toward which we request every province to strive. This ideal is the following, namely that each religious province aim to contribute to Latin America in the next ten years a tithe – ten per cent of its present membership as of this current year. For example, if the present membership is 500, the ideal would be to contribute by the end of this decade fifty members to Latin America.*[2]

1

A Vine Transplanted – Chile

The Dubuque Franciscans, as well as the majority of U.S. congregations, took to heart Rome's call and began serious preparation. A congregational panel presentation entitled The Apostolate in Latin America, offered interesting background information to the sisters:

> Pope Pius XII on April 19, 1958, instituted the Pontifical Commission for Latin America for the purpose of studying the fundamental problems of Catholic life in Latin America which within its population of 190,000,000 embraces some 35% of the total Catholics throughout the globe. Five fundamental fields of assistance will constitute the major goals of this program and by present plans one of each of these five fields will go accentuated in each year's allocations. These five fields are the following:
>
> 1. The recruitment and training of ecclesiastical and lay personnel
>
> 2. The mass organization of religious instruction
>
> 3. The strengthening of the church's social action program
>
> 4. The strengthening of Catholic education
>
> 5. Increased Catholic achievement through mass communication (press, radio, cinema, television)

Chronicling the papal appeal to the North American Church, the panel reported:

> Pope John XXIII, in a special message sent to the memorable assembly of representatives from Latin American, Canadian, and U.S. hierarchies held in Washington, D.C., in November 1959, stated, "We wish to stress our solicitude, trusting ardently that mature resolutions will be made and appropriate measures agreed upon to assist the Latin American Episcopate"... Archbishop Samore, Secretary of the Pontifical Commission for Latin America has pointed out that the Catholics of the Americas are more than 225,000,000 and that together we form almost one half of the total membership of the Catholic Church. "Your potential is enormous," he has said, "so be conscious of your responsibilities, your ability to help one another. You are rich in personnel, and it is from you that personnel is sought, in the confidence that the Lord will reward you for the generosity with which you give, by sending you ever more numerous vocations." [3]

The panel presented to the sisters also gave important historical background about the Church in Latin America. Beginning with the Church in Spain, panel members outlined the history of colonization and described

A Vine Transplanted – Chile

the conditions of the Church and Latin America's current social situation of priest shortage, ignorance of the faith, abject social conditions, unjust agrarian conditions and distribution of wealth, and the need for instruction in Catholic social teaching. The panel concluded that conditions were ripe for revolution.

> *The key question is: Who will guide and direct the changes needed in Latin America? Christians or Marxists? ...At the summit meeting held in Moscow late in 1960 the Communist leaders decided to make Latin America the No. 1 target; accordingly they made a detailed blueprint for Operation Latin America.*

It would seem that the Church's motivation for marshaling broad support for Latin America was pastoral in nature but likely influenced as well, consciously or not, by the political backdrop of the anti-Communist sentiment of the 1950s. Some historians say outright that the purpose of the plan for supporting Latin America was to combat Marxism, Protestantism and secularism.

The panel further instructed the sisters that

> *Those who go must be prepared. Archbishop Helder Cámara, auxiliary of Rio de Janeiro and Secretary of the Brazilian Bishops' Conference, stressed that "It is not sufficient to learn the language. It is necessary to be in tune with the soul of the people to whom you are sent....Only then will you gain all for Our Lord. The approach of Cuernavaca (The Center of Intercultural Formation) is the way you have to choose."*

There appeared to be no question that the community would respond to John XXIII's call to Latin American service. Concrete action soon followed study and community education. In 1963 a letter was sent to all sisters announcing the congregation's intent to open a mission in Latin America and asking for volunteers. Eighty seven sisters offered to go! In November of that same year Mother Matilda and Sister Margaret Francis made a trip to Peru, Bolivia, and Chile to make contacts and assess possible mission sites. They had already received a letter of invitation from Chilean *Renato Poblete*, SJ, formalized through the Jesuit Provincial, *José Aldunate*, SJ. Mother Matilda's October 3 letter of response makes clear the intent of the invitation:

> *I have presented to my council your invitation to our community to staff the Preparatory Section of the Colegio Seminario in Chillán.*

A Vine Transplanted – Chile

All view with favor the prospect of relieving several Jesuit fathers of teaching, thus freeing them for social action work. Naturally, however, we need further information… Two of us will plan to visit Chillán before the end of the present school term. Tentatively, we hope also to visit several other missions in which we have special interest.

The late November trip of Mother Matilda and Sr. Margaret Francis took place just days after the assassination of John F. Kennedy and at every stop they were greeted with condolences and commemorative gestures of appreciation for the president. Sr. Margaret Francis' December letter recounts:

> *Everywhere we went we saw pictures of President Kennedy, his wife and his family. Apparently all of South America was in mourning… Chillán and Santiago declared the same period of mourning which would be extended to any hero of their own country. The schools we visited had pictures of the first family posted. At Sunday Mass in Chillán his name was announced publicly for prayers.*

In both *Chillán* and *Santiago*, U.S. women religious extended a warm welcome to Mother Matilda and Sister Margaret Francis, encouraged them to send sisters, and showed them a number of ministry settings. In *Chillán* visits were also made to Franciscan and Maryknoll men, as well as to the Jesuit *Colegio Seminario* where our sisters would eventually work. In *Santiago* the two sisters met with Chilean Jesuits *Renato Poblete* and provincial *José Aldunate*. Conversations with them proved to be pivotal. Mother Matilda and Sister Margaret Francis continued their travels to *Lima*, Peru and then to *La Paz* and *Cochabamba*, Bolivia. Sinsinawa Dominican sisters and Father Ray Herman from the Dubuque archdiocese met them at the airport in *Cochabamba* and served as their hosts and guides while in the country. The altitude in Bolivia was particularly difficult for Mother Matilda, of frail health. She and Sr. Margaret Francis returned three weeks earlier than anticipated. It was not long afterwards that Mother Matilda underwent heart surgery. The aborted travel plan is probably why no mention is made in congregational communications of contacts in Peru during the trip. However, the archives contain letters from the Papal Nuncio of Peru with concrete offers of a variety of ministry sites.

Following the exploratory trip much discernment took place to confirm a place of mission and to choose the first missioners. In 1964 Mother Matilda attended a meeting for major superiors with Ivan Illich in *Cuernavaca*, Mexico.

A Vine Transplanted – Chile

That gathering provided orientation for congregations considering sending sisters to Latin America and was an aid in clarifying criteria for choosing a mission site. Mother Matilda also spoke with a number of major superiors who already had sisters in Latin America. In her letter announcing to the congregation that the place chosen was *Chillán*, Chile, she mentioned criteria for the choice. She had been advised to consider the pastoral plan of the diocese and how the sisters might fit in as well as the possibility for sisters to work in an area in which they already had some proficiency. It would be helpful to identify with some ongoing work with native clergy which reflected a Church of the poor. Other considerations were tolerable climate and peer support from other American and English-speaking religious. A prevailing philosophy among Latin American Jesuits at that time was that educating middle and upper class young men likely to be the country's future leaders was a way to make a significant impact on the future of the country. The Jesuit boys' school in *Chillán* seemed a good fit. Appropriate communications were exchanged with the Provincial of the Chilean Jesuits and the bishop of *Chillán, Eladio Vicuña,* with enthusiastic responses of acceptance and welcome on the part of both. The Jesuits committed to the construction of a new house for the missioners adjoining a new elementary wing to be added to the *Colegio Seminario*.

Uprooting

Sisters Shaun, Ida, and Mary Albert in front of MSFC

A Vine Transplanted – Chile

The three sisters chosen to go, Sisters Mary Albert (age 41), Ida (age 34), and Shaun (age 28), were instructed to keep the news confidential until it was announced to the entire congregation. Each would need to conclude her ministry in Portland, North Buena Vista and Le Mars respectively and to tell her family. Amelia related her experience in a 2014 interview:

> *Sister Matilda wanted me to tell my mom and dad myself, so in May, Sr. Benett and I drove to Manchester. Mom had had a stroke and was not able to talk. She cried, squeezed my hand and smiled, letting me know she was happy for me. My dad, in his gentle loving way said, "Oh, where they have all the earthquakes," but then he added, "We have tornados in Iowa!" He seemed happy, if I really wanted to go, and I was of course happy and privileged to be chosen.*[4]

Sister Mary Shaun's mother responded to her news in a letter saying:

> *Congratulations and God bless you in your great assignment. I have had the feeling all along that you would be chosen and yet when the news comes it gives me somewhat of a jolt. As you say, we are human and the thoughts of a long separation leaves one with a heavy heart, but knowing it is what you want and will be happy in doing makes it less difficult.*

Mother Mary Matilda had written to Sister Mary Albert in February 1964, saying:

> *I asked Father Albert to come up yesterday afternoon so that I could tell him our plans for you…Although I did not give any reason for wishing to see him, he suspected what it was. In fact, he almost went to South America last summer but decided to delay "just in case" you might be sent. He will be with you all the way, in encouragement and prayerful support.*

The three were uncertain if or when they would return to the United States for a visit which made leaving family and friends particularly difficult. Their departure would, however, be in two stages. The first step of their Latin-American adventure was in *Cuernavaca*, Mexico, where they were to participate from August through December in CIF (*Centro Intercultural de Formación* — Intercultural Formation Center). They were to return to Dubuque in December until their formal departure to Chile in February of 1965.

CIF came into being in 1960 in response to the call of John XXIII that the Catholic world share personnel with Latin America. Associated with CIF

A Vine Transplanted – Chile

was also CIDAL (*Centro de Investigación para el Desarrollo de América Latina*-- Research Center for Latin-American Development) and CIDOC (*Centro Intercultural de Documentación*-----Intercultural Documentation Center). The CIF program to prepare missioners had two locations. Those being prepared for work in Spanish-speaking countries studied in *Cuernavaca*. Those preparing to work in Brazil studied intensive Portuguese in *Petrópolis*, Brazil. In addition to concentrated language study, both programs included cultural orientation and field work two weekends a month, during which students lived in local family homes, convents or rectories. During the mid-term break students were encouraged to visit other parts of the country and experience sites of cultural interest. As part of the program, a variety of evening workshops on themes related to changing realities in Latin America exposed students to an impressive international staff of presenters including Ivan Illich, the director; Archbishop *Sergio Mendes-Arcéo*, Mexico's most forward-looking bishop; Sister of Loretto Mary Luke Tobin, freshly back from Vatican II; Uruguayan liberation theologian *Juan Luis Segundo* together with other theologians from Latin America, the U.S., Belgium; and a host of religious who had been working in Latin American settings.

The program had a progressive spirit, reflecting the Vatican II atmosphere of openness and questioning, yet with a distinctively Latin-American tone. CELAM (Latin-American Bishops' Conference) had not yet taken a more conservative turn and gave input to the program with a view toward preparing missioners for a Church of the poor. Ivan Illich was the philosopher, theologian and ideologue whose ideas shaped the program. He was an Austrian priest incardinated in the Archdiocese of New York where he had worked with the Irish and Puerto Rican communities. Before going to *Cuernavaca* he had been the vice-rector of the Catholic University of Puerto Rico. The program he initiated would expose our first missioners to a large and renewed view of the Church of Latin America.

Sister Amelia Thole described her *Cuernavaca* experience in a 2014 interview:

> *There were 110 language students, sisters, priests, lay men and women, all preparing for Latin American service… Native college students were our teachers through all the day, and excellent speakers after supper. Lots of practice in the Spanish language. Drill, drill, drill every day! … We couldn't wear our habits in the language school except on Fridays when we had a special student Mass. That proved*

to be interesting as all the sisters wore their habits representing their congregations. [5]

Sisters Mary Albert, Ida, and Shaun in Cuernavaca, Mexico

Sister Mary Albert wrote from *Cuernavaca*:

> *Our daily sessions of Spanish are beginning to show fruit. Even I can manage to speak a few sentences. The first two weeks were my trial. I seriously questioned whether or not I would be able to do it but the army of people praying for me got me through.*

Sister Mary Shaun:

> *I could write a book on the events and emotions of my first week-end assignment in a nearby parish…We were on a second class bus… We hadn't gone too far from Cuernavaca when the inevitable second class cargo began coming on board! Under my feet sat the chickens, over my head the garden stuff… We did arrive safely in Fetelcingo…in a barren church where we knelt on the bare floor (no pews) and joined in the rosary… Barefoot boys and girls kneeling, sitting ,standing, crawling, talking, walking and looking at us… It is futile to attempt to describe the poverty of the people.*

In December the three returned to Dubuque with a much larger vision of Latin America, tongues more adept at Spanish, and a great deal to think about. Word had come from *Chillán* that the house being built for them was not yet ready. As a consequence, their departure was delayed, eventually

A Vine Transplanted – Chile

scheduled for February 8, 1965. It was a significant congregational event, with press releases and very formal invitations sent to family members of the missioners and chosen clergy of the archdiocese. Archbishop Byrne was the celebrant who presented mission crosses to the three sisters and Msgr. Daniel Tarrant the homilist. Sister Marie Therese composed a special song for the occasion: "How blessed are the feet of them that bring glad tidings of good things," which remains for the community an ongoing reminder of the call to mission we all share. For the congregation the missioning ceremony stirred great pride and provided enduring inspiration.

Franciscan
FOOTPRINTS

Sisters of St. Francis of Dubuque, Iowa -- Vol. XXIII, Nos. 2 and 3   **February/March 1990**

Dubuque Franciscans in Chile ————
25 AÑOS DE PRESENCIA Y SERVICIO

"How blessed are the feet of them that bring glad tidings of good things." With the strains of the departure song still echoing in their ears and hearts, three Dubuque Franciscans, Srs. Albert (Anna Marie) Manternach, Ida (Amelia) Thole, and Shaun (Peggy) Moran walked down the front steps of Mount St. Francis to a waiting car. Their destination: Chillan, Chile, South America. The date: February 8, 1965.

In a recent letter from S. Amelia in Arica, Chile, she writes, "These 25 years of giving service to God's people here in Chile, in Chillan, Portezuelo, Santiago, Bulnes, Arica, have been years of growing, suffering, rejoicing, sharing and loving. I would do it all over again without one bit of hesitation!"

During the course of these 25 years, ten Dubuque Franciscans have ministered and lived among the Chilean people. The original three were joined the following year by Srs. Elaine Gehling and Rosa Lyons. In subsequent years Srs. Darleen Chmielewski, Jean Hurley, Carol Hawkins, Nancy Meyerhofer and Pat R. Farrell lived and worked in various Chilean locales.

Ironically, the three pioneers have served that entire time in Chile, but two of them, Srs. Anna Marie and Amelia will return to the U.S. in March. After the past 12 years of pastoral ministry in Arica, S. Anna Marie believes they have "helped the people come to a realization of their own capabilities.

But one can't be 25 years in a country without roots. The uprooting will not be easy."

Peggy will continue in her ministry at Casa Sofia Women's Center in Santiago. She has been in the capital since 1969 and initially worked with the Maryknoll sisters in developing basic Christian communities. In 1980 she and Maryknoll S. Carolyn Lehmann began working with women in the *poblacións* on basic mental health issues and therapy sessions. They established their own Center in 1985 and the programming expanded. Sessions now cover a range of issues -- sexuality, health and child care, literacy, communication, music therapy, a theater group, women's rights, politics and current news events.

Peggy comments, "I want to continue in this work because it is such a viable, productive ministry. I remember in my earlier years of returning to the U.S., it was really hard coming back to Chile. Now I have a foot in both places. I still get upset by the glaring materialism whenever I return to the U.S."

Memories of the past 25 years are legion and many bear re-telling:

--The decision to begin the Latin American apostolate in 1965 at Chillan's Colegio Seminario was made after Mother Matilda Adams and S. Margaret Francis Brockamp returned

- cont. p. 2

A Vine Transplanted – Chile

For the missioners the actual leave-taking was gloomy, at best, and difficult for their families. They processed out of chapel directly to the big, black convent car where they were whisked away with Mother Matilda, Sister Maureen Wilwerding, and the driver, Mr. Birch, directly to O'Hare airport. They walked to the car in silence without being able to say goodbye to anyone. Years later they would still recall that it felt to them like a funeral, the big black car like a hearse. The scene at O'Hare was, however, a happier event. Many sisters from the Chicago missions created a festive and supportive environment, waiting to see them off at the airport.

By mid-afternoon the missioners were in the air and touched Chilean soil by noon the following day, greeted by Sr. Stephanie Marie, Regional Superior of Maryknoll, and Jesuit Edwin Hodgson from the *Colegio Seminario* in *Chillán*. They stayed for a week with the Maryknoll sisters in Buzeta, a section of Santiago near the international airport. The time with them was the beginning of a long-term camaraderie with Maryknoll sisters, who during that week showed them lots of ministry sites and toured them around *Santiago*. The three missioners saw their first movies in Chile, *The Sound of Music*, and a film with the Mexican comedian *Cantinflas*, before finally traveling the six hours south to *Chillán* by train a week later.

New Soil: The Chilean Context

Chile in 1965 and the years following was, indeed, a new land where the Dubuque Franciscans were to be transplanted. It could not be more different from Iowa! This string bean country, bordered by the Andes on the east and the Pacific Ocean on the west, is unique geographically. The northern extreme is the *Atacama* Desert, one of the most arid places in the world. The southern extreme is that portion of Antartica which belongs to Chile. The far north and far south of the country are both isolated and sparsely populated, while over half the country lives in the capital city of *Santiago*. One main road, the Pan American Highway, traverses the country north to south. Copper mines dot the northern desert. The central valley is verdant with Chile's own grape-growing wine country. The rural, picturesque south supports farming and fishing. A large number of *Mapuche* indigenous people are concentrated in the south and south-central area, and a smaller number of *Aymara* indigenous people live in the mountains of the north. As in all of Latin America, there are glaring disparities between the wealthy and the impoverished, in rural areas, between those who own land and those who do not. Everywhere, women and indigenous peoples struggle to find their way beyond historical marginalization.

Chile has enjoyed nearly 150 years of democracy, albeit interrupted by the *Pinochet* dictatorship. This is far more than most Latin American countries. Though education is woefully inadequate, especially in the rural areas of the country and urban *poblaciones*, Chileans have a relatively high level of education compared to other Latin American countries, with literacy levels that rival some countries in the global north. Chileans are also fairly politically educated, familiar with ideologies on the right and on the left. Political persuasions in the country traditionally have fallen into thirds, with fairly even distribution of thought at the right, left, and center. Those groupings generally, though not exclusively, correspond to economic levels, the wealthiest on the right, the poorest on the left.

When the sisters arrived in 1965 there was widespread popular support for the new president, elected in 1964, *Eduardo Frei*. He was a member of the Christian Democrat Party, a center-left group espousing ideals of social reform reflecting Catholic social teaching. He promoted educational reform, social programs, and neighborhood committees. Most notably, he continued previous efforts at agrarian reform with a bold program of expropriation of large land and water trusts which had concentrated those resources in the hands of a small minority of the wealthiest. Convinced that such an arrangement was retarding the economic, political and social development of the country, he launched a program to enforce better land distribution. He continued the work of the president before him to lay the necessary groundwork for nationalizing Chile's copper mines.

It was also a new moment for the Chilean Church in 1965. Vatican II was just concluding. In 1968 the Latin American bishops' meeting in *Medellín*, Colombia, produced a watershed document applying the council's teachings to the reality of poverty and oppression in Latin America. The document was nothing short of revolutionary, and Latin America was a powder keg of misery and economic disparity ripe for revolution.

The Catholic Church in Chile had a progressive and cohesive hierarchy, providing noteworthy leadership after the Council. Nonetheless, it was a daunting challenge to transition from a model of Church identified with those who were wealthy and powerful to a Church with a preferential option for those who were poor. This challenge continues. The traditional priest shortage gave added impetus to post-conciliar training of religious and lay leaders. Often parishes covered such enormous geographical areas and served such large numbers of people that they were subdivided into a series of small "chapels," each with its attendant group of people.

There was abundant enthusiasm for forming Base Christian Communities. The process proved tedious and difficult, but in-depth and long-term effort went into promoting this model of Church. Nationally, the bishops approved a process for preparation of children for First Communion that, in fact, supported the structure of Base Christian Communities. Weekly classes were given to parents over a period of two years who in turn prepared the children at home. Such a demanding process was able to be implemented only because all the bishops agreed to it, and there was no alternative. A hope was that after two years of faith formation together, enough of a community would have formed that the parents would want to continue meeting as a Base Christian Community.

Chile went through the same polarization and confusion in implementing Vatican II and *Medellín* as did other countries. On the one hand there was a growing commitment to social action and study of Catholic social teaching. Catholic Action groups such as the Young Christian Worker (JOC) and a similar student movement (JEC), flourished and were nurtured with particular expertise by European missioners. Christians for Socialism was born in Chile. The worker priest movement attracted a number of the clergy. On the other hand, there were those who wanted nothing to do with change. This was the Chilean Church our sisters found upon their arrival.

A Vine Transplanted – Chile

Sprouting: The Early Days in *Chillán*

Sr. Mary Albert Manternach with students

Sisters Ida, Albert, and Shaun were met at the train in *Chillán* by the rector of the *Colegio Seminario* and other representatives of the school. Since their new house was not yet ready they stayed for several weeks with Maryknoll sisters who taught in the parish school of *San Vicente*. Once classes began they walked back and forth to school until the house was ready for occupancy in April.

> *A weed is a plant that has mastered every survival skill except for learning how to grow in rows.* – Doug Larson

March 19, the first day of school, was memorable indeed! To these three teachers seasoned in the discipline of U.S. Catholic schools, it seemed that chaos reigned. They had not been shown the inside of a classroom, didn't know which room they would use, had no list of students or books for either students or teachers. Each room had an average of fifty boys, with two seated on each wooden bench. Annals say of the occasion:

> *First of all, the units of Spanish memorized in Cuernavaca just didn't seem to supply us adequately with the words and expressions needed or wanted. Secondly, benches seemed to be made to be out of, aisles to be milled in, and classrooms to be talked in. And by 11:00 when the boys were all out we were all in!* [6]

A Vine Transplanted – Chile

As the days wore on it became clear that the boys would have only notebooks and pencils. The expected style of teaching was for the teacher to write information on the black board and the students to copy. The grading system was also very different, as the sisters quickly learned after issuing report cards for the first time. They had given many red marks for conduct, thinking the students talked too much in class, and generally were not well behaved. However, in the Chilean school system that kind of mark was reserved for immoral behavior.

> *What an uproar when the parents came for report cards! We knew the parents were upset. They had us cornered in the classroom, talking fast and furious. We, with our limited Spanish, just listened, smiled until Father Hodgson made the rounds and all chattering stopped. He told them he would have a meeting with them the next evening. He had not explained the marking system to us beforehand. (Interview with Amelia)* [7]

The three missioners were quite discouraged and that night Sister Mary Shaun confessed that if she had a ticket she'd go home the next day. But she didn't, of course, and eventually realized that she could vent her classroom frustrations with a few unmentionable expressions in English and the boys would have no idea what she was saying!

Sr. Mary Ida Thole with children from Colegio Padre Hurtado

A Vine Transplanted – Chile

On April 10 the sisters moved into their new house with few of the essentials for making it a home. Milk and butter were kept on the windowsills until they could buy a refrigerator. The first Sunday they were there, Sister Mary Shaun celebrated by serving the other two breakfast in bed. *"It couldn't be done as desired, on a silver platter. In fact, due to the absence of a simple tray it was delivered in the drawers of the kitchen cupboard."* [8] Everyone was delighted that the new house had a fireplace since the cold and damp of southern Chile's winter season was soon to be upon them. It was very unusual for homes to have central heating. By the end of May, Sister Mary Ida had a serious cold that turned into pneumonia. The local hospital didn't seem a good option and the Maryknoll sisters took her into their home in a small room with an electric heater that was reserved for those recuperating. A doctor came daily for nearly two weeks to give her a shot of penicillin. The sisters later obtained an oil burning stove for their house in addition to the fireplace.

The first year in *Chillán* was filled with challenges, adventure, and a fair amount of loneliness, as the three adjusted to language, customs, the school system, their surroundings, and to one another. There were many funny mishaps with language. Frustrations abounded for the first three missioners, as well as those who came after them, in dealing with Chilean port authorities to get their trunks out of Customs.

The Jesuits contracted a woman, *Adriana*, to clean and cook for the sisters. Though not liking the idea at first, they appreciated her help, especially in their first years of adapting to so much. She was an excellent cleaner, priding herself on very shiny floors, and turned out to be a great help to the sisters with their Spanish. She and the missioners had much to learn from each other about customs related to food and cooking. She never did master pies, and the sisters finally decided that when they wanted their own special *gringo* dishes they would prepare them themselves.

Sister Mary Albert writes in October of 1965:

> *One night we were sitting at recreation when the doorbell rang and the empleada (hired homemaker) announced that it was for Sister Mary Ida. After a short time sister came to tell us that she had something for us and carried in a basket. We uncovered the basket and you'd never in a lifetime guess what it contained! There was half a little pig---the head on it and looking like it was sleeping. There was a*

sudden burst of surprise with a bit of squealing---and this didn't come from the basket! When we talked to the gentleman we told him we were glad it was dead. One of the boys was a pupil of Sister Mary Ida's and Sister Mary Shaun had taught a few of them English on Saturday. It was our supply of pork for the week.

In short, there was much to deal with both in and beyond the classroom. But with faith, humor, and the resilience of a missioner's first fervor the Franciscans came into their stride. By the time they began the 1966 school year, Sister Mary Shaun's letter expressed:

> *We have begun and completed three weeks of school. This time we approached the task with more self-assurance and it seems last year's admonitions and guidance yielded fruit. At least the majority found a desk and <u>sat</u> in it, listened to our still faltering but more secure Spanish, used the aisles for getting in and out and not for standing room, etc. But it seems that the bread munchers, the wrigglers and the marble droppers will always be with us.*

Later in the year the rector of the *Colegio Seminario* confirmed their progress in a report to Mother Mary Matilda:

> *They are doing really well. Sister Albert is very prudent and everybody loves her (people here say she is "un encanto", that is, charming). She is gradually taking care of everything that is her matter as the principal in elementary school. ... Sister Ida is so humble and saintly. She has gained our affection and respect, while at the same time you see her busy in apostolic works. She has improved a lot in Spanish. As teachers, the three of them are doing very well. Sister Shaun is a bestseller. All her pupils wish to be her friends. She is simultaneously kind and serious. I asked her this year to take some English classes in high school, which she willingly and effectively has done.*[9]

Sr. Mary Albert Manternach

A Vine Transplanted – Chile

A major factor contributing to the growth and adaptation of the sisters was the friendship and support of so many other religious and priests, mostly other missioners. They often stayed with and visited the Maryknoll, Mercy, Notre Dame, Holy Cross and John the Baptist sisters. Jesuit, Franciscan, and Maryknoll men had become friends. Fairly early in their time in Chile they had a variety of visitors from the U.S., including Archbishop Byrne, Fathers Joe Herard, Tom Manley, Al Manternach, Ken Gehling, Jack Paisley, Marty Pfab, and the Williams family from Webster City. The Dubuque Franciscan community faithfully supported them substantially through multiple communications. But the one who was a particularly significant encouragement for them was Mother Mary Matilda. She was their confidant and wise guide through many difficulties and they had great love for her.

Mother Matilda Adams' visit at Christmas

Mother Matilda came to spend Christmas with them toward the end of that first year in Chile, bringing presents and mail from home. The sisters were naturally very eager to have her experience as much of their new world as possible during that time. There were also lengthy conversations about the learnings of first year in Chile as well as projections for the future.

Mother Matilda encouraged Sister Mary Ida to take extended time for rest and recuperation, which she did at the Maryknoll vacation home in

A Vine Transplanted – Chile

Pucón. While Mother Matilda was there Sister Mary Albert got word that her brother, Peter, father of ten, died. It was an opportune moment for Mother Matilda's comforting presence.

Growth: New Arrivals

Mother Matilda returned home from her 1965 Christmas visit by way of *Cuernavaca* where she attended a workshop for major superiors sending sisters to Latin America given by Ivan Illich, "Alternatives in Missionary Policy for U.S. Religious Communities in Latin America." On her return to Iowa, plans continued for growth of the Chile mission. Another letter asking for volunteers for mission went out to all sisters. This time forty-four sisters responded, either as new or repeated volunteers. During the course of the year Sisters Rosa (age 28) and Sister Bibiana (age 26) were chosen. Plans were made for a send-off ceremony on August 21, 1966. From there they would attend the fall program in *Cuernavaca* and then go directly to Chile, arriving in time for Christmas in *Chillán*.

Srs. Bibiana Gehling and Rosa Lyons

Sister Rosa's diary says of the departure: *"Tears were shed outside and in. We felt the tremendous force of love that supports us as we begin our new work. Sadness and happiness have a way of blending on a day like this, and the resulting feeling is indescribable."* In Chicago, about seventy sisters missioned in the area came to see them off. Wide-eyed at that fully-habited group, the airline attendant at the gate asked if they would all be getting on the plane! Sisters Bibiana and Rosa's time in *Cuernavaca* was similar to that of the first three missioners and their letters from Mexico were filled with gratitude for the opportunity to learn and experience so much. They spent their mid-term vacation in *Acapulco* where, unfortunately, they were robbed. One of Sister Rosa's early letters to the congregation describes their experience:

> *Sister Mary Bibiana and I live in a small casa about ten minutes' walk from the center. We share our facilities with a Belgian sister, five Belgian padres, two Canadian padres, one cat and one dog, and oh yes, about two hundred mosquitoes per square foot.... Our meetings with Msgr. Illich have led us to believe that our future work in Latin America entails essentially the task of contemplating the face of Christ in what is today the reality of that very promising nation. It is constantly brought home to us that our life is one of involvement – we must get very close to the people. They have a saying here... "the dead die peacefully when at a distance."*

Both Sisters Bibiana and Rosa talked about the richness of visiting professors (one being Bernard Haring), contacts with other missioners, and cultural orientation as well as language learning.

They arrived in *Chillán* just two days before Christmas, almost feeling compelled to put a bow around their heads and sit under the Christmas tree. It was a very happy Christmas for the five Franciscans. Sister Rosa's first letter from Chile says:

> *We went to bed in peace that first night in our new adopted homeland, thinking that we could sleep until noon. However, at 7 am the next morning we were awakened with a blast from the record player in the hallway. I jumped out at the sound of the familiar <u>Mexican</u> music and the rest of the community descended upon my bed. There we sat for I don't know how long---with breakfast in bed, we told the sisters of our travels, troubles, trivials, and the news from Iowa that we knew. We've been talking ever since.*

The talking only intensified when, on December 27, Sr. Anna Marie's brother Fr. Al Manternach and Sr. Bibiana's cousin, Fr. Ken Gehling, arrived for a visit.

A Vine Transplanted – Chile

Srs. Rosa and Elaine at cathedral in Chillán

The fun-loving spirit in this community, now expanded to five, is evident in S. Bibiana's letter of January 1967, to Mother Matilda: *"Chillán is truly a great summer city but the sisters keep dropping little hints about the winter. We are taking everything they say with a grain of salt as we occasionally fall for some of their stories and this only adds to their enjoyment!"*

Sr. Rosa says of her early impressions of *Chillán*: *"Chillán seems to be a city of contrasts...the old and the new. It is much more "Americanized" than is Mexico. And yet, it is very common to see a car going down the road with a team of oxen and a cart close by. Yes, there REALLY are oxcarts here, and they are drawn by real live oxen!"*

Since classes in Chile did not begin until mid-March, there was ample time for the two new missioners to explore *Chillán,* including the impoverished *población* where they would begin visiting homes every Saturday. Already

A Vine Transplanted – Chile

Sisters Albert, Ida and Shaun had been involved with a host of pastoral activities in addition to their work in the school. All volunteered in the hospital, where Sister Ida had taken special interest. It was common for nurses to go on strike for higher wages. The sisters filled in, spending time especially with young children with burns all over their bodies as a result of falling in the open, unprotected cooking fires in their homes. Sisters Shaun and Albert did a lot of work with catechesis in *Chillán* parishes during the school year, and through rural missions during summer vacation. All three visited the jail as well as homes in poor neighborhoods. Eventually Sister Ida spent considerable amounts of time helping with classes in a poorer school in *Chillán* run by Franciscan men, and at the nearby rural parish in *Portezuelo* working with Maryknoll Dick Sammon. In early 1966, newly arrived Sisters Rosa and Bibiana became familiar with these apostolates before beginning their work in the school. From the beginning of their time they spent Saturday mornings visiting homes in a *Chillán población*. Sr. Rosa quickly got involved in playing the guitar in parishes in both *Bulnes* and *Portezuelo*, noting that the collection basket passed at the liturgy typically included things like an egg, a nickel, a peso, a few string beans.

Srs. Rosa Lyons and Elaine Gehling visiting the neighborhoods

A Vine Transplanted – Chile

For Srs. Rosa and Bibiana the first year of teaching in Chile was as much of a challenge as it had been for their three predecessors. Sr. Rosa recalls:

> *In March of 1967, we greeted at least 45 little students, restless, normal full-of-life boys. When taking roll call on the first day I called Sr. Anna Marie to my room telling her I was in the wrong room. She knowingly smiled, read off the names, and everyone answered "presente". As class began I asked the boys to put their hands on their desks and immediately they all put their heads under their desks! So much for four months of intensive language studies in Mexico!* [10]

Srs. Rosa Lyons, Peg Moran, and Elaine Gehling with a group of boys

Summers were also filled with courses and workshops, mostly in *Santiago*. In the late '60s and '70s the country was abuzz with post-Vatican II and *Medellín* enthusiasm for updated theology, new methods for catechetic and pastoral activity, and with renewed vision of both Church and religious life. Our sisters took advantage of many educational and renewal opportunities. Workshops in *Santiago* exposed them to priests and religious from all over the country, to their work and lifestyle. The cross pollination of experience was fertile ground for forming friendships and expanding visions. The questioning, searching and creative restlessness typical of those transitional post-Vatican II years was the air everyone breathed. Our own missioners were assessing their lives and ministries, and in that environment coming to new understandings of religious life as well.

A Vine Transplanted – Chile

The sisters' experience in the progressive Chilean Church environment was both similar to and different from the renewal process the rest of the community was living in the U.S. The physical distance from the congregation made the U.S. process feel very removed from them. They were probably influenced by their time in *Cuernavaca*, the contact with theologians and an array of other mission congregations, and the less structured life in Chile. These experiences aligned them with those sisters in the U.S. for whom the changes in religious life could not come soon enough and who were taking liberties and experimenting on their own. There are a number of archived letters from their early days in *Chillán* exchanged with Mother Matilda asking for permission to shorten their veils, to live without an appointed superior, to pray Lauds and Vespers privately, etc. Already in 1965 there were letters advocating for laying aside the habit. They had not worn it in *Cuernavaca*, with Mexico's anticlerical laws, and already the Maryknoll sisters were in suits. A December 1965 letter from Sister M. Shaun to Mother Matilda explains:

> We got a letter from Mexico today and Sister Bibiana said, "Since we received your letter we are very busy cutting our habits apart and remaking them into suits, skirts and what have you." … Mother, I had only told them I asked for your permission. …I hope it's only a joke, but anyhow I wrote a letter back saying that if what she said was true, they would have to explain to you. And I added that we are wearing our habits until you give us permission to change.

In March of 1967, Sr. M. Albert again writes to Mother Matilda on the issue of habits:

> We had a group discussion on habit changes. …Positive reasons such as the repeated instances related by the Maryknoll Sisters or Humility Sisters of experiencing a deepening of confidence and an easier dialogue which they feel is responsible for a more personal involvement in the life of our people. … If you feel it is better to continue wearing our habits may we please eliminate our veils? In your letter you told us to keep our experimenting in the realm of speculation. We want to be obedient, Mother, but we come to ask for permission to experiment in the realm of reality. We would like to use the material we have from habits in a two-piece suit very similar to the one we use in Mexico.

In April of 1967, shortly after the beginning of the school year, the sisters received word that they could return to their baptismal names and did so eagerly. From here on in this text the sisters' baptismal names will be used:

A Vine Transplanted – Chile

Sr. Mary Albert: Sr. Anna Marie Manternach

Sr. Ida: Sr. Amelia Thole

Sr. Shaun: Sr. Peg Moran

Sr. Rosa: Sr. Rose Lyons

Sr. Bibiana: Sr. Elaine Gehling

The Sisters with Padre Roger LaPointu

The questioning and controversies so integral to the 1967 milieu are reflected in a highly publicized article by Ivan Illich that appeared in the January 21, 1967 edition of *America* magazine entitled, "The Seamy Side of Charity" (See end of chapter). It is worth reading in its entirety because of the impact it had. The sending of missioners to Latin America slowed, though probably for additional reasons beyond Illich's writings. In the article Illich questions the initial missioning motivation, saying *"A pointed finger and call for 20,000 convinced many that 'Latin America needs you.' Nobody dared state clearly why, though the first published propaganda included several references to the 'Red danger' in four pages of text."* Illich criticizes the potential for foreign missioners to create increased economic and cultural dependency and implant a new form of colonial imperialism, stating that *"The U.S. missioner of necessity is an 'undercover agent' – albeit unconscious – for U.S. social and political consensus."* He also questions whether a hardy injection of foreign church personnel into Latin America might have the negative effect of shoring up an old system and aborting the Vatican II/*Medellín* transformation process underway. He says: *"Exporting church employees to Latin America masks a*

A Vine Transplanted – Chile

universal and unconscious fear of a new Church." The article caused a maelstrom of criticism. Ivan Illich fell into disfavor with the Vatican, among others. The program in *Cuernavaca* closed in the early 1970s.

Sisters Rosa Lyons and Elaine Gehling, still very close to the *Cuernavaca* experience, commented on the article in letters dated March 7, 1967:

> *Illich brought out the desperate need for serving the poor in his controversial article in America, didn't you think? He sent us a beautiful letter concerning this article and said it was written with the hope of presenting a true picture of misguided aid and unused people power. He said he felt those of us who were in Cuernavaca would understand him when he felt saddened that the message had more of a sour than a sweet impact. I feel that in many ways he is right, but it is quite a bit to swallow. "The whole course of our dedication should be to direct our forces in conscience to the wholehearted work we are going into", writes Illich in a very fatherly way to us who've just completed the course. He stresses humility first, generosity and faithfulness to our vocation. (Sr. Rosa)*

> *Yesterday we received a letter and a copy of "The Seamy Side of Charity" from Msgr. Illich. He has given the world many thoughts to think about and I am certain that much good will come out of it. In his letter he said that he had hoped that it would be taken in a little more constructive light. He does have a point on the great foreign structures that have been built by other countries and that when we leave it will be impossible for the native clergy and people to retain it. One can really see evidence of this in Chile, even though I have been here a short time. We really have an obligation to help the people help themselves. (Sr. Elaine)*

The remaining months of 1967 unfolded with intense pastoral work and continued adaptation of all the missioners. In July Sr. Amelia Thole's mother died. Though it was difficult, she did not return to the U.S. for the funeral. She did, however, receive a great deal of support from the other sisters and from those with whom she worked. Sister Matilda and Sister Georgia attended the wake service in Manchester, Iowa and led the rosary.

In November of 1967, Sister Matilda again visited the sisters in *Chillán*. There was much to discuss with them. In a prior letter, she had sent questions for them to consider.

A Vine Transplanted – Chile

What do you see as the next work we should move into?

Will all of you need further study next summer or have you some apostolic work in mind?

What are your candid opinions about the preparations to be given to the next Sisters to join you? You perhaps know better than I about the changes that have taken place at Cuernavaca. Is this where you think our Sisters should continue to go? Or to Ponce? Or to a language school within the country itself?

They spoke of the work in the school, a possible mission in a rural area, other ways of working more closely with those who were poor, health, home visits, community, personal adaptation, emotional and spiritual support. The community did want to continue to send more sisters to Chile. Who should come? What age, abilities, and temperament? There was growing support for sending sisters to the Maryknoll language school in *Cochabamba*, Bolivia. What did they think about that? And on and on.

It seems that by the 1968 school year some personal questioning and restlessness deepened. Sr. Peg Moran no longer wanted to teach English at the school in *Chillán* and at the suggestion of Jesuit *Renato Poblete* was approved by the community to enroll in the ICLA program (pastoral study and orientation) in *Santiago* for 1969. However, the program was filled and registrations closed, so she was accepted in a program at the Catholic University. Both Sisters Rosa and Elaine were questioning their ongoing presence in the *Colegio Seminario*, attracted to work in the *poblaciones* or in a rural area. On Easter Sunday, Sr. Elaine had an emergency appendectomy and later in the year surgery in *Santiago* for gallstones. Sisters Amelia and Anna Marie had their first home visit in the States. En route to the U.S., Anna Marie stopped in *Bogotá*, Colombia to visit Sr. Jean Hurley who was studying in an international linguistic university on a Fulbright Scholarship, hoping that Jean would join the sisters in Chile. The following year, 1969, was one of even more transitioning. Sr. Peg Moran had begun her year-long course work at the Catholic University in *Santiago*, living at the Maryknoll sisters' center house. Work in the *Colegio Seminario* continued to be intense and lively, with ongoing unrest among some of the sisters about teaching primarily English classes and desiring more direct pastoral work.

A Vine Transplanted – Chile

Sr. Mary Ida Thole with young women

Though their teaching schedules were full time, each of the sisters was involved in other ministries. Sr. Anna Marie did follow-up work with *Cursillo* groups and worked with the Legion of Mary in *Purén..* Sr. Amelia did catechetical work in the Cathedral Parish and spent a lot of time visiting the homes of impoverished children in *Población Santa Elvira*. Sr. Elaine was involved in preparing future catechists in *Población Santa Elvira*. She was also part of a social action group dedicated to meeting the material and spiritual needs of youth in the *Chillán* jail. She began the school year after having had a very significant summer mission experience near Santiago which intensified her desire to do full-time pastoral work in poor areas. Sr. Rosa spent weekends in the rural area surrounding the town of *Bulnes*, near *Chillán*. She worked with the Catholic Action groups of JOC (*Juventud Obrera Católica*—Young Catholic Workers) and JEC (*Juventud Estudiantil Católica*---Young Catholic Students). During the week in *Chillán* she was the advisor for ANECAP, a national association of domestic workers.

A Vine Transplanted – Chile

Sisters visiting the Maryknoll Center

A very important part of the year was Sr. Margaret Francis' six-month visit with the sisters in *Chillán* and *Santiago*. Her extended visit was very timely, both in updating the sisters on recent Chapter proceedings as well as in helping them to navigate the waters of a lot of personal and community transition. Her hope was to experience the life lived by the sisters in Chile in order to better understand them and their world, to learn more of the Church in Chile in order to help the community discern its future ministry there, and to come to a clearer understanding of the qualities needed in those sisters choosing to work in Latin America.

Shortly after Sr. Margaret Francis arrived, Sr. Rosa discovered a lump on her breast and was in need of imminent surgery. After much consideration, it was decided that she would teach until late July and then travel to Dubuque to have the surgery at Xavier Hospital. Departing on August 9, she did not return to Chile after recovering from her surgery and eventually decided to withdraw from the congregation.

On August 3 Sr. Jean Hurley, (age 35) who had been studying in Colombia, arrived in *Santiago* to do pastoral work in one of the economically deprived areas of the city with Sr. Peg Moran. Jean joined Peg in living at

A Vine Transplanted – Chile

the Maryknoll center house and taking classes at the Catholic University in preparation for doing pastoral work in *Santiago*. During that time they were also exploring where and with whom they would work the following year. They elected to work in *San Alberto*'s, a huge parish in a very poor neighborhood, quite spread out, with several smaller chapels as subdivisions and a population of 123,000. They would be joining a team of Maryknoll priests and sisters, Providence sisters, permanent deacons and a large group of lay catechists. The Maryknoll priests, especially Fr. Dick Smith, provided a great deal of support to the team's work, both financially as well as in the effort to establish Base Christian Communities. Sr. Jean was enthusiastic about the new venture and in 2014 wrote of her memories: *"We were fortunate to be in Chile and working with the Chilean Church, as Chile was more progressive than many other Latin American countries and the Church was very advanced, with progressive Bishops interested in reaching out to the many poor areas in Chile."*

In September Sr. Darleen Chmielewski (age 27) arrived to work in the *Colegio Seminario* in *Chillán*, after a simple send-off from Mount St. Francis. She describes her arrival in a first letter to Sr. Matilda: *"I spotted a band-strip of brown on the airport deck before the plane even landed – which I surmised was the whole gang!"* That gang was delighted to welcome her and took her to the Maryknoll center house for lunch where already they began to talk about plans. During the remainder of September, she would get acquainted with a bit of *Santiago* and a lot of *Chillán*. She would begin to observe classes in the school and take over some classes as she felt ready to do so. The hope was that she would take over Sr. Elaine's classes by November, so that Elaine could visit her brother in El Paso before he left for Vietnam. Having been a high school Spanish teacher, Darleen had a head start with language skills, though spoken Spanish was still a challenge, especially given the difficult Chilean accent.

Darleen had hopes of living with a Chilean family or community initially to absorb more of the language and culture. Ultimately it turned out to be more practical to live with the community at the *Colegio* in *Chillán*, which she did. By January she would go to the Maryknoll language school in *Cochabamba*, Bolivia, during the school's summer vacation. In an October letter Darleen writes of an attempt to overthrow President *Frei* by a military general. *"Even though it has been more or less resolved, it may pave the way for others to occur."* She had no way of predicting then how right she was.

A Vine Transplanted – Chile

Srs. Jean, Peg, Anna Marie, and Darleen with Frs. Brosius and Al

Amid all the comings and goings in the eventful year of 1969, several U.S. priests came, also visiting the Dubuque archdiocesan mission in *Cochabamba*: Fathers Leon Connolly, Ray Herman, John Smith, Al Manternach, Bob Vogl, and Fr. Brosius. In November Elaine left for a home visit. On December 21 Margaret Francis completed her six-month time with the sisters and returned to the States (See end of chapter: her letter summarizing what she learned during her extended visit). Her visit had been mutually supportive, though the sisters teased her about trying to "fatten them up" with the homemade bread she loved to bake for them. The Chilean people had made their way into her heart, and with her love for education, she dreamed of returning to help further develop the work in the school. She left the airport misty-eyed, declaring that she would be back. The day after Margaret Francis left, Amelia received word of her father's death and returned to the U.S. for the funeral. By the following January, Darleen went to language school in *Cochabamba*, Bolivia, accompanied by Sr. Anna Marie who took advantage of the time to improve her own language skills.

When Elaine, Darleen, Amelia and Anna Marie returned, early 1970 found four Franciscans in *Chillán* and two in *Santiago*. Jean Hurley and Peg Moran were now settled in the enormous parish of *San Alberto*, part of a large team charged with forming Base Christian Communities as the basic structure of local Church. They shared a home with two Maryknoll sisters on the team, a simple but adequate fenced-in house heated by a kerosene stove in the living room during the colder months of the year. The neighborhood was very poor and very densely populated, with no paved streets, limited water access, and with many houses made of cardboard. Jean Hurley Redmond, writing in 2014, recalls:

> Many Chileans and others who lived in middle class neighborhoods of Santiago (and really weren't even familiar with life in a poor neighborhood) would often ask us if we weren't afraid walking around in the parish we lived in, especially at night. Of course, we weren't, since all knew us and would come to our aid if there ever was a problem. The only fear we had was of the dogs, allowed to roam about freely and at times not friendly.

Two things that left a lasting impression on Jean were the damp cold of the winters and the strong earthquakes, most notably the one that occurred in 1970. She remembers awakening to see furniture floating around as if made of cardboard, and her first impulse of trying to crawl under the bed. Many people in their neighborhood lost homes, and some were even electrocuted from live wires brought down in the quake.

The work of Peg and Jean followed the pastoral priorities of the Archdiocese of *Santiago*: evangelization, formation of Christian communities, and insertion of the Church in the world. Each of them was in charge of a sector of the parish that covered about forty blocks. After visiting each home to invite and organize people for the two-year adult small-group formation program, groups were established. They then spent almost every night of the week and a good portion of the day-time accompanying groups. It was a lot of work, but the sisters were very motivated with this model of Church: going to the people, gathering them into communities, and putting leadership and responsibility in their hands.

Meanwhile, in *Chillán*, the sisters negotiated a teaching schedule that began at 8 am and ended at 1:30 pm, allowing time in the afternoon and evenings for other apostolic endeavors. Conversation and discernment about future work was a common topic. Sisters Darleen and Elaine accompanied Amelia to *Portezuelo* each week to teach English to grades 1-12. *Portezuelo* was a more rural parish and it was too far for some students to walk to their homes in remote hills. Therefore the parish had a dorm for boarders. Amelia usually went to *Portezuelo* from Wednesday afternoon to Saturday morning.

A Vine Transplanted – Chile

She would stay in the dorm, accompanied by 100 boarders, where teachers and students ate together before going to their bunk beds.

Behind the scenes of such an outpouring of pastoral energy, the political climate was moving into high gear. In fact, our sisters witnessed a period of profound political transition which affected all strata of society, including the Church and their own individual apostolates. In July the *Chillán* school had mid-term vacation earlier because of student riots in *Santiago*. In November of 1970, *Salvador Allende*, a socialist, was elected president of Chile, and ushered in a new and challenging era.

Amelia writes of the occasion in a November 8 letter:

> *Tuesday, our great President Frei handed over his responsibilities to our new Chilean President Allende. Truly it was a most impressive ceremony. Both television and radio carried in detail this historical event in Chilean history… Everyone believes he is sincere and are showing much confidence already. He said he would respect everyone's beliefs no matter to which religion they belong or if they belong to none. We must continue to pray that he will be enlightened from above. On Wednesday the new Minister of Education declared a free day in honor of the new Socialist Party.*

The innovative government structured participation of the populace, particularly of those of few economic resources, to participate in the construction of their own future. Many projects and programs were initiated. Eventually government-sponsored health care was accessible to all and public university education was available with no tuition to qualified students. Foreign-owned companies were nationalized in order to keep profits within the country. In particular, the nationalization of U.S.-owned copper mining industries caused panic in international economic circles and at CIA headquarters. Though groundwork for such nationalization was already in progress from two presidents before him, *Allende* finalized the process and suffered the resulting public fallout. Reactions to the new government were mixed, and grew more and more polarized. All of this began in late 1970 with *Allende*'s election and crescendoed during the following three years of his presidency.

On the one hand, 1971 in the *Colegio Seminario* seemed to continue in the mode of "business as usual," though no one could ignore the changing political climate. Parents of the students fell on both sides of the growing controversy. It is understandable, given the reality reflected in Margaret Francis' letter to the community in March of 1970, after her six-month visit in 1969.

> *Beginning in March 1970, 35 percent of the students in the Colegio-Seminario will come from poor families; the remaining 65 percent of the students from the homes of wealthy families and a rising middle class. It is worthy of note that these 65 percent have opted the payment of a higher tuition so that the 35 percent may attend the Colegio free of tuition. This, I feel, is to be commended. …The Jesuit Father feels this was possible because of their work and the work of the Sisters with the parents, helping them to become responsible Christians. I wish to add that the Sisters are contributing one scholarship for a poor child through their assumption of their own house work, cleaning, washing, cooking.*

In the U.S., the press was following closely the historical situation in Chile where a socialist president had been democratically elected rather than coming to power through military force. Sister Matilda wrote to the sisters in Chile in a letter dated August 7, 1971:

> *Our paper continues to carry articles about what is happening – or believed to be happening, or could happen – in Chile. Our Catholic papers carried an article on the stand the Chilean Bishops took recently – how they pointed out that the real evil to be feared is not capitalism or Marxism as such, but the materialism that infects both of them. I must say that the articles carried by Catholic news service, though cautious in their optimism, are more hopeful than those of the secular press. Concern for American capital invested in Chile rather than for the free exercise of religion is the thrust of many of the news items in the daily press.*

In *Chillán*, Darleen and Elaine both decided that at the end of the 1971 school year they would conclude their work in the *Colegio Seminario* and move into full-time pastoral work in an impoverished location. Such decisions were the fruit of personal discernment, community processes and much conversation. In an effort to do long-range planning for the Dubuque community in Chile, the four sisters wrote Sister Matilda and the congregation as a whole. June 4, 1971, they wrote:

> *As we gathered for a house meeting this week, we came to the conclusion of the need to write to you now. Both Sister Amelia and Sister Anna Marie see the need and want to stay in the Colegio so there*

arose the possibility of having to live only as a two-Sister house. The political situation of Chile right now is such that we cannot be positively certain of the school being able to function under Jesuit direction next year. However, we cannot wait until December to write and ask if it would be possible to send another Sister with the destination being the Colegio for the new school year beginning in March.

The letter went on to detail the qualities the sisters thought essential in someone coming to work at the *Colegio Seminario* in *Chillán*. No additional sisters came, however, and in 1972 Anna Marie and Amelia were joined by Sister Louisa, an Ursuline from Maple Mount, Kentucky.

Also in 1972, as anticipated, Elaine and Darleen discontinued their work in the *Colegio Seminario*, the name of which was changed during 1972 to *Colegio Padre Alberto Hurtado*. *Padre Hurtado* was a revered Chilean Jesuit who tirelessly served the poor and has since been canonized. They began visiting parishes in *Chillán* to explore pastoral need and work possibilities. When visiting the parish of *La Merced*, the pastor immediately said that he would love to have sisters working in the chapel area of *San Ramón* in the two *poblaciones Mardones* and *Río Viejo*. The parish was subdivided into chapels, each surrounded by a geographic area and a corresponding population to be served. The area was about two miles beyond *Chillán*, a 45-minute bus ride from the *Colegio*. He could offer no housing and very, very minimal financial support, but the area was poor and the work compelling, and the choice was obvious to the two sisters. The pastor took them to a meeting with the people from that area who were very welcoming. Before the meeting was over two unmarried twin sisters had invited them to come immediately to live in their house. They would make an infrequently-used dining room available to them as a bedroom. They accepted, and in short order moved into a single room where they lived with two small beds, a table, and a place to hang clothes. The house had running water, but only an outhouse since there was no sewage hook-up yet in that part of the city.

Elaine and Darleen found the arrangement a fortuitous beginning. Word quickly got around the neighborhood that they were living happily in a home like everyone else's, eating the kind of food others in the *población* typically ate. The sisters spent four months visiting homes and getting to know the people and their reality. Their pastoral work was first and foremost one of presence with a simple lifestyle, both at this beginning stage and throughout their ministry. The twin sisters suggested that they take someone from the

A Vine Transplanted – Chile

neighborhood with them on visits to introduce them to the people, which they did. One of their two companions was Eloisa who became a long-term friend and who, at one point, expressed interest in entering the congregation, though at the time the community was not opting to receive vocations in Chile.

After four months living in the dining room of the twin sisters, an eighty-five year old woman in the *población, Mercedes Vásquez,* offered the parish a small vacant lot adjoining her home where a house could be built for the sisters.

Señora Mercedes Vasquez

The parish did build a very small, simple house. The sisters asked that the kitchen be very small in order to have a larger space for the living room so that they could have meetings there. Initially they had no bathroom, just a hole outdoors with a toilet over it. Parishioners put boards up around it later. When a sewer system was put into the *población* they built an outdoor bathroom with a shower. Over time they were able to build on two other little rooms, one with a sawdust stove. Someone from Darleen's youth group went to the lumberyard every week and brought them a sack of sawdust to burn. They did some cooking on that stove, but were invited to peoples' homes to eat so frequently that they didn't do much cooking at home. They never had a refrigerator but eventually had a two-burner stove with a bottle of gas.

A Vine Transplanted – Chile

In a letter dated April 11, 1972, Darleen and Elaine describe their situation:

> *Although the construction of the three-room house is progressing slowly due to strikes and scarcity of materials and finances, it is really a proof of Christ performing miracles today through communal efforts. Saturday, April 15, we will have the blessing of the house, not yet resurrected, and a fund-raising talent show and lunch to pay for the cost of the roof... The community is basically composed of rural people that now have occupations ranging from driving taxis to peddling herbs in the open market. The lack of modern living and conveniences and the darkness of dirt-floored huts are overshadowed by the beautiful simplicity of the people, the panoramic scene of golden fields backed by white-capped mountains, and the remnants of a romantic past such as ox-carts, horses and sheep herds.*

The backyard of the house in Mardones

Gradually the two sisters developed youth groups, organized family catechesis, formed Base Christian Communities, and worked with the sick and the elderly. Elaine and Darleen were very happy in their lives and work in the población. Darleen described her experience in a 2014 interview as:

> *...a complete conversion! I was a public school Catholic and the Chileans made the Gospel come alive for me. Everything in Chile centered around the Church. People would come for the activities of the Mes de María (the month of Mary) without even inviting them. So many things came alive for me! We would gather to study the Bible in their homes and that became the beginning of natural Base Christian Communities. Before I went to Chile I had studied a bit about Vatican II but it didn't have much of an impact on me. In Chile, Vatican II and*

A Vine Transplanted – Chile

Medellín came alive! In their group reflections, people in Chile had such wonderful applications. It was wonderful to be able to share in their lives and living conditions. Their faith was alive and real.

Meanwhile, in *Santiago*, Jean Hurley and Peg Moran initiated the 1971 pastoral year with continued work in *San Alberto's*. Sometime during that year an invitation was extended to them from a Precious Blood priest to work in a large and even poorer area with no sisters, *Pudahuél*. Peg Moran initiated work there with two Maryknoll sisters while Jean Hurley returned to the States for a visit. While in the U.S. Jean came to the decision to leave the congregation. Peg then continued to live and work with the Maryknoll sisters she had been living and working with as part of the team in *Pudahuél*, assuming responsibility for 5,000 families in that *población*. The work there was almost exclusively in the formation of Base Christian Communities.

1973 Coup D'état and Its Effects

The Day Will Come, from *Canto General*, by Pablo Neruda, Chilean poet

> *Don't renounce the day bestowed on you*
> *by those who died struggling. Every spike*
> *is born of a grain seeded in the earth,*
> *and like the wheat, the innumerable people*
> *join roots, accumulate spikes,*
> *and in the tempest unleashed*
> *they rise up to the light of the universe.* [11]

As 1973 began, international opposition was exerting a great deal of pressure on the socialist government of Chile. With the hindsight of history we know that the CIA was involved in helping to destabilize the country from within, to bring down *Allende's* government, and to encourage a coup. This has been well documented, including in papers released by the CIA itself. Ten million dollars in U.S. money was poured into that effort. However, at the moment the destabilization was taking place, the experience on the ground was very confusing, frustrating and unclear. The final straw that broke public support for the socialist government and paralyzed the country was a prolonged truckers' strike. In a country as long as Chile, with one north-south highway, stopping the transportation of food and other supplies was an effective strategy.

A Vine Transplanted – Chile

Peg Moran's letter, Aug. 20:

> *The truckers have been on strike for almost a month and other groups are joining in sympathy. This has caused a scarcity greater than the normal lack of necessities and prices are way out of proportion. Potatoes jumped 100% in a week's time. Saturday I talked to a woman whose husband still hadn't come home after being in a bread line for* seven *hours. That is becoming the normal scene on weekends when they can get bread for two days (provided big families put several people in line). During the week it takes hours to get in line and then wait for the batches to be produced. People have been coming asking us for just enough sugar to take with coffee for breakfast. We got that item two weeks ago – four pounds. It is desperate for some of these large families and I would be the first to admit it affects us as well, in a different way of course. Transportation into the city and out of the city if not impossible is accomplished only after long waits. We stood one and one half hours in line to get a bus to class Friday and got there as it ended and then ended up walking over an hour to get home, partway home that is, and then got a lift in a car. These are the things that work on one and are such a waste of time for these people. …During this time there have been threats from outside groups, supposedly armed, who were to be coming in to this población to occupy houses that aren't finished being built (there are many) and/or plots of unoccupied land. Men were keeping guard at night and when they wanted to warn of imminent danger they rang the school bell to get the neighbors out to help. That went on for over a week and then a meeting with a delegate of the government cleared up the matter.*

In a 2014 interview Darleen mentions that her accompaniment of the people in the *población* in *Chillán* included joining them in their protests. *"Their welcoming of us meant that they expected us to be with them. I remember walking with the women beating on pots and pans. Once, in the center of Chillán the protest got violent and I had to find a way to escape."*

Amelia, in a 2014 interview:

> *Before the coup there were so many strikes, protests, and lack of merchandise in the stores. Only plastic and paper goods could be found in the grocery stores. Many people, knowing something would happen, had stored up food supplies in their pantries. (These were the more well-to-do people.) We, along with the majority of people in Chillán, stood in long lines to obtain a can of instant coffee, sugar, meat, or other so-called necessary items, along with soaps and toilet paper. Vegetables and fruits came to the open market, so although not as plentiful, they*

were able to be had. We stood in line for hours for the above items and kerosene for our little heater to keep us warm in a curtained-off small area near our bedrooms. …

In confrontation in the streets outside our school and home, the two sides would clash…. One afternoon quite close to September 11, one of my pupils got up, said "I need to go" when there was a protest outside. His dad was a taxi driver. He was out of the room, out of the school building in seconds. Tear gas bombs were thrown into the school patio over the outer walls of the Colegio Padre Hurtado. We led our pupils, over a thousand, into the patio, where the principal, teachers and all pupils gathered. …After some time all the students were taken out through our home's front door, two or three at a time. Luckily all got home safely that day. School was called off for two days to insure safety of all the pupils and teachers.

Some of our pupils were taxi cab drivers' children. The dads had been off work for several weeks, but the families were getting paid in American dollars. One day one of the pupils flashed a $20 bill. I said, "Where did you get that? I don't even have one." He said proudly, "My dad is paid in dollars." That proved that the U.S. government was in on getting rid of President Salvador Allende as legal president of Chile. …

One night, shortly before the coup, I looked out of my bedroom window. A protest was going on in the street. Young men were scaling a wall to get into the government building across the street. Once they got into the building's office, they took papers and strewed them all into the streets below. I thought, this is it! I took my dresser drawers with passport, identification papers and other things important to me, crawled on my hands and knees out into the corridor where Anna Marie had just come out of her bedroom. She was frightened to see me do this, as usually I kept quite calm, but this was too close for comfort. We were safe, though, all night.

That night I listened to my little radio. As I told Anna Marie, there was something happening in Santiago. All of a sudden the radio stations were all off the air. The next morning at 7 o'clock the whole country was under one radio station broadcasting what was happening. The military under General Augusto Pinochet had taken over the presidential palace in Santiago and each governor from the north to the south of Chile had been arrested and taken from their offices. Some were killed outright. We heard lots of gun shots from morning through the night of September 11, 1973. We were not allowed to leave our homes until September 14 in the afternoon, for one hour! During that hour I walked to Srs. Darleen and Elaine's little home in the población where they ministered and lived. Their precious neighbor was fine, no problem and not afraid. Elaine and Darleen were both in the U.S.A. for their home visits. I came back from their home, bought some freshly baked bread on the way. The stores seemed to have food supplies again, showing that it had all been hoarded and hidden to break the government of Allende!

Immediately after the September 11 coup, the dictatorship declared a *"toque de queda"* or "curfew" which meant that everything was closed down and no one could leave his or her home. Anyone doing so was shot on sight. During that time, many were taken prisoner, tortured, killed or disappeared. The national soccer stadium was used as a holding place for leftists or those suspected of being leftists. Prisoners held there were routinely tortured. Many disappeared from there or did not survive the experience. When the state of siege was lifted some days later, an ongoing curfew was put in place every night for several months. In effect, that meant that anyone who was not in their home after the designated hour could be arrested or shot on sight. At the very least, noncompliant persons were made to face a wall, hands up, feet apart, and searched by the police.

When the coup took place, Darleen and Elaine were in New York on their way back to Chile. The Chilean borders were closed and they were not able to return. In the meantime, they remained in New York with Mercy sisters. Having no idea how long it would be before they could get back into the country, the Mercy sisters helped them find work to do in the interim. Elaine did cleaning and housekeeping work in a nursing home. Darleen helped as a tutor in a pre-school. As it turned out, just ten days after the coup they were able to get a flight to Chile. Upon arriving they stayed with Mercy sisters in *Santiago*. It was disconcerting to hear so much shooting during the night. When they returned to their *población* in *Chillán* they found their youth groups shattered. Some of the youth had been tortured, killed, others disappeared. One had hung himself in jail. The evening curfew was in place and the sisters could hear lots of shooting at night. A neighbor was in jail. The nearby river where children often swam had a sign posted not to swim there after one of the children found a human hip bone in the water.

In *Santiago*, Peg Moran and the Maryknoll Sister Carolyn Lehmann, with whom she lived, were horrified. Carolyn's diary written on September 11, as the coup was taking place (Maryknoll archives):

A Vine Transplanted – Chile

> *On a very poor transmission of the government station, the president came on to talk to the people. He was very calm, and explained that only yesterday the generals had pledged their allegiance to him, and today they have turned traitors. He said he would pay with his life rather than resign from the presidency. He said those would probably be his last words to the country – because the radio was being cut off. Shortly after, all the radios were ordered closed down. The only one giving news is the official station of the armed forces. After the president talked, I just cried. We have arrived at a very sad day in Chile. It may prove to be worse than the sufferings we have seen so far.*

Peg Moran's September 29 letter describes the continuing saga:

> *I thought the preceding days had been tough ones, but they couldn't compare with those that have followed the 11th until now. The tension has been more than any of us has been through....Two Maryknollers, one a seminarian and one a brother, and a Holy Cross priest were held from 7 to 11 days... in the stadium where all the captives are sent and today they are leaving the country – by order of the new regime. ...A man up the street went to work on the 17th and his wife doesn't know yet where he is. Yesterday, after almost two weeks of standing in line at the stadium to find out if he were on the list, she went to the morgue to see if he might be there! She is of course a wreck.*

She later learned that he had faced a firing squad on the 17th of September. His crime? Supporting the party of President *Allende*. Peg continues in an October 20 letter:

> *I am wondering where the physical, emotional and psychic stamina will keep coming from. This week... prices went up 300 to 400%... Our people are sick and desperate. They can't afford the needed bread now, to say nothing of clothing....They have been assured there will be no more lines. True. The majority of the people won't be able to afford what they need.*

The work Peg Moran was doing in *Pudahuél* underwent a major shift at the time of the coup. In a 1984 personal history account she writes:

> *Groups flourished until 1973 and the military coup in Chile. The subsequent oppression, night curfews, prohibitions of meetings, arbitrary arrests and threats instilled fear in our people and curtailed our work. Our work and presence took on new forms of solidarity with specific concrete responses to situations of hunger, unemployment and other results of the cruel dictatorship. The number of communities diminished with these commitments of the communities as people*

feared possible consequences of their involvement being interpreted as political. The Gospel message lived out in these circumstances became revolutionary and dangerous. The option for the poor challenged us to walk in their shoes.

In *Portezuelo* where Amelia frequently worked with Maryknoll Fr. Dick Sammon, soldiers had been coming to the school to assess the effects of the pastor's rumored support of *Allende*'s government and outspoken defense of local groups. Fr. Sammon asked Amelia to remain in the principal's office during a few school days in place of the pastor and administrator. He feared for himself and the principal. Armed military did come to the office looking for them while Amelia was there and she diverted them.

Such repression and intimidation were continuous, marking the entire time of dictatorship. The sisters' work was altered substantially by the climate of fear in the country. In the *Colegio*, military personnel sometimes asked the children what the sisters were saying and teaching. They had to measure their words. A neighbor and friend of Amelia and Anna Marie's, the mother of an army captain who worked at the *Chillán* jail, told them one day that because of their weekly visits to prisoners they were under suspicion. *"They think you're Communists because you visit all these people,"* she told them. Anyone who worked with the poor was considered subversive. Though in different settings in the *Colegio,* and in *poblaciones* in *Chillán* and *Santiago*, all of the sisters lived under very stressful circumstances and were affected by the intense suffering all around them. It was impossible for them to communicate the experience to sisters, family and friends in the States. Nonetheless, life in Chile went on. The sisters adapted and did what they could to meet the challenges of an environment of fear and repression under the dictatorship. Asked in a 2014 interview if one ever gets used to living in such circumstances, Anna Marie replied: *"You never get used to it but you build yourself up to it. This is what you've got to do. You've got to walk with the people. You are here. Again, it's grace."*

Post-Coup Growth of the Community

In July of 1974 Elaine received word that her mother was dying of cancer. She left as soon as she could, hoping to be home before her mother died. Given the limitations of communication at such a distance, she didn't know how close to death her mother actually was. Her mother lived, in fact, for nine more months. During that time Elaine took a job with Catholic

A Vine Transplanted – Chile

Charities in Waterloo, Iowa, and spent weekends with her mother. When full-time care was needed, Elaine went to be with her. After her mother's death, Elaine continued working in Waterloo and did not return to Chile.

Darleen stayed alone after Elaine left, continuing as she was able with the pastoral projects they had begun together. In a 1984 personal history account she writes:

> *The experience of living and working alone so closely with the Chilean people was very enriching as I became more intimately inserted in their lives and reality. At the same time, it was a very painful experience to bury youth and accompany mothers searching for their husbands, sons and relatives after the military coup, to watch families sell their meager belongings to fight off unjust political and economic systems as well as experiencing the frustrating impotency with a pastoral work that was not adequately responding to the needs of the people.*

After about a year of being alone, she felt a need for more contact with the other sisters so she offered to teach a class in the *Colegio*. She providentially found her way to a course in *Lima*, Peru on the Better World Movement's plan to make the parish a community of smaller communities. It was another conversion experience for Darleen and an opportunity for her to understand so many things in a new way. The Better World vision was one she found inspiring, convincing, applicable to a variety of pastoral realities. It was the right thing at the right time for her and shed new light on the work she was doing in the *población* in *Chillán*.

The sisters in Chile were encouraged by the 1976 arrival of Sister Carol Hawkins (age 32). The summer prior to her arrival she had attended a month-long Maryknoll orientation experience for new missioners in New York where she met sisters who had been in Chile at one time. Her leave-taking from Dubuque followed the pattern of the other missioners. There was a send-off Mass and departure ceremony at the motherhouse, and a gathering of Chicago sisters at O'Hare to see her off. After an en-route visit with her mother in Miami, she arrived in *Santiago* March 10, met by all the Franciscans in the country. Typically, as well, she toured a bit of *Santiago* before going to spend a week in *Chillán*. She returned to *Santiago* for another week of exploration before flying from there to *Cochabamba*, Bolivia where she would study Spanish from April through September.

A Vine Transplanted – Chile

Sisters at waterfall at Salto del Laja

When Carol returned from *Cochabamba* she lived with the community at the *Colegio* in *Chillán* for a time and eventually joined Darleen in the *población*. There she began to visit homes and acquaint herself with the people and their reality. In 1977 Carol and Darleen discerned that together they would initiate pastoral work in *Bulnes*, a country parish of 20,000 inhabitants 25 kilometers from *Chillán*. Ever since the sisters began in the *Colegio* in *Chillán*, it had been a desire of the bishop that they have a second house in *Bulnes*, to be a pastoral presence there. The town itself had about 10,000 inhabitants of whom 99% were farmers working in the surrounding area forming about 30 dispersed Christian communities. Letters about their new ministry reflected the sisters' desire to support Chile's rural poor whose situation had been altered under the dictatorship. Years of concerted effort at agrarian reform were set back an estimated 30-40 years under the *Pinochet* regime. After movements of farming cooperatives and expropriations of large tracks of land concentrated in the hands of a few wealthy landowners, 50% of those lands had been returned to large land owners or to the military. Many farmers in the area were impoverished anew. Within this context Darleen and Carol were beginning their work in the villages surrounding *Bulnes*, traveling by foot, by horse, horse cart, and if really lucky by truck. They were enjoying the simplicity of the people and their receptivity to the Gospel, and had begun implementing the Better World Movement's plan for parish development.

A Vine Transplanted – Chile

However, in 1977 other winds were blowing in *Chillán*. The Jesuits in Chile were discerning their future commitments in light of their 32nd General Congregation and the shifting pastoral urgencies in Chile. They decided to leave the *Colegio* in *Chillán* and turn it over to the diocese in January of 1978. Knowing that their decision would impact the Dubuque Franciscans who had served with them for 13 years, they were quick to communicate with both the sisters in *Chillán* as well as the congregational leaders in Dubuque. The Jesuits offered the sisters, as a gift, the house they had built for them, attached to the new primary wing of the *Colegio*. The Jesuit provincial knew from conversations with the sisters that they considered the Jesuits' leaving the *Colegio* as an opportune moment for them to do so as well and to discern where they might begin more direct pastoral work. He therefore invited them to work with Jesuits in other places. His primary encouragement was *Arica*, a territory that had been entrusted to the Jesuits by the Holy See. The Chilean bishops had recently encouraged religious congregations nationally to consider the work of evangelization in the sparsely populated and poorly served northern desert.

The bishop of *Chillán* was quite unhappy to know that the sisters were considering leaving the *Colegio* and possibly the diocese as well. He proposed to them that they all work in *Bulnes*. He saw it as a place of great need, Carol and Darleen were already working there, and the parish had recently purchased a house where they could live.

Discernment, once again! Anna Marie was leaving for a home visit and planned to stop in *Arica* as part of her travels back to *Chillán*. Amelia, Carol and Darleen made an exploratory visit to *Arica* after the school year ended at the *Colegio*. When Anna Marie returned, Sister Margaret Clare came with her. Together they visited *Arica* and then traveled to *Chillán* to join the others in trying to pray and discern their way into a decision. Carol and Darleen were just getting started in *Bulnes*, were motivated in their work there, and were not eager to uproot and begin again in *Arica*. Yet the need in *Arica* was great. Amelia (2014 interview): *"It was a difficult, prayerful time. Very taxing and decisive, with much prayer, dialog and giving and taking with each other."* In the discernment process Margaret Clare asked for the Spirit's guidance and opened the Scriptures, as St. Francis had done, to a page that read: "I will lead them into the desert." *Arica*, in the *Atacama* Desert of northern Chile, was chosen.

A Vine Transplanted – Chile

Arica, Chile landscape

The sisters informed the Bishop of *Chillán* that they were leaving and formally gave their house at the *Colegio* to the diocese. After communications with the bishop of *Arica, Ramón Salas*, SJ, it was agreed that the sisters would work in *Población Once de Septiembre* and that the diocese would provide and maintain a house for them in that neighborhood. The congregation was to cover living expenses. Darleen was feeling personally called to work with the Better World Movement and wanted more in-depth preparation work. She committed to one year in *Arica* to help the others launch their ministry after which she would pursue work with the Better World Movement. Back in Iowa, Margaret Francis had been following very closely the unfolding of the lives and ministries of the sisters in Chile, always hoping to return more permanently. Around this time she decided not to go. She had recently had heart surgery and her background in education and school administration would be less critically helpful now that the sisters were leaving the *Colegio* and moving to *Arica*.

At the beginning of 1978, Carol went to the new missioner orientation in *Santiago* while the others in *Chillán* finished their remaining commitments. Farewells were bittersweet for everyone. Thirteen years of ministry in *Chillán* were filled with many relationships and happy memories for Amelia and Anna Marie and there was much leave-taking to do. Darleen and Carol were in the ambivalent situation of ending what they had so recently begun,

A Vine Transplanted – Chile

with a different set of ending tasks. By March they were ready to go and Anna Marie, Darleen and Carol arrived in *Arica*. Amelia was delayed until mid-April due to a surgery in *Chillán*. After just two weeks in *Arica* she left for a home visit, timed so that she could attend to other health concerns, and remained at Mount St. Francis for 15 months, returning in August of 1979.

Transplanted in Arica

The house in Población 11 de Septiembre

The first three had arrived via a very long bus ride and were met at the depot by two Jesuits, the bishop *Ramón Salas* and the superior of the Jesuits in *Arica*, *Pepe Corréa*. Anna Marie writes:*"After lunch…they took us to our HOME. To our delight it was a very simple house made from the wooden boxes that had served in importing cars, and a tin roof. The first night we felt like the three little pigs – the wolf could have easily blown the house down, and not too many puffs."*

People gathered in the Arica desert (blessing of site for chapel)

A Vine Transplanted – Chile

The *Arica* annals say of their beginnings:

> The first night the three sisters slept at the convent of the Lourdes sisters in Holy Family parish. The following night the three anxious women wanted to sleep in their own convent. Luckily they had sent their beds and mattresses and their personal belongings up earlier by truck. They managed to find sheets and a blanket and so slept healthfully in their own home. There was no stove on which to heat water, so by God's loving providence they managed to uncover an electric skillet which was their means of preparing their meals for two days until they found bottled gas for the stove.

On April 25 the small community of about 30 people which had begun to grow in *Población Once de Septiembre* gathered with the sisters and two Jesuits to bless the house.

Those first months in *Arica* were ones of comings and goings, with Darleen leaving for a home visit, Carol spending some time in Spain, and Anna Marie receiving a number of visitors during her months alone. When the group was reassembled, there was a great deal of exploring to do in order to assess how to focus their work. *Arica* was very different from *Chillán*. Situated on Chile's northern border with Peru, the port city of *Arica* is in the heart of the *Atacama* Desert, which is made up of about a 600-mile extension of some of the most arid land in the world. *Arica* has not had measurable rainfall for over 100 years and water in the city is permanently rationed, with each neighborhood having access for one hour each day. The region is very sparsely populated, the next city (*Iquique*) being a five-hour drive south. However, to the east of *Arica* all the way to the Bolivian border, nestled in high altitudes of the Andes, the Chilean *altiplano*, are a number of villages of native *Aymara* people.

The north of Chile was traditionally the country's mining territory, consequently characterized by the strong leftist leanings remaining from years of the labor struggles of miners. In fact, the political parties of the left in Chile, including the Communist party, were born in the miners' process of organizing for their rights. The large copper mines were many hours south of *Arica*. Closer were the ghost towns where silver nitrate mines used to be before becoming unprofitable after silver nitrate was able to be produced synthetically.

A Vine Transplanted – Chile

In a November 1978 letter the sisters described their new situation:

> *We live in a población called Once de Septiembre (September 11, the date of the coup) inhabited by approximately 10,500 persons. It is a relatively young settlement of people in two aspects:*
>
> 1. *It came into existence in the late '60s, composed mainly of leftists and therefore was called Venceremos or We Shall Overcome. After the change of government in 1973, it was renamed Once de Septiembre. It is a good example of what has happened in Arica during this time. People from all over Chile came looking for jobs in the numerous factories favored by the free port that has recently been discontinued, and consequently many factories have closed down. They settled or squatted on the land – first living in whatever type of shelter they could manage – tents, cardboard houses or simply in open air.*
>
> 2. *Seventy-five percent of the inhabitants are 50 or younger with a high concentration of children and young adults. In a study we did of this población, we found that there is an interesting mixture of origins and cultures. Since most of them come from other parts, they find themselves uprooted and unstable; because life in the north is difficult, they find it impossible to adhere to the traditions of their origins. The primary problem is that many are without work since the large factories have closed or have cut production. Being in a strange land and having lived through abrupt political changes, the people mistrust one another and prefer not to know their neighbors.*

After the military dictatorship came to power there was a change in economic policies, inviting greater foreign investment and welcoming imports without customs fees. National industries that had sprung up rapidly when *Arica* was a free port could not handle the competition and were forced to close or downsize. Empty factory buildings were converted into military quarters and unemployment in *Arica* became the highest in the country.

The sisters' description of the pastoral reality of *Arica*:

> *Another characteristic is the high percentage of non-Catholics since the north has long been poorly attended (pastorally) and since there is a tendency in a military government to promote non-Catholic sects in order to weaken the efforts of the Catholic Church in social commitments that promote liberation of the whole person. Also evident is the high concentration of military in Arica, due to the continuing dispute of the boundaries between Peru, Bolivia and Chile. The presence*

of 30,000 military (in the area) adds to problems of prostitution, an atmosphere of fear and a transient population.

After making a diagnosis of the area in which we are working, we have discovered that the fundamental pastoral problem is the gap between the institutional Church and the Church as a People, which is dramatized by the fact that we have contact with only 2% of the baptized Catholics in the parish. So we have opted for the Better World's New Image of the Parish as a plan to organize our new parish. That is, by a slow, progressive global process, we hope to arrive at decentralization and an organic, dynamic Ecclesial Base Community in the local Church. This takes into account the five pastoral thrusts of Latin America after the Vatican Council II and Medellín: 1) team ministry, 2) Ecclesial Base Communities, 3) pastoral of liberation, 4) evangelization, and 5) popular religion or traditional piety....

Arica was not yet formalized as a diocese, but was, rather, a prelature with a very minimal number of native clergy. It was mission territory in Chile, and most of the sisters' pastoral companions were other foreigners. Columban missioners and Jesuits predominated among the men. Most of the women religious, though few in number, were Chilean. With the exception of one Jesuit from the Baltimore, MD, province, the Dubuque Franciscans were the only U.S. pastoral workers in the city of about 120,000. Others were from Chile, Italy, Ireland, Scotland, New Zealand, Australia, and Malta. During the first year in *Arica* the sisters got to know these pastoral companions. More importantly, they set out visiting homes in *Población Once de Septiembre* to get to know the people they were sent to serve.

During the same year, 1978, *Santiago* was intensely experiencing the effects of military rule and the Church was responding with many gestures of solidarity. Peg Moran and Carolyn Lehmann represented one face of solidarity through their involvement in a hunger strike undertaken by family members of the detained and disappeared. It began after the military junta's April decree of amnesty proclaiming freedom to political prisoners and allowing for the return of Chileans living in exile for political reasons. It was deceptive. Its scope was extremely limited for prisoners and exiles, but offered total exoneration for government and military personnel from prosecution for human rights abuses. After the decree, the courts closed all cases of investigation of persons missing after the coup.

A Vine Transplanted – Chile

In response, four groups of relatives of disappeared persons, with about twenty per group, occupied three Catholic churches and the UNICEF building in *Santiago* to begin a hunger strike, till death if necessary, until the government was willing to undergo a full investigation of the disappearance of their relatives and provide information. Three days after the hunger strike began, several priests and women religious joined it, among them Peg and Carolyn. Peg's testimony (from Maryknoll archives):

> *I have assumed over the years of living in the población many of the problems of our people. I have felt a part of their friendship, joys and also their sorrows. This was a deeper step in the process. Now, how much better I'll be able to understand when someone comes to our door and says he hasn't eaten for many days.*

From Carolyn's diary (Maryknoll archives):

> *Everyone is weak, but under the circumstances, this is of course normal. All have a great desire this will end soon. With spirits good, we continue convinced that truth and justice will triumph. At Mass tonight I felt I understood for the first time the words: "This is my Body which will be given up for you."*

Other hunger strikes began in sympathy in more than 20 countries, and in Chile the solidarity was widespread. Church groups around the country held vigils and fasts, and 30 political prisoners in *Santiago* joined the hunger strike from their cells. There were finally more than 200 people in Chile on the long-term hunger strike. The relatives of the disappeared asked Cardinal *Raúl Silva Henríquez* to mediate between themselves and the government and ultimately the Minister of the Interior pledged that within a short time the government would give account of the fate of each one of the missing persons whose disappearance had been documented before Chilean authorities. The cardinal pledged the Catholic Church's ongoing intervention in the process, and in the following months it was announced that Chile would allow a UN human rights commission to enter the country, after years of blocking such an entry. After 17 days the hunger strike ended. Peg and Carolyn had participated for 14 days.

A Vine Transplanted – Chile

"Morir sin haber hecho mal a nadie
y bien a todos,
desfallecer por ayudar a otros
a llevar su carga
consolando, instruyendo
haciendo el bien."

P. 11

Srs. Peg Moran and Carolyn Lehman on hunger strike

A poem written for the hunger strikers as they left: *"You have sown a tear that shouts until it flowers in the morning. You have sown a network of hands, so united, so soft, so blue, so great and so strong..."*

During 1979 Peg Moran and Carolyn Lehmann found themselves to be the remaining members of the household that had begun as a larger Maryknoll community. They decided to begin phasing out their work in the *población* where they had been since 1972. Though there was still much work to do they felt that they had done what they could as women religious. There had never been a consistent presence of a priest and the community had grown to the size that warranted the presence of a sacramental minister. Peg found the leaving difficult, saying that her work in that *población* had been the most challenging, demanding and rewarding years of her presence in Chile. Of their newly-chosen ministry site, *Población Lo Amor*, Peg says:

A Vine Transplanted – Chile

After having had the pastoral and institutional responsibilities of eight years, we opted for an area where there were no religious, to go there and be present, with a special desire to work with women, who as the documents of Puebla say, are doubly oppressed: because they are poor and because they are women. As women religious, we had also experienced that oppression within the church structure. During this first year, we supplemented our small bishop's salary by doing craft work, rather than depend on our congregations for support. Eventually, work in mental health therapy groups with women took us to eight poblaciones in the deanery, in answer to the growing statistics of neurosis among the people. ... Because of the potential dangers of living in a military dictatorship and the great distance from the other Franciscans in Chile, I asked at this time to be associated formally with the Maryknoll sisters. (1984 personal history)

Peg signed a contract in 1980 as a Maryknoll Associate.

Darleen's one year of working in *Arica*, helping the other Franciscans to initiate the Better World Movement's pastoral vision, gave her practical experiential preparation for later work at the national level in promoting the Better World Movement in Chile. In 1979 she left *Arica* and returned to *Chillán* to join the team promoting the program throughout the country. She lived in a *población* with a French Canadian sister, Lucy Larouche, of the Daughters of Jesus, also on the team. A priest from Spain, *Jose Antonio Ortega*, was the third member of their group.

Sr. Darleen and the Better World Team

A Vine Transplanted – Chile

Together they promoted structural change in both Church and Society. She describes the work:

> *We organized our efforts into projects or processes to renew by creating concrete models in four areas: Organic Pastoral Plan for forming Church into a communion of communities that could organize and give identity to the People of God that opt for Jesus and live according to the values of the Kingdom; renewal of religious life with Chilean congregations with courses and orientation of chapters; promotion of human dignity and rights in grassroots consciousness raising and organization; and education in schools which forms a critical and political conscience so as to promote liberation. (1984 personal history)*

Darleen found the work with Better World very motivating, and she continued to work as part of the national promotional team during the remainder of her time in Chile.

With Darleen's Better World pastoral orientation, the sisters had begun to organize their work in *Arica*. They were off to a good start. In May of 1979 Darleen moved back to *Chillán* and Carol went to the U.S. for a visit and for a surgery at Xavier Hospital. In August Amelia returned to Chile and joined the others in *Arica*. Her arrival was a comedy of errors. Peg Moran had traveled from *Santiago* to welcome her back. However, Amelia's flight had been delayed. She missed a connection in *La Paz*, Bolívia, and had to wait another three days for the next flight. Peg returned to *Santiago* without seeing her because of scheduled commitments. Anna Marie was expecting her a few days later, but Amelia decided to take the train from *La Paz*, sitting on a wooden seat amidst Bolivian, Peruvian and Chilean women bringing items to sell in the open markets of *Arica*. Her early arrival was a total surprise!

With Carol's return in November, each of the three began to settle into specific areas of responsibility. The parish of *Once de Septiembre* had three smaller chapels, and each of the sisters took overall responsibility for the community in a given area: Anna Marie in *Cristo Hermano de los Hombres*, Carol in *San Pedro*, and Amelia in *San Esteban*. Each of them assumed areas of responsibility in the overall parish as well.

Carol, as the youngest of the group, was encouraged to develop youth ministry in the parish, so that is where she began. She later took up the support of a children's "dining room" already organized by the people. During the years of dictatorship, people in economically stressed areas all over the country had begun to organize a united effort to feed at least young children, knowing that malnutrition at an early age can retard brain development. Carol helped the group to secure supplemental food supplies and to support those local leaders who kept the dining room functioning. It eventually became clear that entire families, not just children, were in need of food, so Carol helped with their organization of *ollas communes* or collective soup kitchens. Much of Carol's pastoral activity developed in response to the needs of those who were the poorest in *Once de Septiembre*. She organized a number of self-help groups for women, teaching a variety of crafts, enabling them to make simple things to sell. Some women sewed. Others spun wool, knitted, and wove garments of *llama* and *alpaca*. The households most in need were those in which neither parent had work. She helped women with unemployed husbands organize, build and run a small laundry as a source of income. A new building was constructed to house the laundry and other self-help projects. Carol's chapel area was the most distant from the sisters' house and she came and went on a bicycle. A Jesuit, *Ignacio Vergara*, lived in that area, and Carol worked with him in supporting some of the Base Christian Communities formed there.

Sr. Anna Marie Manternach with a group of children

A Vine Transplanted – Chile

Anna Marie began organizing family catechesis in each chapel, the two-year adult formation program which was a launching pad for Base Christian Communities. It was easily a full-time endeavor, which mushroomed in scope in direct proportion to growing church participation and increasing population in *Once de Septiembre*. New housing units were continuously being built and more and more people arrived in the neighborhood. It was very difficult to keep up with the demand for catechesis and for training leaders. Once small community groups were formed, Carol and Amelia continued them in their corresponding chapel areas. Anna Marie became the principal resource person in the diocese for promoting the program not only in *Once de Septiembre* but in other parishes as well. Anna Marie accompanied the Franciscan Third Order and the Charismatic Movement in *Arica*. Particularly significant for her was being chosen as one of two sisters to officially represent the Diocese of *Arica* in greeting Pope John Paul II in *Antofogasta* (northern desert city) on his visit to Chile.

Sr. Amelia Thole with one of the Base Christian Communities

Amelia initiated work with senior citizens in each area of the parish. She also worked with groups of children, ages 7-12, using an international program called MOANI that teaches working together, and she did some volunteer teaching in the one Catholic school in *Arica*. She visited those in prison as well as the homes of parishioners. She helped the sick as she

A Vine Transplanted – Chile

was able, with an occasional trip on a crowded bus to *Tacna*, Peru, a 14-mile trip across the border, to buy less expensive medicines for people than could be found in Chile. There were Maryknoll sisters in *Tacna*, and the trip was always an occasion for a visit. As did the others, Amelia continued working with the Base Christian Communities that resulted from the family First Communion preparation program. She describes that work in a 2014 interview:

> *These communities were very important for the people in the years of Augusto Pinochet, the dictator of Chile for 18 years. It was a place where the people felt they could discuss freely their problems with the Bible as their basis. Singing, Bible discussion, and airing fears and problems, socializing, and ending with tea and hard toasted bread made up the schedule. Some nights I took part in three or four different Base Communities, sometimes getting back to our little home at 1:30 am. The Base Communities were very supportive of each other.*

As 1979 was drawing to a close, the sisters were eagerly anticipating having Sisters Nancy Meyerhofer and Pat Farrell, join them in Chile in January of 1980. Their missionary call had been developing over a long period of time. Nancy was inspired to minister in Chile when she was a postulant in 1966 and met Peg Moran who was in the U.S. for her first home visit. Nancy's desire to be a missioner in Chile never wavered from that time on. Pat had worked in a Mexican-American parish in San Antonio, Texas, for five years prior to coming to Chile. When she spent time in Mexico learning Spanish, she fell in love with the kind of Church she saw in *Cuernavaca*, where Base Christian Communities flourished. She returned to the U.S. saying to the community that she wanted to go to Latin America sometime in the future. The sisters in Chile had advised the Dubuque leadership not to send any sister alone, but rather to wait until two could come together. Nancy spent a year in San Antonio synchronizing her timing with Pat's for them to go together. They represented a sort of second generation of missioners in the community, inspired by those who had gone before them.

From August through September 1979, Srs. Pat and Nancy participated in a training program for Latin-American missioners, sponsored by the United States Catholic Conference and held at MACC (Mexican American Cultural Center) in San Antonio. It had three six-week segments. The first was an immersion experience in Mexico, with two weeks in a middle-sized city, two weeks in Mexico City, and two weeks in very isolated rural areas.

A Vine Transplanted – Chile

It was designed to give them an exposure to ministry in a variety of settings. The second six weeks were intensive Spanish classes at MACC. The third segment was input from Latin American theologians and scholars, including Brazilian liberation theologian *Leonardo Boff* and *Samuel Ruiz*, the bishop from *Chiapas*, Mexico, known to be a champion for the indigenous peoples.

Shortly before the two were scheduled to leave on January 13, Sr. Matilda died. The timing was providential. They were able to attend her wake and funeral and bring a first-hand account of that to the sisters in Chile who had such love for her. They chose an assortment of momentos for the Chile sisters from among her personal belongings before their send-off ceremony from Mount St. Francis.

Srs. Pat Farrell and Peg Moran

On the day of their departure there was a serious ice storm. Very few people ventured the treacherous drive to the airport. Only one flight left Dubuque on January 13, before the airport shut down. The two sisters were on it. Within hours, however, they were enjoying the sunny warmth of Miami where they remained for three days to negotiate a temporary resident visa from the Chilean Embassy. Entering the country with only a tourist visa seemed too risky during the time of dictatorship. On January 17 they arrived in *Santiago*, met by Peg Moran and Carolyn Lehmann.

A Vine Transplanted – Chile

Interested in learning about the community's presence in Chile, Pat and Nancy spent time in *Santiago*, staying in the *población* with Peg and Carolyn. It was assumed that Pat and Nancy would work in *Arica*, but they also wanted to explore *Santiago* before making that decision. They met many other missioners and saw the variety of apostolates in which they served. Maryknoll Sr. Ita Ford was a frequent visitor to the house in those days. Recently returned to Chile after time in the States, she too, was looking for a place to settle and work.

They then took a scenic train ride to *Chillán* and spent time with Darleen and Lucy, hearing about their work with the Better World Movement. Darleen gave them a history tour of the *Colegio*, the *población* where she and Elaine worked, and the town of *Bulnes* where she and Carol had been. After days of touring, conversation, popcorn and Chilean wine, they returned to *Santiago* and got on a bus for the 36-hour ride through the northern desert to *Arica*.

There was a warm welcome in *Arica*, from both Franciscan enthusiasm as well as the elevated temperatures. Nancy and Pat spent a month shadowing the sisters and learning a great deal about their lives and work. Community was a clear priority. Each Tuesday morning one of the Jesuits came to the house for an intimate Eucharistic celebration followed by breakfast. Many card games took place when a break in the evening meetings allowed. There were many, many instructive conversations about the situation in the country under the dictatorship and the style of Church operative in the diocese.

Srs. Nancy, Pat, and Carol singing

A Vine Transplanted – Chile

Pat and Nancy's first letter to the community:

We'd like to share some of our first impressions of the Church in Chile. It seems to have made an option for the poor and put emphasis on justice through such activities as: dining rooms that provide one meal a day for poor children; organized solidarity with workers, with those whose family members have been detained or have disappeared since the coup in 1973, with families of political prisoners, and with other such groups that need a powerful voice to speak for them. In a country where the press is very controlled, Church-sponsored publications seem to be the only ones able to get by with any kind of critical, prophetic message. We felt privileged to have the opportunity while in Santiago to participate in a romería (pilgrimage, rally) held in a cemetery where more than 300 unmarked graves from the time of the coup were recently discovered.

From March 9-14 all the Franciscans in the country gathered in *Arica*. Sister Matilda's death was the event around which they first came together, with the two recently arrived missioners recounting details and delivering personal keepsakes of hers. The time together was significant in other ways, too. It was a general chapter year, and the sisters gathered input and suggestions from Chile. One was that Chile should have a delegate and also an on-going contact person. Since no one had been elected as a delegate from Chile, the leadership team in Dubuque approved a non-voting representative and Anna Marie was chosen since the timing coincided with an already-planned home visit. The leadership team also approved having a contact person and Elaine Gehling was chosen, with the understanding that she would visit every two years to be in touch with the sisters, their needs and concerns. This gathering in *Arica* was important in that the group decided that they would all meet annually. The geographic distances were great enough that coming together had to be very intentional or it was not likely to happen.

Later in March, Nancy and Pat returned to *Santiago* and had directed retreats at the same time, both ultimately discerning to go to *Arica*. While they were in *Santiago*, Archbishop *Oscar Romero* was assassinated in El Salvador, and they attended a commemorative Eucharist in *Santiago*'s cathedral where the impact was manifested in the enormous crowd, outpouring of emotion, and prophetic homily by Cardinal *Raúl Silva Henríquez*. In April they participated in a new missioner orientation (prepared and facilitated by Peg Moran, and Maryknoll Sisters Carolyn Lehmann, Ita Ford, and Connie

A Vine Transplanted – Chile

Popsilil). Before returning to *Arica* to settle in, they attended a farewell party for Ita Ford who was leaving for El Salvador. At the prayer service that evening, Ita's friend Carolyn prayed that she would have the courage to give her life if that should ever be asked of her. Little did they know that before the year was over that would be a reality.

Once back in the north, Nancy and Pat set about the work of becoming acquainted with the world of *Arica* and finding a focus for ministry. They chose to work in *Población Chile,* an impoverished neighborhood that was a chapel subdivision of a larger parish, *El Carmen,* staffed by the Jesuits. For six months they visited homes, listened and learned. Pat recounts part of that experience that had an important influence on her.

> *Nancy and I visited one home where a teenager invited us to go with her to a party that evening. It was a family celebration and her uncle was driving. That sounded like a great idea---to socialize with Chileans and get a taste of what that was like. We went. We ate. We danced. At some point we noticed that the uncle driver was drinking rather heavily and thought it best to ask him to take us home early, while he was still in condition to drive. On the way he wanted to stop and walk along the beach. It didn't seem like a great idea, but he was the driver, so we walked along the ocean, in the semi-dark. Suddenly he burst into tears and then began recounting that he had tortured a lot of people and now couldn't live with himself and knew that he drank too much. I was on high alert, sensing the potential danger of the moment. More importantly, however, I saw how terribly the military, especially those who tortured, were affected by what they did. During the years that followed I could never demonize those who committed such atrocities, knowing that many of them were left as traumatized as the victims.*

During 1980 when all five of the sisters lived together in *Once de Septiembre,* Carol and Anna Marie both got hepatitis. Their brief stay in the *Arica* hospital was a logistical challenge for everyone, since the sisters had to buy and bring any needed medicine, supplement meager hospital meals, and wash the hospital bed sheets. Carol and Anna Marie's recovery at home was a three-month period of rest, much of it in bed. A doctor friend who was also the head of *Arica*'s Human Rights Commission, came at least once a week to check on them. He also taught all of the sisters how to give injections, which they reluctantly practiced on one another with injectable vitamins!

A Vine Transplanted – Chile

Pat and Nancy continued to learn the complexities of working in a very controlled environment of dictatorship. The fear and mistrust of the people were palpable. There was continual and open conversation among the sisters and other pastoral companions, however. The focus was always on how to be Church and how to embody the Gospel under those restrictive circumstances. In December of 1980, the *Arica* sisters received a call from Peg Moran with the first news of Ita Ford's assassination in El Salvador. It was sobering, yet somehow strengthening at the same time, each person praying to be faithful to the end as Ita was.

Front of the house in Población 11 de Septiembre

Among the pastoral priorities of the bishop was that of tending to the *Aymara* population in the mountainous section of the diocese, an area woefully abandoned by church personnel, with no means of transportation to get there. The sisters in *Arica* had expressed that need to the two newest missioners before they came and through a providential set of circumstances they were able to get a used jeep in San Antonio.

When it arrived by boat, two teams were formed to work in the villages. Nancy was part of the team that worked in the highest (15,000 ft.) *altiplano* area near the Bolivian border. Pat was on the team that worked the mid-level mountain area, an elevation of about 10,000 ft. Several times a year each team would make the rounds in their respective areas for ten to fourteen days.

The conditions in the villages were rustic and overnight accommodations often involved sleeping on the floor somewhere. The trips were too infrequent and the contact with the people too little to do much in-depth pastoral work, but over time the missioners gained some trust with the people. They were invited to be part of a few *Aymara* rituals and celebrations, very rich in symbol and tradition. Each village had common land and the profit from any crop planted and harvested on that land was used to finance the annual fiesta of the village. Ancient community rituals, chants and dances accompanied the group planting and harvesting, always concluding with a community meal of animals sacrificed for the event.

Sr. Pat with Aymara women at a planting ceremony

A Vine Transplanted – Chile

The people were mostly shepherds of herds of sheep in the mid-mountain ranges, and of llamas and alpacas in the *altiplano*. Diet was very sparse; the people were isolated and poor. The mid-range mountain people grew oregano as a cash crop. Other than potatoes grown throughout the area and meat from the herds, there was little other variety of food. Coca (from which cocaine is derived) was grown freely. Chewing coca leaves was often part of rituals, but also common in daily life since it reduced hunger and gave a certain kind of energy. Each trip the teams made afforded some measure of education and enculturation, and usually the adventure of some travel mishap.

Altiplano village where Srs. Nancy Meyerhofer and Pat Farrell worked

Apart from these regular trips into the Andes, Nancy and Pat worked mostly in the city of *Arica*. At the beginning of their second year, they found a house in the neighborhood where they worked in the Chapel of *Cristo Obrero*, parish of *El Carmen*. A family who had lived in the house was moving for a time to another part of the country and let them stay in the house. It was small and Pat and Nancy shared the one bedroom. As with other houses in the neighborhood, it was a flimsy structure with a flat, plywood roof. Since it never rained, nothing more substantial was needed, though it didn't keep a cat from falling through once!

A Vine Transplanted – Chile

Cristo Obrero Chapel   *Sr. Pat Farrell in front of their house*

Nancy and Pat began together to form youth groups in *Cristo Obrero* but eventually each found a more individual focus. Nancy continued working alone with youth and she gradually was involved with training and organization at all levels: local, deanery, diocesan and national. She and a Chilean psychologist invented a program called PROFA (*Programa de Formación Afectiva*—Program for Affective Formation) to help young people in the areas of affectivity and sexuality, very much needed as the dictatorship and its effects made it difficult for young people to become mature and independent. Many delayed marriage because they couldn't afford to support a family, or lived with their parents/in-laws, often indefinitely. In her later years in Chile, Nancy helped to start a drug rehabilitation program in *Arica*, which developed into a large operation with a residential facility able to accommodate 40 persons at a time. In addition to her long-term commitment to youth work, she helped form mental health promoters for impoverished neighborhoods.

Pat got involved in work similar to what Sr. Carol did in *Once de Septiembre*. She set up women's self-help groups in which participants spun wool, wove and made garments of *llama* and *alpaca* to sell. She helped organize *ollas communes* (soup kitchens) and worked with Base Christian Communities in the neighborhood. With one of the Jesuits she did some campus ministry, forming groups that used Ignatian spirituality as a framework for their meetings. She brought a few university students to *Población Chile* to do literacy classes in the neighborhood. On the city level she supported and accompanied groups of recovering alcoholics.

A Vine Transplanted – Chile

After moving to *Población Chile*, Nancy and Pat maintained weekly contact with the other sisters in *Arica*, participating in the Tuesday morning home liturgies and breakfast, traveling back and forth and everywhere by bicycle. Often on Sundays one house or the other would invite the whole group for dinner.

One commonality between the two sectors where the sisters worked was the practice of popular religiosity. The most common expression was that of the dance communities, which were even more widespread in parts of Peru and Bolivia. Since the north of Chile had historically been part of Peru at one time, many cultural characteristics of life in the north reflect that influence. The dance communities trained and organized themselves to raise money for the annual pilgrimage to a Marian shrine, where they would dance before an image of the Virgin Mary for hours at a time (often until entering a trance-like state). The sisters often accompanied the pilgrims to the nearest shrine in the interior of *Arica, Nuestra Señora de Las Peñas (Our Lady of the Rocks)*, and occasionally to the more distant shrine of *La Tirana* near the city of *Iquique*.

Fiesta dance groups

In 1991 Peg Moran returned to Dubuque to accompany her dying mother. Amelia and Anna Marie also visited the U.S. at that time and were able to be with Peg, the first time since their 1965 missioning from the

A Vine Transplanted – Chile

motherhouse that the three had been together in the United States. Peg's mother died in November, after which Peg returned to *Santiago*.

In 1982 both Darleen and Elaine visited *Arica*. Darleen was en route to the U.S. for surgery. In May Elaine made her first visit to Chile as the sisters' designated contact person with the congregation. In *Santiago*, Peg Moran and Carolyn Lehmann were joined by Maryknoll Linda Donavan who came to live and minister with them. During December Sr. Susan Seitz visited. Traveling through Peru en route to *Arica*, Susan's delayed flight was met in *Lima* by Fr. Perez, one of Darleen's co-workers in the Better World Movement. In Chile, she visited the sisters in all three ministry locations, experiencing their lives and work and bearing Christmas gifts and greetings to all from Dubuque. Except for a bit of altitude sickness in the *altiplano*, she seemed to enjoy the trip.

Sister Susan Seitz (OSF President) visit with the Sisters

During 1983 a noteworthy shift took place in Chile. The dictatorship had maintained the Chilean peso at an artificially stable exchange rate in order to attract international investment to the country. By 1983, however, it was no longer feasible to sustain that strategy and the Chilean currency was devalued significantly. From one day to another people's money was worth much, much less, without a corresponding raise in income or adjustment of the cost of base commodities. People were desperate and outraged. It was a tipping point in grassroots sentiment toward the dictatorship, turning the tide away from the pervasive climate of fear. There were, of course, other factors contributing to the change, not the least of which was the growing underground opposition movement now beginning to surface. The miners in the north began to call for open demonstrations.

The government was quick to try to contain the increasing unrest. *Pinochet* declared that no meeting of any kind with more than three people would be allowed anywhere in the country without written permission from the military. The next day Cardinal *Raúl Silva Henríquez,* already a brave public spokesperson against the human rights abuses of the military regime, sent a letter to all dioceses of the country with instructions that the Catholic Church would never ask permission for any meeting. It would be impossible to continue effective pastoral work otherwise. As a result, parishes became the only semi-safe haven for groups to meet. Church groups in poor areas tended to be in sympathy to the opposition movement, and Catholic Church leadership had been the most outspoken force against the dictatorship, particularly through the voice of the cardinal and the structure of Vicariate of Solidarity in the Archdiocese of *Santiago.* The Catholic Church was an increasingly prophetic defender of human rights. As a result, it was also vulnerable to repression by the military.

A national movement of non-violent resistance gained momentum through the organization of massive but low-risk mobilization. People opposing the dictatorship were invited to turn off their lights at 8 pm. Massive blackouts resulted nationally, affecting the electric company. On a designated day, Chileans were called to beat on pots and pans in their own back yards. No one could ignore the large-scale participation. On the 11th of every month, chosen in opposition to the coup that happened on the 11th of September, the directive was to not purchase anything. As peoples' courage grew, so also did the collective activities carried out on the 11th of each month. Soon children did not go to school on the 11th. Adults did not go to work. Then many businesses closed on the 11th. It quickly became evident that there was widespread opposition to the dictatorship and that the Chilean people were shedding their fear of expressing it. Open protests subsequently began, met with severe repression.

> *They can crush a few flowers, but they can't hold back the springtime.*
>
> --Pablo Neruda, Chilean poet [12]

A Vine Transplanted – Chile

What did all of that look like in *Arica*? On the one hand, life and work proceeded more or less as usual, with the pervasive heaviness and generalized fatigue resulting from the environment of dictatorship and the insecurity of hand-to-mouth living. On the other hand, protests took place, though on a smaller scale than in *Santiago*, with both caution and vigor. Not surprisingly, there were consequences. In *Once de Septiembre*, two of the three chapel buildings where our sisters worked (*Cristo Hermano de los Hombres* and *San Pedro*) were attacked during the middle of the night by a right-wing group called, "Comandos Defenders of the Fatherland." They broke into the two chapels at about the same time, threw gasoline all over and then tossed in a fire bomb, setting both structures on fire. Neighbors immediately rushed out and put out the fire before the buildings could be burned extensively, though there was damage in both places. They found pamphlets everywhere saying: *"For the fatherland, I condemn you. For the fatherland I denounce you. Leave, Communist priests!"* Another read *"Priests, protestors, terrorists, Communists, agitators of the people: Leave!"*

A few years later there was a serious attack on the main church of the *El Carmen* parish. Nancy, in a 2014 interview, recalls that it was a Monday night. The parish was full (an estimated 120 people), as that was the night all levels of coordinators would meet, youth group leaders, etc. At the time she was in her office behind the church and heard what sounded like a car backfiring. Soon she realized it was the sound of gunshots. Nancy ran toward the front of the parish against a flood of people running in the opposite direction to take shelter behind the brick church. In the process she found some of the youth carrying a young woman, *Soledad*, out of a meeting room. She had been shot when she stood up to turn off the lights so the group wouldn't be seen. Everyone else had hit the ground. Nancy ran out into the street to look for a car, and finding none went to a neighbor, explained the situation, and borrowed a car to take *Soledad* to the hospital. The young woman had two surgeries that evening, eventually two or three more, leaving her with a colostomy.

The parish had been attacked by a paramilitary group called "Armagedon." Most of the parish structure was made of *cholguan* (a sort of plywood) so some bullets penetrated four or five walls. A Molotov cocktail set an outside wall on fire. A group of university students, eating in a soup kitchen that the parish organized for them, put out the fire.

A Vine Transplanted – Chile

There was no running water in the neighborhood at that hour so they used containers where vegetables were soaking. The "Armagedon" group left pamphlets claiming responsibility for the attack, intending to intimidate. The parish responded with a week-long series of non-violent actions: including a way of the cross, pamphlets to denounce what had happened, a candlelight vigil, a fast, a procession through the streets of the parish with a large cross, and so on. (Nancy recalls running off copies of the pamphlets.) The week of events ended with a Mass well attended by a throng of people in support of the parish. The Jesuit pastor was so moved by the show of solidarity that when he tried to speak at the end of the liturgy, he couldn't. He put his head down on the altar and wept. After the week of protest, a young man told Nancy he was leaving his armed resistance group. *"I've become a man of peace because of this experience,"* he said.

New Callings

Just as noticeable changes were taking place in the country in 1983, so, too, major shifts were beginning among the Franciscans in Chile during 1984. In February all the sisters gathered in *Arica* and prepared together for the 1984 Chapter in Dubuque. Darleen spoke of her desire to initiate conversation in the congregation about a new mission in another country. She had spent 15 years in Chile and her 25th jubilee was on the not-too-distant horizon. She felt called to a sabbatical year in the States. In her words (1984 personal history), the sabbatical would be to:

> ...celebrate my gratitude for my life thus far and to ratify and rectify my vocational and life options. I am sincerely grateful to our community for the faithful spiritual, affective and financial support that I have felt during these years of trying to be attentive to the Lord within me and in the signs of the times, in order to love and serve the people of God in Chile.

She dreamed of beginning again in another country as she had begun in Chile: called by the congregation, entering a new culture, learning a new language.

During the gathering in *Arica*, the sisters spoke of possible countries. Haiti? Central America? Darleen had some thoughts of Guatemala after having seen pictures of suffering faces of Guatemalan people in the human rights office in *Santiago*. The images stayed with her. Darleen was chosen

A Vine Transplanted – Chile

as the Chile delegate to the 1984 Chapter where she could bring the issue to the congregation.

Peg Moran had discerned a move to accompany an Australian Mercy sister, Monica Hingston, who was planning to live in a small house in *Santiago* near where Peg had been working. It would make it possible to maintain a presence in a house that otherwise would have been closed. She moved in March of 1984.

Peg also explained to the sisters her involvement in *Santiago* in the *Sebastian Acevedo* Movement against Torture. The movement took its name from a man, *Sebastian Acevedo*, whose son and daughter were captured by the military. Since he was aware that during the first 72 hours after detaining someone the military would give no information and routinely torture people, he insisted on knowing of his children's whereabouts and their safety. When no information was forthcoming he set himself on fire in the middle of the plaza in the city of *Concepción* to call attention to the torture he knew his children were undergoing. He lived a few hours, was interviewed and his story inspired the coalescing of the *Sebastian Acevedo* Movement against Torture. It was a non-violent resistance movement that did clandestine planning and carrying out of lightening demonstrations in *Santiago*, hoping for a quick getaway since no public demonstrations of any kind were permitted under the dictatorship. It was a highly organized and disciplined group whose members agreed that if anyone was arrested everyone else would go, too. A solitary person was likely to be tortured or to disappear, but not an entire group. The movement was effective in calling public attention to the use of torture by the military. Peg Moran was part of the movement from its inception.

Later that year Pat also felt the need for a change, to step out of being overly-extended in the work in *Arica* and to continue to discern her calling. She moved to *Santiago* in July of 1984. She committed herself just for a year to work as bi-lingual secretary and translator for *Sergio Torres*, founder and then treasurer for EATWOT, The Ecumenical Association of Third World Theologians. In *Santiago* she lived with Odile Loubet, a French woman, and former Dominican sister, in *Población Violeta Parra II*, not far from Peg Moran's house. During that year Pat also participated in the lightening protests of the *Sebastian Acevedo* Movement against Torture and became part of the movement's middle-level organizing group. Once during that year in

A Vine Transplanted – Chile

Santiago, Pat and Odile's house was raided by the military. Helicopters came swooping down over the area just before dawn. The neighborhood was cordoned off and all men and older boys were taken from their homes and frisked. Some were taken prisoner. Pat's house was thoroughly searched and the military pulled materials from shelves which they considered subversive. First among them was the Latin American translation of the Bible. The military filled the dining room table with "subversive" materials and filmed Pat and Odile standing with them. The two never knew how the film would be used or why their house was ransacked.

A more gradually-developing new call to the sisters in Chile was a beginning awareness of women's theology and issues. Educational programs and focused attention on the needs of women were in very early stages. The sisters in Chile were typically less exposed to feminist thought in Latin America than sisters in the U.S. A New Jersey Sister of Charity, Barbara Aires, doing work in Chile with socially responsible investment, became aware of that and offered to send their Sister Marilyn Thie, who taught women's studies at Colgate University in New York, to *Santiago* to do a workshop for women religious. Marilyn, insisting on the need to begin with theology, brought another sister from her congregation, theology professor Peggy O'Neill, to teach feminist theology and ritual. Anna Marie attended the workshop from *Arica* and Peg Moran from *Santiago*. The following year, the two presenters returned to *Santiago* to do a second workshop. Pat was in *Santiago* by then, attended the workshop, and got to know Peggy. Afterwards, Peggy O'Neill stayed for a six-month sabbatical, living in *Santiago* with Maryknoll Carolyn Lehmann. Peggy's connection with the Dubuque Franciscans in Chile would later lead to a partnership in Central America.

Peg Moran had already been working with women in *Santiago* together with Maryknoll Carolyn Lehmann. Now, in her new living and working arrangement, she and Monica Hingston established a women's center, *Casa Sofía, Un Centro para la Mujer Pobladora* (House of Wisdom, A Center for Marginated Women). They continued working with a mental health program for women which Peg and Carolyn had begun. The program used a popular education model and formed instructive support groups for women from the *poblaciones,* emotionally affected mostly by the stressors of dictatorship, poverty and violence. From each group that was formed, they selected two women who demonstrated leadership qualities and trained them to form and facilitate other groups. The program multiplied in a very effective way, placing leadership and responsibility in the hands of the women participants. Peg and Carolyn had published a manual to make the program accessible and replicable in other areas, *Haciendo Conexiones* (Making Connections). Peg and Monica, as they continued to develop the work, put together a second edition, co-authored with Carolyn Lehmann, *Rehaciendo Nuestras Conexiones* (Remaking Our Connections), with an additional nine chapters on issues related to sexuality. Within a short time, 300 copies were sold in 26 countries.

After a trip to Nicaragua to explore government-sponsored literacy programs there, Peg and Monica developed a program based on the methodology of Paulo Freire and piloted it with women from the *población*. They wrote a manual for leaders, *Mañana Será Distinto* (Tomorrow Will be Different), which was also soon in demand from others working with grassroots women's groups. In a congregational newsletter, Peg says of the effort:

> The "alfabetización" (literacy) book contains full-page illustrations from the daily life of Chilean women ... it's great to have the finished work in our hands. This work without phones, computers, cars---to say nothing of wash machines and microwaves and in a situation of psychological war and blackouts – is a real achievement. We're happy and excited about what a significant contribution it is to work with women, especially those living in poverty.

The ongoing work of literacy and mental health groups occupied their best energies for the remainder of their time in Chile.

The beginning of 1985 found *Arica*'s three sisters in *Población Once de Septiembre* intensely engaged in work that only kept multiplying as both the resistance movement and the repression and kept growing. Nancy helped to organize a local group of the *Sebastian Acevedo* Movement against Torture in *Arica*. She, Amelia and Carol all participated in the demonstrations.

The new calls of the previous year were moving into concrete action. Conversation continued about the possibility of beginning a mission in another country. The 1984 Chapter had taken up the issue, and a group called "Border Crossing" was set up to explore concrete options. This process will be described in greater detail in the section of this book on Central America. Darleen and Pat were already anticipating being part of the new mission.

A Vine Transplanted – Chile

Darleen was in the U.S. on a mini-sabbatical and later in 1985 returned to *Chillán*, living with Kentucky Ursuline Sister Elizabeth (Mimi) Ballard. There she awaited further action on the Border Crossing endeavor. Mimi would also eventually join the project in Central America. Also anticipating a move to another country, Pat left Chile in June of 1985 and returned to the U.S. for an interim sabbatical at Weston School of Theology.

Sr. Nancy Meyerhofer in her parish office

Nancy Meyerhofer's efforts moved to a concentration on mental health work with women and drug rehabilitation with young addicts. With the help of two women psychologists from a center in *Santiago*, she organized and directed a popular education program of mental health for *población* women. It was similar to the program Peg Moran had developed in *Santiago*, inspired by a few of the same practices, but elaborating a different set of materials. She put great energy into the development of a drug rehabilitation program during this time. Having raised money in the States, she helped buy a structure in the neighborhood and opened a center staffed by a young ex-addict and his wife, with the support of a psychologist and two pro-bono physicians volunteering as needed. Initial success was not apparent, but the program was developed little by little, maturing after Nancy's time in Chile, into a very successful venture.

A Vine Transplanted – Chile

In a return trip to Chile after she had left the country, Nancy was told a moving story about a middle-aged man who came to the rehabilitation center for services. Once received into treatment for addiction to both drugs and alcohol, he asked to speak to *Pedro*, the director, and confessed to him that he had been part of the group that attacked the parish. He had discovered later that both his mother and brother were in the parish that evening. That was disturbing to him as well as the knowledge that a young woman had been shot and nearly killed in the attack. He told *Pedro* that his life had been hell ever since, and that all the members of the group had taken an oath never to talk about the incident nor give names. He knew that while he was at the drug rehab center he was being watched, but he needed to ask pardon of the girl. *Pedro* got in touch with *Soledad* and asked if she would listen to the man. At first she didn't want to, but realized that her resistance indicated that she really hadn't pardoned the persons responsible for her suffering and that she needed to meet with him. They met in a chapel and he told her what his life had been like since then and crying, asked her forgiveness. She wept as well and forgave him. She told Nancy: *"I have my children, my job, my faith: I thought I had suffered, but he suffered so much more."*

By 1988 the sisters in *Arica* were beginning to evaluate their length of stay in Chile and to envision their eventual return to the U.S. The three sisters in *Población Once de Septiembre* gave verbal notice during the year that they intended to conclude their pastoral work in *Arica* in the near future. Sr. Carol went to Dubuque to celebrate her 25th jubilee in 1988, and returned for another year in *Arica*.

Even in the midst of their leavings, the sisters found themselves immersed in very eventful days in Chile. The growing movement of resistance to the dictatorship drew international attention and pressure for a return to democracy in Chile. In response, a national plebiscite was scheduled for October 5, 1988. A "Yes" vote would approve *Pinochet*'s continuation in power for another eight years. A "No" vote would end the dictatorship and bring about a return to democratic rule in Chile. Both sides were allowed 15 minutes of national television time each evening during the month before the vote, allowing a voice in opposition to the military regime to be heard for the first time since the coup. The campaign was quite determining of the outcome. The "Yes" campaign tried to inspire fear of a return to chaos if "No" won and to improve the public image of *Pinochet*, seen as arrogant and authoritarian. The "No" campaign was upbeat and optimistic, meeting the challenge of making "no" positive and appealing. The "No" group was both critical of the dictatorship while inspiring hope in the future. Their campaign was superior in both argumentation and appeal. On September 22, the "No" side called for a 10-day "March of Joy" in *Santiago*, gathering participants from all parts of the country. Many of the demonstrators were attacked. The "Yes" group held a huge rally on October 2, which was widely covered by the still-controlled media. On October 5, 1988, with 97% voter turnout, the "No" vote won with 56% of the votes, ending 16 ½ years of dictatorship. The election of a new president and congress took place on December 14, 1989. The Christian Democrat candidate, *Patricio Alywin*, was elected president and took office on March 11, 1990. The newly elected Congress was sworn in that same day.

Despedida (farewell) for Sr. Carol at the airport in Arica

Such was the backdrop while the sisters in *Arica* were considering new directions. In 1989, Carol Hawkins returned to the U.S. permanently. She narrated in a 2014 interview that she had experienced a significant shift over the years in her understanding of what it meant to be a missioner. Rather than being the one to offer help to people in need, she had received much inspiration from them on both the human and spiritual level. She wanted her presence to be supportive and empowering and didn't want to do for people what they could do for themselves. There was by 1989 good leadership among the people and she determined that it was time for her to go. In Iowa she initially cared for her mother during recuperation from surgery, and then worked as a community outreach worker at *Casa Latina* in Sioux City. For nine years she continued doing similar work for the diocese, residing in Storm Lake, before eventually being accepted into a degree program in marriage and family counseling in San Antonio.

In July of 1989 Nancy Meyerhofer left Chile. She had replaced herself in youth ministry through years of training leaders. Though she loved that work, she too determined that her presence was no longer needed. She had lived alone since Pat left. She was also aware of wanting to live in community again and to be close to her aging parents. After some rest, family visits, a Ministry to Ministers sabbatical program, and Common Venture volunteer experience in McAllen, Texas, she ultimately decided to begin a new ministry with other Dubuque Franciscans who by then were in El Salvador.

Anna Marie and Amelia left on March 4, 1990. They, too, sensed that there was sufficient local leadership to continue the work they had begun. They also wanted to adjust to life in the United States after so many years in Chile, and wanted to make that change before retiring.

In the end, the first three sisters to go to Chile, Anna Marie, Amelia, and Peg, were the last three to leave and were there to celebrate together their 25 years in the country. In a 1990 letter, Amelia wrote: *"These 25 years of giving service to God's people here in Chile, in Chillán, Portezuelo, Santiago, Bulnes, Arica, have been years of growing, suffering, rejoicing, sharing and loving. I would do it all over again without one bit of hesitation!"* Similarly, Anna Marie wrote that she believed they have *"helped the people come to a realization of their own capabilities. But one can't be 25 years in a country without roots. The uprooting will not be easy."*

A Vine Transplanted – Chile

Srs. Anna Marie, Peg, and Amelia at Santiago airport

The day before Amelia and Anna Marie left Chile, the bishop of *Arica* and many religious, priests, parishioners and friends gathered with them in *Población Once de Septiembre* for a Mass of Thanksgiving for their 25 years in Chile and bid them farewell. On March 4, 1990, they left from the *Arica* airport. When they arrived at the front door of Mount St. Francis, a number of sisters met them and accompanied them to chapel to give thanks for their 25 years of ministry in Chile and their safe return.

Peg Moran continued her work in Santiago until the end of 1990. In July she requested and received dispensation from her vows, and returned to Chile intending to stay for a longer time. However, before the end of the year she and Monica decided to move to Australia where Peg died in March of 2011.

A congregational proclamation, signed by President Mary Clare O'Toole commemorates 25 years of congregational service in Chile:

> *Whereas the first Dubuque Franciscan Sisters arrived in Chile on February 9, 1965, to begin a quarter-century of work among the Chilean people;*
>
> *Whereas during this time the community had sisters in several places in Chile, namely: Chillán, Santiago, Bulnes, Portezuelo, and Arica;*

A Vine Transplanted – Chile

Whereas the Sisters adapted to the language and culture of the country and made friends as they did pastoral work, formation of youth groups, education of children and adults, visits to the sick and elderly, formation of Base Christian Communities, work on the Better World Movement, formation of women's groups, popular education, construction of laundry and common soup kitchens, rehabilitation of chemically dependent and other projects during these twenty-five years;

Therefore, we proclaim 1990 as the Twenty-Five-Year Anniversary of the Chilean Missions for the Sisters of St. Francis of Dubuque, Iowa

Given this 9th day of February, 1990
Sister Mary Clare O'Toole, OSF

February of 2015 marked the 50th anniversary of the beginning of the congregation's mission in Chile. With the exception of Peg Moran, all the Franciscans who served there were still alive. Each of them was invited to include in this account a very brief statement of what her time in Chile has meant to her. This segment on Chile ends with each person's own words about her experience.

Darleen Chmielewski

When I recall my years in Chile, I remember the people who opened their arms to me in friendship and taught me so much. For example, I was teaching the Nativity story to 30 Colegio first graders. At one point, I asked them who was our savior (Salvador in Spanish). Like spontaneous combustion they all stood up, pumping their hands and chanted "Salvador Allende!" Those young voices opened my eyes to a people very actively engaged in directing their destiny. And maybe they were wise because after Allende was elected, the marginated people, who had been living in huts with dirt floors, could buy homes and gas stoves. Leonardo Boff wrote that the oppressed peoples were sacraments of God in our midst. And the Chileans became that to me. When we celebrated the month of Mary with rosaries and scripture meditations, they evangelized me with their dynamic, lived faith: we're never too poor that we can't share; never too busy or tired that we can't help; never too oppressed that we can't hope; never too sad that we can't celebrate; and never too communist that we don't believe in God. Most of all I remember many hours of listening to their life stories and realized that they gave new meanings to the words: people, solidarity, community and friendship. Sharing their joys and sorrows, they invited me to walk with them. At the peñas (folk and protest songfests with empanadas) I got glimpses

A Vine Transplanted – Chile

of their spirit and soul. Violeta Parra's "Gracias a la Vida" echoes in my heart as I give thanks for all the life I lived in Chile and all the people I met: Mercedes, Eloisa, Luzmira, Sergio, Ida…..

Pat Farrell

In my research for this writing I ran across my own words. They still capture what I carry within as a nourishing memory: I "have been roused by the faith and solidarity of the people. The Church seen from this corner of the world gives me hope. Mass has never meant more to me than when celebrated in the humble wooden chapel that houses what I know to be a real community. As I see the faces of those who enter, I picture the activities of each during the week – the visiting of sick neighbors, the meeting of the local human rights group, the rebuilding of an earthquake victim's fallen home, the cooking in the olla común ("common pot" or soup kitchen), the struggling to nurture a beginning Comunidad de Base, the preparing of parents of First Communion children, the gathering of youth, etc., etc. There is a momentum in all of that I sense to be so of the Spirit that I'm convinced not even the injustices within the Church or heavy-handed hierarchical defence mechanisms can alter its liberating course. And it has been liberating in these years of ministry to accompany rather than lead, to listen more than to speak, and to give and receive so interchangeably." The Jesuits we worked with were brothers and friends, visionary spiritual companions. The Chilean Church was courageously prophetic, faith and justice a seamless whole. To participate in the country's process of non-violent transformation from dictatorship to democracy was an amazing historical privilege. It has all shaped me. Because of Chile, I know what church can be and I carry that image within as a template and guide. I am grateful.

Elaine Gehling

My eight years living and walking with the people of Chile awakened in me a great respect for the Chilean people as they struggled to maintain their dignity after losing their freedom and democracy. I learned to listen to the people and their ideas and share in their life experiences as they found ways to advocate for themselves.

¡Viva Chile!

I left Chile with a deeper advocacy awareness that I used in my work in Waterloo and Des Moines, Iowa, and currently in Napa, California with a special emphasis on treating people with gentleness and kindness.

A Vine Transplanted – Chile

Carol Hawkins

My desire to be a missionary had its first stirrings in high school when I heard a missionary from Peru speak about Latin America — its poverty, oppression and the need to support its missionaries. In the novitiate this desire was reawakened when our community sent sisters to Chile. I felt a strong urge to serve with them. With a spirit of adventure I set out in 1976 on my first international flight to South America. I felt capable of adjusting to challenging situations, but never imagined what a life altering experience Chile would be for me.

It wasn't difficult for me to do without, to live more simply and rely on my personal resources. What I learned in Chile was to trust in the providence of God, to share what I have without concern for tomorrow. This was a huge leap in faith for me.

My upbringing taught me to concentrate on work. I learned that in a Latin culture relationships are the priority. I tended to move immediately to the task at hand and miss the importance of relationship building and making each person feel valued for who they are and what they can contribute to the common good.

I became aware that the Chilean people were poor economically but not poor in their remarkable human and spiritual resources. I learned to recognize their gifts, to empower, to accompany, to support and to stand with them in solidarity rather than offering right answers and ready solutions.

Reading and sharing Scripture with God's favored ones -- the oppressed, the poor, powerless, the sick, the widow, those suffering injustice, was an experience for which I deeply grateful. Standing with and among the poor opened me to a dimension of God I had not had previously known.

I am grateful for the move from North to South which shifted my perceptions and transformed me in my experience of God, self and the reality.

Jean Hurley Redmond

My experience gave me an appreciation for how the poor have to struggle to get adequate work, maintain a family, acquire sufficient food and meet the health and other basic needs for survival, even though often they were in debt, lacked work, or had difficult problems like alcoholism or health issues to deal with. The people showed

A Vine Transplanted – Chile

me how much their Catholic faith was able to encourage them and help overcome the many difficulties they faced. Their appreciation for their faith strengthened and increased mine.

My time in Chile made me very conscious of the many excesses and luxuries in food, clothing, health care, and entertainment that we often took for granted simply because we had easy access to them, and made us want to do with less. Even having enough kerosene for heating their home in the winter was a luxury some couldn't afford and had to use many layers of clothes to adjust to the cold.

The generosity of the poor toward each other and their willingness to share what little they had was a continuous, motivating example. Frequently a family would be raising a child who was not theirs, simply because his/her parents were dead, ill, or otherwise unable to raise the child.

I learned the importance of community, prayer and sharing for those who are working with the poor.

Rosa Lyons Crispo

Santos (child from Chile)

When I think of Chillán, one story always comes to mind, and always will. Coming back from organ practice at the cathedral on a cold, rainy winter day, I came upon a big box in the middle of the sidewalk. Upon inspection I found a small child, perhaps five years old, crouched down in fetal position. He told me his name

A Vine Transplanted – Chile

was Santos. "Where do you live, Santos?" "This is my home," he answered with a smile. "Come home with me, Santos, and I'll give you some bread." He answered, "Sí, Madre Rosa," so he was from the población, I reasoned. Santos was so dirty that I tried to give him a bath. Since he had never experienced such a thing he thought he was dying, and so did I! We both survived and every day after school that year Santos would wait by the kitchen window for some bread. We became good friends and he was a master guide in the población.

It was hard to leave Mount St. Francis as we set out for unknown places and new adventures. Three years later, it was much harder to return and see so many cars, so many food choices, and such a quick pace of living. When I returned Mother Matilda pointed out a group of inter-faith priests, ministers and lay people working for social betterment in Chicago. I joined the group and once again met Msgr. Ivan Illich. We had become good friends in Cuernavaca, and frequently corresponded.

My experience in Chile changed my life, my attitudes and resulted in an ever-growing love and admiration for the poor. I taught in the "Skid Row" area of Chicago for a year and marvelled at the poverty of spirit I saw there. After years of teaching in the city of Boston I still am amazed at the resiliency of the people, their struggle and their love for each other. The opportunity of serving in the missions of Latin America is one that I will forever be grateful for.

Anna Marie Manternach

One event that made me aware that we were a long way from home was during the Pinochet dictatorship when Sr. Margaret Clare was visiting us in Chillán and got very sick. It had been declared a law that no car or any means of transportation could move without permission. The hospital advised us to have the lights on in the inside the car so the authorities could see who was inside and have just one person accompanying her. I wish you could have seen the bed they put her in! And the walls were decorated with blood and dirt. I'm happy to tell you that she recovered! Sr. Susan Seitz also visited when we were going out to work in poorer areas, which seemed relaxing after trying to get forty or more boys into a teachable environment.

Our classrooms had cement floors and the only heat we had was a small sawdust stove. The floors never warmed up so the little boys had cardboard under their feet and wore a couple of coats. They looked as round as they were tall. What a lively bunch! I loved them!

A Vine Transplanted – Chile

I can honestly tell you I appreciated my years in Chile. The people were very good to us and the Jesuits always ready to help us in any way. My grateful thanks to the Maryknoll sisters and priests. If I hadn't gotten so old I'd be ready to return.

Nancy Meyerhofer

The near-decade in Chile was for me enormously significant with a huge learning curve. Working closely with Jesuits Chago Marshall and Pepe Correa, both Chileans and excellent mentors for me in pastoral work, and with Jim Hosey (U.S.) and Hector Mercieca (Malta), I learned to accompany a people struggling with conditions of life under a cruel and intelligent military dictatorship. The people taught me so much, some of that being: that the Bible was written from the viewpoint of the poor and when read from that perspective there are many new meanings; that humor is a way to maintain hope and battle oppression; that the solidarity of poor people knows no limits; that I had undiscovered gifts which they called forth. I feel I grew up and matured with the Chilean people and am so grateful for all that I lived there.

Amelia Thole

To me, my most rewarding time of life was my ministry in Chile! First of all, the privilege to be missioned by the community, to walk and share with the Chilean people, were years of growth in many ways. They were years of confiding in God's love and compassion. I learned so much from the children and adults and their eagerness to help us wherever possible, especially in learning the Spanish language as well as their acceptance and confidence in us, and becoming part of their culture ourselves. I always felt welcomed in their homes. The Base Communities were such an inspiration, as the members opened their homes for the group to participate each week.

Leaving Chile was very difficult for me, as I felt it was home to me. Receiving and writing letters to friends in Chile keeps the special bond going. My heart is still in the gracious, loving people I was able to journey with as we got together for our spiritual needs. God bless each one!

A Vine Transplanted – Chile

Chronology of Franciscan Sisters' Service in Chile

1964   Sisters Anna Marie Manternach, Amelia Thole, and Peg Moran are selected to go to Chile

1965   February 8, the three leave Mount St. Francis, arriving in Santiago February 9 to work at the *Colegio Seminario* in *Chillán*. Mother Matilda Adams visits at Christmas.

1966   Sisters Elaine Gehling and Rosa Lyons arrive just before Christmas and join the staff at the *Colgeio Seminario.* Mother Matilda Adams again visits.

1968   Peg Moran requests to study theology at the Catholic University in *Santiago* in preparation for doing pastoral work.

1969   Sister Margaret Francis Brockamp visits for six months.

Sisters Darleen Chmielewski and Jean Hurley arrive.

Darleen Chmielewski settles in *Chillán* while Jean Hurley joins Peg Moran in working with Maryknoll sisters in an impoverished parish in *Santiago*.

1970   Rosa Lyons returns to the U.S. for surgery, subsequently choosing to leave the congregation.

1972   Jean Hurley goes to the U.S. for a visit and withdraws from the congregation.

Peg Moran begins work in a different area of Santiago with Maryknoll sisters.

1974   Elaine Gehling leaves *Chillán* to accompany her dying mother. She does not return to Chile.

1976   Sister Carol Hawkins arrives in Chile, joining Darleen Chmielewski in *Chillán* after language studies.

1977   Sister Margaret Clare Dreckman, travels to Chile with Anna Marie Manternach, guides the sisters in a discernment process that leads to a decision to move to *Arica*.

A Vine Transplanted – Chile

1978 Darleen Chmielewski arrives in *Arica*, followed by Carol Hawkins and Anna Marie Manternach.

1978 Amelia Thole arrives after surgery in *Chillán* and two weeks later leaves Chile for medical attention in the U.S., remaining at Mount St. Francis for eighteen months.

1979 Darleen Chmielewski returns to *Chillán* to work with the Better World Movement.

Peg Moran and Maryknoll Sister Carolyn Lehmann phase out their work in *Pudahuél* and begin work in Lo *Amor*.

Carol Hawkins goes to the U.S. for medical attention and Amelia Thole returns to *Arica* after medical clearance.

1980 Sisters Nancy Meyerhofer and Pat Farrell arrive, eventually working in *Población Chile* in *Arica*.

Peg Moran begins a formal, three-year association with Maryknoll and does mental health work in the deanery.

All the Franciscans in Chile gather in *Arica* for their first annual meeting.

Carol Hawkins and Anna Marie Manternach spend months recovering from hepatitis.

1981 Peg Moran goes to the U.S. to accompany her dying mother and returns following her death.

1982 Darleen Chmielewski returns to the U.S. for surgery.

Elaine Gehling makes her first official visit as community contact person for Latin America.

Sister Susan Seitz visits all the sisters in Chile.

Maryknoll Sister Linda Donavan joins Peg Moran and Carolyn Lehmann in *Santiago*.

1984 All the sisters in Chile gather in *Arica* for pre-chapter meeting and preparations.

A Vine Transplanted – Chile

Peg Moran moves to another neighborhood with Mercy Sister Monica Hingston.

Pat Farrell moves to *Santiago* for an interim year, working with EATWOT.

Darleen Chmielewski initiates a sabbatical time in the U.S., anticipating a move to another country.

1985   Pat Farrell leaves Chile and begins a sabbatical in preparation for work in another country.

Darleen Chmielewski returns to *Chillán* awaiting finalization of plans for another country.

1986   Darleen Chmielewski leaves Chile.

1988   Verbal notice is given of the intention to conclude Franciscan ministry in *Arica*.

1989   Carol Hawkins and Nancy Meyerhofer terminate their work in Chile and return to the U.S.

Written notice is given of the Franciscans leaving *Arica* in 1990.

1990   March 4, Amelia Thole and Anna Marie Manternach leave Chile, concluding twenty-five years of service.

Peg Moran leaves Chile, also after twenty-five years, returns to the U.S. and is dispensed from her vows. She moves to Australia at the end of the year, where she dies in 2011.

A Vine Transplanted – Chile

SISTER MARGARET FRANCIS' LETTER TO THE COMMUNITY

AFTER SIX MONTHS IN CHILE

March 26, 1970

Dear Sisters,

Since it is impossible for me to meet with all of you personally, I am writing to share some of the experiences I had during my recent time in Chile.

You will recall that I left for Chile in July in order to live for a time with our Sisters in *Chillán* and *Santiago*. This extended visit was undertaken for three reasons: 1) to experience life as it is lived by our Sisters, thereby gaining a deeper understanding of their needs, joys, and hardships; 2) to learn to know the present role of the Church in Chile (made evident to me through my visits with bishops, missionary priests, sisters, and laymen and women); to consider with the Sisters the direction of our continuing role in the work of the Church in Latin America, and 3) to arrive at a better understanding of the qualities needed in Sisters choosing to work in Chile.

In the October 14 Secondary Bulletin, I shared with you the work our Sisters are doing at the *Colegio Seminario* in *Chillán*, and in the community of *Chillán*. A group of Sisters desire to continue their work in the school, believing that the school is one of the most effective agents in promoting social transformation through the fostering of attitudinal changes which in turn will make Christian social change possible.

Beginning in March 1970, 35 percent of the students in the *Colegio Seminario* will come from poor families; the remaining 65 percent of the students from the homes of wealthy families and a rising middle class. It is worthy of note that these 65 percent have opted the payment of a higher tuition so that the 35 percent may attend the *Colegio* free of tuition. The Jesuit Fathers feel this was possible because of their work and the work of the Sisters with the parents, helping them to become responsible Christians. I wish to add that the Sisters are contributing one scholarship for a poor child through their assumption of their own housework, cleaning, washing, cooking. In doing this, they are likewise witnessing to the mothers that work has dignity, and the mothers have commented that if the Sisters can do this, they should be able to do likewise.

This year the Sisters' school day will end at 1:30 pm, enabling them to do more home visiting, adult education, catechizing, and other apostolic works, besides providing them with time to improve themselves spiritually and professionally.

Two of our Sisters, Sister Jean Hurley and Sister Shaun Moran, are working in *Santiago*, part of a team of Maryknoll Fathers, Maryknoll Sisters, Providence Sisters, lay catechists, and married deacons. They live with the Maryknoll Sisters in St. Albert's, a *población* of 123,000 people. This includes the poorest of the poor who live in cardboard houses, and a very low middle class. The streets, for the most part, are unpaved; there are few sidewalks; there is no water except from midnight to 7:00 a.m. from December through February. The work in this large parish follows the pastoral priorities of the Archdiocese of *Santiago*: evangelization, formation of Christian communities, and insertion of the Church in the world.

The team helps to form Christian communities operating without priests, having Scripture readings, prayer, and discussion on faith preparing the people for sacramental living, which will come, hopefully, as deacons are prepared and more priests are available.

In catechesis, the prominent note at St. Albert's is that of evangelizing the parents, who in turn, over a supervised two-year period, prepare their own children for the sacraments. Last year some 800 mother-catechists were involved, many of whom, the priests feel, grew appreciably in their adhesion to Christ, thanks to a deeper knowledge and reflection. As a result, many of these women now sense a new responsibility not only toward their own homes but also toward their neighbors. Many, too, are on their way to a more sacramental life.

In the hope of interesting more men, the team will attempt the "*Renca* Plan" involving fifteen meetings in private homes with obligatory attendance on the part of some eight homogeneous couples.

A Vine Transplanted – Chile

In preparation for Confirmation, courses for pre-teens and teenagers are given by the Sisters. Much is also done in youth work through meetings, discussions and study.

The entire effort of the team is to take the Archdiocesan pastoral plan, with its spelled-out priorities, seriously.

As early as January 1969, Bishop *Gonzales* called a Synod of 330 laymen, 28 Sisters, 45 priests, 3 teaching brothers, and 3 seminarians. The Synod adopted resolutions under the general titles of 1) Pastoral Priorities, 2) Liturgy, 3) the Image of the Church, 4) Base Christian Communities, 5) the Insertion of the Church in the Region of *Maule*, Chile. Father Maney has been appointed episcopal vicar of *Talca* Diocese and is assisted by a Pastoral Council of 5 laymen, a Maryknoll Sister, and a diocesan priest. There is a catechetical council.

The goal of the Pastoral Council here is Christian renewal as presented by Vatican II and as clarified and adapted to the local situation by the Synod of *Talca*. It is being brought about by:

1. Unification of personnel into a team effort

2. Formation of Christian communities, with special emphasis in seeking married deacons for each active community

3. Formation of centers for adult information

4. Special attention to the priorities of the *Talca* Diocese which insists on evangelization over sacramentalization and emphasizes work with adults and youth in contrast to school children. Another important decision of the Synod was to place the country (*campesinos*) apostolate as top priority in the diocese.

With this new plan, all the personnel will be involved in team work with a view toward the whole zone.

The Latin American world is a world in a process of revolution, where violence is present in various ways. The root of much of the violence lies in the serious situation of injustice and alienation affecting life in Latin America. The Latin American Bishops' Conference; it means participating fully in the salvific process that effects the whole man, and it is the Latin American Church that will have to put into effect this theological vision.

A Vine Transplanted – Chile

The Church will need to purify itself of the ambiguous social prestige it now enjoys. It will need to make the message of love it bears credible by lining up clergy on the side of the oppressed peoples.

The Church realizes that *Medellín* is a clarion call and that only a beginning has been made. It is no easy task, for the experience of the Church in Latin America is intimately linked with the history of the people who belong to it, and it reflects all the people's vicissitudes. Added to this is the dimension that because Latin American peoples are culturally dependent, they have never thought of themselves except with patterns borrowed from other peoples. Many leaders in the Latin countries feel that dependence is perhaps the fundamental fact in Latin America's underdevelopment; and since the Church is intimately bound to the social structures, it too is dependent.

These factors and a multitude of others face the Church in Latin America. The great hope of the Church lies in the application of the *Medellín* conference in which the Latin American bishops set out to have the Council's findings adapted for Latin America and by Latin America. It was the most important event of the century for the Church there.

Our Sisters working in cooperation with the pastoral plan for Chile are, hopefully, aware of the social forces reshaping the lives of people today. With an attitude oriented toward the future and rooted in the belief that the Lord is always at work rebuilding and renewing the world, they are happy to share in this mission.

Needless to say, my stay in Chile was one of the most marvelous experiences of my life, and I am grateful to Sisters Matilda, Gertrude Ann, and the other members of the Executive Board for making this possible.

Sincerely,

Sister Margaret Francis Brockamp

A Vine Transplanted – Chile

THE SEAMY SIDE OF CHARITY, by Ivan Illich

America, January 21, 1967, Vol. 116, No. 3 - Used with permission

Five years ago, U.S. Catholics undertook a peculiar alliance for the progress of the Latin American Church. By 1970, ten per cent of the more than 225,000 priests, brothers and sisters would volunteer to be shipped south of the border. In the meantime, the combined U.S. male and female "clergy" in South America has increased by only 1,622. Halfway is a good time to examine whether a program launched is still sailing on course and, more importantly, if its destination still seems worth-while. Numerically, the program was certainly a flop. Should this be a source of disappointment or of relief?

The project relied on an impulse supported by uncritical imagination and sentimental judgment. A pointed finger and a "call for 20,000" convinced many that "Latin America needs YOU." Nobody dared state clearly why, though the first published propaganda included several references to the "Red danger" in four pages of text. The Latin America Bureau of the NCWC attached the word "papal;" to the program, the volunteers, and the call itself.

A campaign for more funds is now being proposed. This is the moment, therefore, at which the call for 20,000 persons and the need for millions of dollars should be re-examined. Both appeals must be submitted to a public debate among U.S. Catholics, from bishop to widow, since they are the ones asked to supply the [personnel] and pay the bill. Critical thinking must prevail. Fancy and colorful campaign slogans for another collection, with their appeal to emotion, will only cloud the real issues. Let us coldly examine the American Church's outburst of charitable frenzy which resulted in the creation of "papal" volunteers, student "mission crusades," the annual CICOP mass assemblies, numerous diocesan mission and new religious communities.

I will not focus on details. The above programs themselves continually study and revise minutiae. Rather, I dare to point out some fundamental facts and implications of the so-called papal plan – part of the many-faceted effort to keep Latin America within the ideologies of the West. Church policy makers in the United States must face up to the socio-political consequences involved in their well-intentioned missionary ventures. They must review their vocation as Christian theologians and their actions as Western politicians.

Men and money sent with missionary motivation carry a foreign Christian image, a foreign pastoral approach and a foreign political message. They also bear the mark of North American capitalism of the 1950s. Why not, for once, consider the shady side of charity; weigh the inevitable burdens foreign help imposes on the South American Church; taste the bitterness of the damage done by our sacrifices? If, for example, U.S. Catholics would simply turn from the dream of "ten percent," and do some honest thinking about the implications of their help, the awakened awareness of intrinsic fallacies could lead to sober, meaningful generosity.

But let me be more precise. The unquestionable joys of giving and the fruits of receiving should be treated as two distinctly separate chapters. I propose to delineate *only the negative* results that foreign money, men and ideas produce in the South American Church, in order that the future U.S. program may be tailored accordingly.

During the past five years, the cost of operating the Church in Latin America has multiplied many times. There is no precedent for a similar rate of increase in Church expenses on a continental scale. Today, one Catholic university, mission society or radio chain may cost more to operate than the whole country's Church a decade ago. Most of the funds for this kind of growth came from outside and flowed from two types of sources. The first is the Church itself, which raised its income in three ways:

1. Dollar by dollar, appealing to the generosity of the faithful, as was done in Germany and the Low Countries by Adveniat, Misereor and Oostpriesterhulp. These contributions reach more than $25 million a year.

2. Through lump sums, made by individual churchmen – such as Cardinal Cushing, the outstanding example; or by institutions-such as the NCWC, transferring $ 1 million from the home missions to the Latin American Bureau.

3. By assigning priests, religious and laymen, all trained at considerable cost and often backed financially in their apostolic undertakings.

A Vine Transplanted – Chile

This kind of foreign generosity has enticed the Latin American Church into becoming a satellite to North Atlantic cultural phenomena and policy. Increased apostolic resources intensified the need for their continued flow and created islands of apostolic well-being, each day farther beyond the capacity of local support. The Latin American Church flowers anew by returning to what the Conquest stamped her: a colonial plant that blooms because of foreign cultivation. Instead of learning either how to get along with less money or close up shop, bishops are being trapped into needing more money now and bequeathing an institution impossible to run in the future. Education, the one true of investment that could give long-range returns, is conceived mostly as training for bureaucrats who will maintain the existing apparatus.

Recently, I saw an example of this in a large group of Latin American priests who had been sent to Europe for advanced degrees. In order to relate the Church to the world, nine-tenths of these men were studying teaching methods – catechetics, pastoral theology or canon law – and thereby not directly advancing their knowledge of either the Church or the world. Only a very few studied the Church in its history and sources, or the world as it is.

It is easy to come by big sums to build a new church in a jungle or a high school in a suburb, and then to staff the plants with new missioners. A patently irrelevant pastoral system is artificially and expensively sustained, while basic research for a new and vital one is considered an extravagant luxury. Scholarships for non-ecclesiastical humanist studies, seed money for imaginative pastoral experimentation, grants for documentation and research to make specific constructive criticism – all run the frightening risk of threatening our temporal structures, clerical plants and "good business" methods.

Even more surprising than churchly generosity for churchly concern is a second source of money. A decade ago, the Church was like an impoverished *grande dame* trying to keep up an imperial tradition of almsgiving from her reduced income. In the more than a century since Spain lost Latin America, the Church has steadily lost government grants, patrons' gifts and, finally, the revenue from its former lands. According to the colonial concept of charity, the Church lost its power to help the poor. It came to be considered a historical relic, inevitably the ally of conservative politicians.

A Vine Transplanted – Chile

By 1966, almost the contrary seem true – at least, at first sight. The Church has become an agent trusted to run programs aimed at social change. It is committed enough to produce some results. But when it is threatened by real change, it withdraws rather than permit social awareness to spread like wildfire. The smothering of the Brazilian radio schools by a high Church authority is a good example.

Thus Church discipline assures the donor that his money does twice the job in the hands of a priest. It will not evaporate, nor will it be accepted for what it is: publicity for private enterprise and indoctrination to a way of life that the rich have chosen as suitable for the poor. The receiver inevitably gets the message: the "padre" stands on the side of W.R. Grace and Co., Esso, the Alliance for Progress, democratic government, the AFL-CIO and whatever is holy in the Western pantheon.

Opinion is divided, of course, on whether the Church went heavily into social projects because it could thus obtain funds "for the poor," or whether it went after the funds because it could thus contain Castroism and assure its institutional respectability. By becoming an "official" agency of one kind of progress, the Church ceases to speak for the underdog who is outside all agencies but who is an ever-growing majority. By accepting the power to help, the Church necessarily must denounce a Camilo Torres, who symbolizes the power of renunciation. Money thus builds the Church a "pastoral" structure beyond its means and makes it a political power.

Superficial emotional involvement obscures rational thinking about American international "assistance." Healthy guilt feelings are repressed by a strangely motivated desire to "help" in Vietnam. Finally, our generation begins to cut through the rhetoric of patriotic "loyalty." We stumblingly recognize the perversity of our power politics and the destructive direction of our warped efforts to impose unilaterally "our way of life" on all. We have not yet begun to face the seamy side of clerical man-power involvement and the Church's complicity in stifling universal awakening too revolutionary to lie quietly within the "Great Society."

I know that there is no foreign priest or nun so shoddy in his work that through his stay in Latin America he has not enriched some life; and that there is no missioner so incompetent that through him Latin America has not made some small contribution to Europe and North America. But neither our admiration for conspicuous generosity, nor our fear of making bitter enemies out of lukewarm friends, must stop us from facing the facts. Missioners sent to Latin America can make 1) an alien Church more foreign, 2) an over-staffed Church priest-ridden and 3) bishops into abject beggars. Recent public discord has shattered the unanimity of the national consensus on Vietnam. I hope that public awareness of the repressive and corruptive elements contained in "official" ecclesiastical assistance programs will give rise to a real sense of guilt: guilt for having wasted the lives of young men and women dedicated to the task of evangelization in Latin America.

Massive, indiscriminate importation of clergy helps the ecclesiastical bureaucracy survive in its own colony, which every day becomes more foreign and comfortable. This immigration helps to transform the old-style hacienda of God (on which the people were only squatters) into the Lord's supermarket, with catechisms, liturgy and other means of grace heavily in stock. It makes contented consumers out of vegetating peasants, demanding clients out of former devotees. It lines the sacred pockets, providing refuge for men who are frightened by secular responsibility.

Churchgoers, accustomed to priests, novenas, books and culture from Spain (quite possibly to Franco's picture in the rectory), now meet a new type of executive, administrative and financial talent promoting a certain type of democracy as the Christian ideal. The people soon see that the Church is distant, alienated from them — an imported, specialized operation, financed from abroad, which speaks with a holy, because foreign, accent.

This foreign transfusion – and the hope for more – gave ecclesiastical pusillanimity a new lease on life, another chance to make the archaic and colonial system work. If North America and Europe send enough priests to fill the vacant parishes, there is no need to consider laymen – unpaid for part-time work – to fulfill most evangelical tasks; no need to re-examine the structure of the parish, the function of the priest, the Sunday obligation and clerical sermon; no need for exploring the use of the married diaconate, new forms of celebration of the Word and Eucharist and intimate familial celebrations of conversion to the gospel in the milieu of the home. The promise of more clergy is like a bewitching siren. It makes the chronic surplus of clergy in Latin America invisible and it makes it impossible to diagnose this surplus as the gravest illness of the Church. Today, this pessimistic evaluation is slightly altered by a courageous and imaginative few – non-Latins among them – who see, study and strive for true reform.

A large proportion of Latin American church personnel are presently employed in private institutions that serve the middle and upper classes and frequently produce highly respectable profits; this on a continent where there is a desperate need for teachers, nurses and social workers in public institutions that serve the poor. A large part of the clergy is engaged in bureaucratic functions, usually related to peddling sacraments, sacramental and superstitious "blessings." Most of them live in squalor. The Church, unable to use its personnel in pastorally meaningful tasks cannot even support its priests and the 670 bishops who govern them. Theology is used to justify this system, canon law to administer it and foreign clergy to create a world-wide consensus on the necessity of its continuation.

A healthy sense of values empties the seminaries and the ranks of the clergy much more effectively than a lack of discipline and generosity. In fact, the new mood of well-being makes the ecclesiastical career more attractive to the self-seeker. Bishops then turn servile beggars, become temped to organize safaris, and hunt out foreign priests and funds for constructing such anomalies as minor seminaries. As long as such expeditions succeed, it will be difficult, if not impossible, to take the emotionally harder road: to ask ourselves honestly if we need such game.

Exporting church employees to Latin America masks a universal and unconscious fear of a new Church. North and South American authorities, differently motivated but equally fearful, become accomplices in maintaining a clerical and irrelevant Church. Sacralizing employees and property, this Church becomes progressively more blind to the possibilities of sacralizing person and community.

It is hard to help by refusing to give alms. I remember once having stopped food distributions from sacristies in an area where there was great hunger. I still feel the sting of an accusing voice saying: "Sleep well for the rest of your life with dozens of children's deaths on your conscience." Even some doctors prefer aspirins to radical surgery. They feel no guilt having the patient die of cancer, but fear the risk of applying the knife. The courage needed today is that expressed by Daniel Berrigan, S.J., writing of Latin

A Vine Transplanted – Chile

America: "I suggest we stop sending anyone or anything for three years and dig in and face our mistakes and find out how not to canonize them."

From six years' experience of training hundreds of foreign missioners assigned to Latin America, I know that real volunteers increasingly want to face the truth that puts their faith to the test. Superiors, who shift personnel by their administrative decisions but do not have to live with the ensuing deceptions, are emotionally handicapped facing these realities.

The U.S. Church must face the painful side of generosity: the burden that a life gratuitously offered imposes on the recipient. The men who go to Latin America must humbly accept the possibility that they are useless or even harmful, although they give all they have. They must accept the fact that a limping ecclesiastical assistance program uses them as palliatives to ease the pain of a cancerous structure, the only hope that the prescription will give the organism enough time and rest to initiate a spontaneous healing. Much more probably, the pharmacist's pill will both stop the patient from seeking a surgeon's advice and addict him to the drug.

Foreign missioners increasingly realize that they heeded a call to plug the holes in a sinking ship because the officers did not dare launch the life rafts. Unless this is clearly seen, men who obediently offer the best years of their lives will find themselves tricked into a useless struggle to keep a doomed liner afloat as it limps through uncharted seas.

We must acknowledge that missioners can be pawns in a world ideological struggle and that it is blasphemous to use the gospel to prop up any social or political system. When men and money are sent into a society within the framework of a program, they bring ideas that live after them. It has been pointed out, in the case of the Peace Corps, that the cultural mutation catalyzed by a small foreign group might be more effective than all the immediate services it renders. The same can be true of the North American missioner – close to home, having great means at his disposal, frequently on a short-term assignment – who moves into an area of intense U.S. cultural and economic colonization. He is part of this sphere of influence and, at times, intrigue. Through the U.S. missioner, the United States shadows and colors the public image of the Church. The influx of U.S. missioners coincides with the Alliance for Progress, Camelot, and CIA projects and looks like a baptism of these! The Alliance appears directed by Christian justice and is not seen for what it is: a deception designed to maintain the status quo, albeit variously motivated. During the program's first five years, the net capital leaving Latin America has tripled. The program is too small to permit even the achievement of a threshold of sustained growth. It is a bone thrown to the dog, that he remain quiet in the backyard of the Americas.

Within these realities, the U.S. missioner tends to fulfill the traditional role of a colonial power's lackey chaplain. The dangers implicit in Church use of foreign money assume the proportion of caricature when this aid is administered by a "gringo" to keep the "underdeveloped" quiet. It is, of course, too much to ask of most Americans that they make sound, clear and outspoken criticisms of U.S. socio-political aggression in Latin America; even more difficult that they do so without the bitterness of the expatriate or the opportunism of the turncoat.

Groups of U.S. missioners cannot avoid projecting the image of "U.S. outposts." Only individual Americans mixed in with local men could avoid this distortion. The U.S. missioner of necessity is an "undercover" agent – albeit unconscious – for U.S. social and political consensus. But, consciously and purposely, he wishes to bring the values of his Church to South America; adaptation and selection seldom reach the level of questioning the values themselves.

The situation was not so ambiguous ten years ago, when in good conscience mission societies were channels for the flow of traditional U.S. Church hardware to Latin America. Everything from the Roman collar to parochial schools, from the CCD to Catholic universities, was considered salable merchandise in the new Latin American market. Not much salesmanship was needed to convince the Latin bishops to give the "Made in U.S.A." label a try.

In the meantime, however, the situation has changed considerably. The U.S. Church is shaking from the first findings of a scientific and massive self-evaluation. Not only methods and institutions, but also the ideologies that they imply, are subject to examination and attack. The self-confidence of the American ecclesiastical salesman is therefore shaky. We see the strange paradox of a man attempting to implant, in a really different culture, structures and programs that are now rejected in the country of their origin. (I recently heard of a Catholic grammar school being planned by U.S.

personnel in a Central American city parish where there are already a dozen public schools.)

There is an opposite danger, too. Latin America can no longer tolerate being a haven for U.S. liberals who cannot make their point at home, an outlet for apostles too "apostolic" to find their vocation as competent professionals within their own community. The hardware salesman threatens to dump second-rate imitations of parishes, schools and catechisms – outmoded even in the United States – all around the continent. The traveling escapist threatens to further confuse a foreign world with his superficial protests, which were not viable even at home.

The American Church of the Vietnam generation finds it difficult to engage in foreign aid without exporting either its solutions or its problems. Both are prohibitive luxuries for developing nations. Mexicans, to avoid offending the sender, pay high duties for useless or unasked-for gifts sent them by well-meaning American friends. Gift-givers must think not of this moment and of this need, but in terms of a full generation, of the future effects. Gift-planners must ask if the global value of the gift in men, money and ideas is worth the price the recipient will ultimately have to pay for it. As Fr. Berrigan suggests, the rich and powerful can decide not to give; the poor can hardly refuse to accept. Since almsgiving conditions the beggar's mind, the Latin American bishops are not entirely at fault in asking for misdirected and harmful foreign aid. A large measure of the blame lies with the underdeveloped ecclesiology of U.S. clerics who direct the "sale" of American good intentions.

The U.S. Catholic wants to be involved in an ecclesiologically valid program, not its subsidiary political and social programs designed to influence the growth of developing nations according to anybody's social doctrine, be it even described as the Pope's. The heart of the discussion is therefore not *how* to send more men and money but rather *why* they should be sent at all. The Church, in the meantime, is in no critical danger. We are tempted to shore up and salvage structures rather than question their purpose and truth. Hoping to glory in the works of our hands, we feel guilty, frustrated and angry when part of the building starts to crumble. Instead of believing in the Church, we frantically attempt to construct it according to our own cloudy cultural image. We want to build community, relying on techniques, and are blind to the latent desire for unity that is trying to express itself among men. In fear, we plan *our* Church with statistics, rather than trustingly search for it. [13]

Central America: The Call to a New Transplanting

> *I myself will take a shoot from the very top of a cedar and plant it;*
>
> *I will break off a tender sprig from its topmost shoots and plant it on a high and lofty mountain. On the mountain heights of Israel I will plant it; it will produce branches and bear fruit and become a splendid cedar.*
>
> *Birds of every kind will nest in it; they will find shelter in the shade of its branches. (Ez. 17: 22-23) (NIV)* [14]

The congregation's General Chapter of 1984 invited the delegates to focus on international missions. Sister Elaine Gehling, contact person for Chile, reported on key activities, trends, and future visions articulated by the sisters in Chile. Sister Darleen Chmielewski, delegate from Chile, addressed the Chapter body, explaining her own decision to leave Chile, take some sabbatical time, and to explore how "to live a simple, radical, Gospel life in a complex world." [15] Her words were heard as a challenge to the community to broaden its horizons and to give corporate witness. The proposal she presented, *Report on Chile and Future Missionary Projections*, recommended a congregational call to begin a mission in another country. Sisters Elaine and Darleen provided further reflection on criteria for discernment for future missioners and missions and on places being considered: Bolivia, Nicaragua, Haiti, Dominican Republic, Guatemala, Uganda, as well as other locations in Chile.

In response to the report, the delegates verbalized support for the congregation's missioners, articulated questions about the continuation of the Chile mission, and expressed encouragement for the ongoing discernment of future options. It seemed to the Chapter body that the proposal and process was not at a concrete enough stage for a vote of approval and suggested forming a support group for sisters interested in ministry beyond the United States to engage in more specific planning. An invitation to the entire congregation remained, nonetheless: to intentionally cross any personal borders that might separate us from others in need.

The group that began to gather included sisters who were interested in going to another country for long-term mission or for short-term immersion experiences, as well as those who wanted to help discern the places and the processes. During their discussion they were in dialogue with those already working in other countries. Participants called the group "Border Crossing" and met several times. Some sisters were personally discerning whether to be available for a new mission, and the group did, indeed, provide mutual support in their decision making. Discernment of place gradually became more focused on Central America, given the violence and upheaval in the region and the fact that the congregation had recently declared a corporate stance supporting sanctuary for Central American refugees.

Sister Carol Besch describes her experience in the group:

> *I remember clearly in one of these "Border Crossing" workshops that we were asked to think of an image of what ministry in another country would mean for each one of us. The image that came to me was that of a bridge spanning the chasm that exists between the U.S. and Central America. I saw the possibility of my very body becoming that bridge. Maybe in the same way that Paul speaks of Christ's mission of reconciliation '...you who were far off have become brought near by the sacrifice of Christ, who is our peace. Christ made both groups into one and broke down the dividing wall of hostility between us... you are no longer strangers and aliens, but you are citizens... (Excerpts based on Eph. 2: 13-14, 19). I saw the possibility of expressing to the Salvadorans another face of the U.S. people – one that was opposed to the military domination of the U.S. in the Central American countries. I also saw our Franciscan presence in Central America as a way to bring to light what the U.S. military presence was actually doing to the lives of the poor.* [16]

The "Border Crossers" ultimately suggested a fact-finding trip through Central America to assess the greatest need and to discern a location. Meanwhile, Darleen had returned to *Chillán*, Chile, awaiting concrete movement on the proposal, and lived with Kentucky Ursuline Sister Elizabeth (Mimi) Ballard. Mimi was personally ready for a change and had asked about the possibility of joining the new venture. Sister Pat Farrell was in a sabbatical program also anticipating being part of the project. Sister of Charity Peggy O'Neill had continued to be in communication with the Dubuque Franciscans, hoping to join the group as well. From the outset there was openness to making the mission to a new country an inter-congregational undertaking. Pat Farrell organized a month-long exploratory trip in June 1986, to *Chiapas* in Mexico, Guatemala, Honduras, El Salvador and Nicaragua. The plan was to bring information back to a gathering of

A Vine Transplanted – The Call to a New Transplanting

those sisters who were ready to be part of the mission and to discern together where and when to begin.

Darleen, Pat, Mimi and Peg set out on what proved to be quite an adventure. The first thing that became apparent to them was that the goal of assessing the greatest need was ill-conceived. In each country the need was overwhelming, varying mostly with cultural and historical factors. Compelling hardship was everywhere. The only place that seemed a little less in need was Mexico. The sisters' primary interest in visiting *Chiapas*, Mexico, was the possibility of working with the large number of Guatemalan refugees who had crossed the border fleeing the genocide in Guatemala. Bishop *Samuél Ruíz*, known as a prophetic advocate for the Mayan indigenous peoples of *Chiapas*, personally hosted them and escorted them around the diocese. There was a great deal of pastoral dynamism evidenced throughout the diocese: clear options for the indigenous and the poor, for team ministry, for formation of grassroots leaders. The morale of pastoral workers, the majority Mexican, was very high. The diocese didn't seem in great need of foreigners as supplemental pastoral workers and expressed a preference for Mexicans to work with the influx of Guatemalan refugees.

In Honduras the poverty was extreme and appalling, but the country was not in the throes of civil war. The violence in Guatemala, though somewhat hidden, was disturbing and directed mostly toward the very vulnerable Mayan indigenous population. The sisters were hosted by the bishop of *Huehuetenango*, among others. In El Salvador they met with liberation theologian *Jon Sobrino* for his perspective on the entire region. El Salvador's Episcopal Vicar for Pastoral Activity showed the sisters a number of locations in need of help. In Nicaragua, church workers told the sisters that the cardinal of *Managua* would not receive anyone sympathetic to the *Sandinistas* or with progressive pastoral tendencies. There was great need in Nicaragua and there would be much the sisters could do, but it would be better, perhaps, not coordinated through official Catholic Church structures.

Later in the summer of 1986 the four travelers shared their findings in a discernment gathering at the Franciscan convent in Niles, Illinois, facilitated by Sisters Susan Seitz and Mary Lenz. It was an unspoken assumption that only one country would be chosen. There was great attraction to working with the Mayan culture in Guatemala, but it was unrealistic to expect of those who had no Latin American experience or comfort with Spanish to

A Vine Transplanted – The Call to a New Transplanting

learn the indigenous language. There were other non-indigenous areas in Guatemala where newer people could work, but in the discernment the group was also drawn to the extreme needs in Nicaragua and El Salvador. The final decision was to send sisters to both Guatemala and El Salvador. Sisters Darleen Chmielewski (age 44) and Mimi Ballard would begin as soon as possible in Guatemala, hoping that Maureen Leach (age 30) and Dianna Ortiz (age 28) would soon be able to join them. Sisters Kay Koppes (age 40) and Pat Farrell (age 39) would begin in El Salvador, with Peggy O'Neill (age 47) joining them six months later and Carol Besch (age 38) within the year.

Family picnic in Waterloo: gathering for mutual support during the war years

Families of those about to leave for Central America had mixed reactions, to say the least. Pat's mother responded saying *"Now that's really crazy! They're killing people over there. Why don't you stay home until I die and then go?"* Wanting to be supportive, she said to Pat the next day: *"I've been thinking about it. I can really understand your wanting to go help people in that war situation. If I were younger I would go with you!"*

A Vine Transplanted – The Call to a New Transplanting

Knowing the worry their decision was evoking in their families, the sisters going to Central America organized periodic gatherings of themselves and their parents during the war years, so that the parents could become acquainted and be an ongoing support to one another. There were, in fact, a number of phone calls among them for mutual updating on news they received from or about their daughters.

Guatemala (3 years of congregational presence, 1986-1989)

Sowing, by Julia Esquivel, Guatemala poet

Because you can't
kill death with death,
Sow life
and kill death with life.
But you can only harvest the infinite, complete, and perennial,
through your own death,
by loving as much as you can.

For you can only
sow life with life
since life, as love,
is stronger than death. [17]

Transplanting in the Soil of Guatemala: Beginnings

With eager anticipation, Dubuque Franciscan Sister Darleen Chmielewski (age 44) and Ursuline Sister Elizabeth (Mimi) Ballard began the inter-congregational mission to Guatemala, arriving by plane on September 10, 1986. They came without a specific commitment of place or work, but with a clear preference for working with Mayan indigenous peoples. They intended to explore concrete options after arriving in Guatemala. Both Darleen and Mimi had been part of the fact-finding trip to Central America during which they had met the bishop of *Huehuetenango, Victor Hugo Martinez.* He had been recommended to Darleen by her contacts at the Better World Movement, and the two newly-arrived missioners sought him out soon after their arrival. During their first month in Guatemala Mimi and Darleen visited other priests and religious and explored some of the country, mostly in the state of *Huehuetenango* which forms Guatemala's western border with Mexico. They stayed in *Huehuetenango's* diocesan center, formerly Maryknoll's Latin American language school, before it was moved to *Cochabamba, Bolivia.*

A Vine Transplanted – Guatemala

The bishop welcomed them to the diocese, assuring them that the situation was less dangerous than it had been in the early 1980s. He supported their interest in working in an indigenous village and suggested two places in the diocese where he hoped to have sisters. Darleen and Mimi visited both places and easily chose *San Miguel Acatán*. The people there had suffered intensely at the hands of the military. They had been in danger simply from their association with the Church and told horrible stories of what had happened to them. Many had fled and in 1986 were beginning to return to *San Miguel Acatán*. The sisters wanted to support them as they returned to begin again.

The church of San Miguel Acatán

With that desire Mimi and Darleen moved to *San Miguel Acatán*. Their new home was a spacious convent on the second floor of the parish center, formerly a school building. The school had been built by Maryknoll priests who began working in *San Miguel* in the 1940s. The priests had also begun a

A Vine Transplanted – Guatemala

clinic and furniture and rug-making cooperatives. The school closed in the 1970s because of the escalating violence in the area. As soon as conditions allowed, a small group of U.S. School Sisters of Notre Dame came, ran the clinic and taught the children. The circumstances in *San Miguel* at that time were those of a typical Mayan village. The overall literacy rate was ten percent. Eighty percent of children under the age of five were malnourished. One in ten children died in infancy. It had been a compelling choice for the Notre Dame Sisters to work in *San Miguel*, but they left in 1980 for personal reasons and because of increasing violence. Darleen and Mimi were the first to inhabit the convent again after the Notre Dame sisters departed. The house was simple but adequate. There was a wood-burning stove for cooking and the people of the parish kept them supplied with firewood.

The sisters' early days were spent visiting homes and becoming acquainted with the *Kanjobal*-speaking people and culture of *San Miguel Acatán*. It was interesting for them to step into the brilliant woven colors, communal values and pageantry evident in the Mayan world. Faith was central to village life, in a fascinating syncretistic blend of Catholic and traditional Mayan practices.

Mayan woman, kneeling in church

A Vine Transplanted – Guatemala

The parishioners were welcoming and responsive to the sisters' pastoral outreach, hoping that they would remain for a long time in *San Miguel Acatán,* but expecting that the new sisters would leave them as the ones before them had. The sisters assured them that they had no intention of abandoning them and expected to be with them for many years.

The Mayan people were also reserved, somewhat closed and very protective of the sisters, not wanting them to go anywhere alone. The sisters began to notice a certain secrecy and intrigue in their new environment, which was understandable given the extreme violence to which the people had so recently been subjected. The guarded demeanor of the indigenous was a contrast, however, to the openness and ready friendships Mimi and Darleen missed from their experience with the people in Chile. It was clear that there was much for them to learn in order to work effectively in Guatemala.

They discovered that Guatemala is a beautiful country. It has a rich variety of landscapes and climates, dominated by high mountains and winding roads, with breathtakingly beautiful panoramas at each turn. It was the center of the ancient well-developed Mayan civilization, dating back thousands of years. The inaccessibility of the remote mountain areas helped the Mayan population survive various waves of colonization with its language and culture intact. But life was hard and poverty extreme among the different indigenous groups.

Doña Juanita making tortillas

A Vine Transplanted – Guatemala

Their agricultural labor provided them with minimal subsistence because the majority, not owning land, had to pay wealthy elite landowners a sizeable portion of their income. The situation of the indigenous was a recipe for social unrest and potential revolution. In the 1940s democratic reformist governments began to address such issues and to make changes. The United Fruit Company, heavily invested in Guatemala and fearing risk to its interests, called the changes "communist" and asked the CIA to help stop them.

Declassified CIA documents report that the U.S. government organized, funded and equipped a coup in 1954, ousting the elected president, *Arbenz*, and setting in place a massive counter-insurgency strategy resulting in four decades of violent repression. In the '60s and '70s the ratio of U.S. military advisors to Guatemalan military was the highest in Latin America, while the development of death squads was simultaneously on the rise in the country. In 1977 the Carter administration cut U.S. military aid to Guatemala based on its scandalous human rights record. Aid was resumed under President Reagan with Israel acting as a surrogate supplier of weapons.

In 1981 a new *guerrilla* group coalesced and a large-scale counter-insurgency campaign was launched, focused in the Departments of *Quiche* and *Huehuetenango*, killing an estimated 11,000, mostly Mayan civilians. Villages and crops were burned and massacres carried out unscrupulously in remote areas where such violence could, to some degree, be hidden and denied. During the 36 years of Guatemala's civil war 1.5 million people were displaced, many fleeing into Mexico, and more than 1 million migrating to the U.S.

In 1982 a coup put General *Efraín Ríos Montt* in power and an environment of fear and terror ruled. The army destroyed over 600 villages during his presidency. In 1982 alone there were 18,000 documented state-sponsored killings. Large numbers of rural civilians were conscripted into the civilian self-defense patrol, essentially civilian paramilitary bands. The military's operating assumption was that anyone living in an isolated mountain village was supportive of the *guerrillas* and therefore to be eliminated, although the *guerrilla*'s military capacity never posed a real threat to the Guatemalan state. There was growing international pressure to condition military aid based on improved human rights conditions. A gesture in that direction was the 1986 election of a civilian president, *Vicente Cerezo*, a Christian

A Vine Transplanted – Guatemala

Democrat. The civil war continued, but its image and tone were changing. Gradually the massacres and assassinations decreased, but the kidnappings and disappearances increased, accompanied by the use of illegal clandestine prisons.

This was the Guatemala of 1986 when Darleen and Mimi moved to *San Miguel Acatán*. Darleen reflects on her experience of it:

> *The people were still oppressed but carrying on with life, doing the best they could. With hindsight, I would say that I was blindsided by the repression and danger, and now I feel betrayed. I'm not sure people were being honest with us about the level of danger. Pastorally, I had started meetings in homes. Now as I look back on it, I think it was pretty dangerous to be in peoples' homes and forming leaders after previous pastoral leaders had fled or had been killed. It didn't seem so risky to me at the time. I thought I was prepared for the dangers of Guatemala from my experience in Chile. Yet we didn't meet a single family in San Miguel Acatán who hadn't lost a family member in the war. I was working with the catechists, affirming them, and was edified by their commitment. If they said they would do something, they did it... No matter what horrors were taking place all around them during the war, they went out to fulfill pastoral commitments, in spite of the danger.* [18]

In September of 1987, just a year after Darleen and Mimi's arrival, they were joined by Franciscan Sister Maureen Leach (age 31) and Ursuline Sister Dianna Ortiz (age 29). Maureen had just made her final vows on August 11. She had been working with farmworkers in the Rio Grande Valley. With her five years in Texas plus her college major in Spanish and semester in Spain, she was already a fluent Spanish speaker. Dianna had been working as a kindergarten teacher. While she was culturally Hispanic and the language familiar to her ears, she did not yet speak Spanish. Dianna met Maureen in Texas and they traveled together by bus to Guatemala. The windows on the bus didn't open, the heater didn't work, and the bus broke down in Mexico and took several hours to fix. But none of that seemed to dampen their eagerness to get to their new mission. Dubuque Franciscans from El Salvador met them in Guatemala City for a welcome and an overnight together. Darleen and Mimi met Maureen and Dianna at the bus terminal in the city of Huehuetenango. From there it was another lengthy bus ride through the mountains to San Miguel Acatán, shortened by much animated conversation.

A Vine Transplanted – Guatemala

Sisters wearing Mayan clothes, gifts from the people

Maureen and Dianna quickly settled into their new home. With the dampness of the rainy season and cold of the altitude, the sisters decided to have a fireplace built. The project, using mostly natural stone, cost $50, including labor and lunches for the workers. It was double what they had anticipated, but all were happy for the warmth provided by the fireplace.

After some accommodation time in *San Miguel Acatán*, Dianna went to *Antigua, Guatemala*, for a few months of language school. Her time there overlapped with two members of the inter-congregational team from El Salvador: first with Sister of Charity Peggy O'Neill, and later with Franciscan Sister Carol Besch. By mid-December of 1987, Dianna returned to *San Miguel Acatán* and the team of four sisters was again complete.

Language was a challenge for all the sisters. *Kanjobal* was the native tongue of the people of *San Miguel Acatán* and its surrounding villages. Women and pre-school children typically spoke only *Kanjobal*, so the sisters were unable to communicate with them in Spanish. Before going to school, children enrolled in a preparatory year of Spanish, the language of formal education. Many of the men spoke Spanish, but the more remote the location of their village, the less that was the case. Much of the time the sisters were accompanied in their work by interpreters. The language does not translate easily because *Kanjobal* is very concrete. For any abstract term, the interpreters would have to invent a concrete example to describe it. Or at times an interpreter would talk about something entirely different in *Kanjobal* when not easily finding words to translate what the sisters were saying in Spanish.

Another difficulty was that one of the few written materials translated into *Kanjobal* was the Christian Scripture (the New Testament). The Hebrew Scriptures had not been translated. When used in the liturgy, they had to be translated on the spot by the lector. There were three versions of the alphabet and no common agreement among linguistic, government and religious groups, or even among the sisters in *San Miguel Acatán* about which to use.

The sisters tried a variety of strategies for learning *Kanjobal*. Darleen had studied with two Spanish-speaking women, *Malín* and *Petrona*, and then practiced with catechists and women in the sewing group. Some of the sisters went to *Jacaltenango*, another town a few mountains away, and studied with a teacher recommended to them by Maryknoll missioners. The teachers there did not know Kanjobal but did know grammar structures of Mayan languages. That proved helpful. The sisters had not received the telegram that told them to bring a native speaker with them for the class. Though the sisters did not come away speaking the language, the experience helped them understand grammatical structures and the thinking of the people, shaped and expressed through *Kanjobal*. In *San Miguel*, some bilingual women, former teachers with the Notre Dame sisters, served as tutors and ongoing guides of both language and culture.

Maureen was particularly determined to learn the language. In a letter she states:

> *I used to carry a notebook around and try to write down new expressions. I also recorded people saying things. I listened to the recordings at night when I was getting ready to go to sleep. I was hoping the language could become part of me. …The study of the language helped shape my understanding of the spirituality of the people and helped transform my own spirituality.*

Planting and Tending: Pastoral Work in San Miguel Acatán

> *The true meaning of life is to plant trees*
> *under whose shade you do not expect to sit.*
> *–Nelson Henderson*

A Vine Transplanted – Guatemala

Working in the garden on steep mountainside in Guatemala

Mayan spirituality is very connected to the earth. Reflecting that cultural value, a young refugee girl gifted the sisters with of a plot of land to use for a garden. Darleen quipped: *"But you know how the terrain is here. We could fall off our land and break a leg!"*

In truth, they were planting much more than a garden. By the beginning of 1989 Darleen and Mimi had established areas of work and Dianna and Maureen were finding how they could best serve. The four of them together with pastoral leaders had identified needs and established long-term pastoral goals:

1.   Formation of animators of the faith and/or community coordinators.

2.   Continuation of the traditional pastoral work of forming and supporting catechists, youth groups, liturgical leaders, Eucharistic ministers, ministers to the sick and elderly.

3.   Promotion of the indigenous Mayan culture by affirming cultural values, developing materials to teach indigenous language and culture, and discovering seeds of the Word in the culture and incorporating them into the faith life of the people.

A Vine Transplanted – Guatemala

4. Promotion of women through literacy, leadership, and incorporating cultural expressions.

5. Promotion of family life through formation of young couples and support for families in crisis.

6. Improvement of health programs, training health promoters and midwives, community education about hygiene and nutrition.

7. Development of adult and youth education centers for literacy and a variety of skills and crafts.

Sr. Maureen Leach with catechists, preparing to visit a village

A letter from the four sisters to the Dubuque congregation describes these visits:

> *The people welcome us very warmly. … When we arrive, the people are gathered, the path to the village is covered with fresh pine needles and flowers, and the people greet us with song, handshakes, knee hugs (from the children) and showers of colorful flower petals. … Our visits to the aldeas enable us to join with the people in living a simple life-style. There is no electricity or running water. Most people sleep on boards or on dirt floors. One often has to let go of modesty because some aldeas have no outhouses, very few bushes, and many young curious eyes!*

A Vine Transplanted – Guatemala

Baptism, San Miguel Acatán

The sisters noted with amusement that when they traveled to the *aldeas* with the priest the communities served them a meal of chicken soup; when they went accompanied by local catechists they were served eggs and tortillas; and when they went to the most remote and extremely impoverished village they were served tortillas with salt and chili peppers. Darleen describes:

> *When we stayed overnight, we slept on boards; in the morning we were allotted a small tin cup of water to wash the sleep out of our eyes, brush our teeth and take a small sip. I was impressed with the peoples' priority to introduce us to all the communities regardless of the distance and poverty. In Chile we were attempting to decentralize parish as a community of communities and I found it already flourishing in San Miguel. Of course it was nourished by the blood of many. The Guatemalan people taught me that water was so precious that for many years I took my showers here in the U.S. seeing the women scurry down steep mountain paths to get water from the spring or river and balance [it] just on their heads as they climbed back up.* [19]

Darleen worked with a cultural group to promote the integration of Mayan traditions and Catholic practices. The group restored an ancient birth rite celebrated 20 days (one month by the Mayan calendar) after the birth of a child. A prayer in Mayan communal style included participation by parents, grandparents, godparents, a catechist, and the midwife. All were invited to bless the child and to bring symbolic gifts. The Mayan custom was to put hot chili on the tongue of the child so she or he would grow up to be truthful. The restored birth rite used salt and a Scripture reading about the salt of the earth.

A Vine Transplanted – Guatemala

Sr. Darleen with newlyweds and their family

Darleen also acquired a sewing machine and taught sewing, with a goal to start a mini sewing cooperative of baby clothes. She worked with the diocesan committee establishing parish coops to obtain fertilizer at a reduced rate. Adult education was a primary focus for her, as well. She worked with catechist formation and taught Spanish literacy and Bible study classes. She used the Bible to teach people to read *Kanjobal*. Much of her work with families was proactive, forming couples as leaders to give classes in their *aldeas* to strengthen family and marriage relationships.

Maureen writes:

> *We also have a committee on evangelization... seeking ways to help the people rediscover some lost cultural activities and to encourage them to reflect on the meaning of customs they continue to follow. It*

A Vine Transplanted – Guatemala

is an uphill climb because past missionaries have condemned many cultural practices. I notice that Darleen finds ways to bring the beauty of the culture of the ancestors into all her ministry.

Dianna began classes in Spanish and *Kanjobal* with young children, aided by an interpreter. She taught basic skills common in preschool, including activities to increase the children's motor skills. When teaching the alphabet, the children studied the letter "D" (*dientes* — teeth). She incorporated dental hygiene skills and sent each child home with a toothbrush. For most of the children it was their first.

Mimi coordinated the parish clinic and the courses for about fifty health promoters. Since much of the medicine used was from the U.S. she translated labels and instructions. Another major focus of her work was with youth groups and youth leaders. She was, in fact, the deanery coordinator for youth ministry and put a lot of energy into leadership training. In coordination with Darleen's sewing classes, Mimi taught knitting and crocheting. She and Darleen also worked together with families. Mimi focused more on counseling. It was common for people to come to the convent wanting to discuss a crisis in the family. Families were experiencing a great deal of stress due to the economic situation and the war which often resulted in separation of family members.

Two young Mayan girls

A Vine Transplanted – Guatemala

Maureen worked with music and liturgy. She coordinated a liturgy committee, supported two existing choirs of men and began a youth choir. Her guitar classes were especially popular with the youth and she found funds to buy additional guitars. Both the youth choir and guitar classes grew to sizeable numbers. With her particular interest in the *Kanjobal* language, Maureen put together a book of church songs in *Kanjobal* and had one of their language tutors make a tape of the songs so the sisters could study the pronunciation. Maureen accompanied a group of midwives and supported them in their work. She also served as a tutor for students trying to complete the sixth grade by correspondence. That led eventually to her becoming the local coordinator for correspondence courses to complete basic educational levels.

Through Mimi's initiative the sisters acquired a jeep for the parish to support the ministry in *San Miguel Acatán*. Funds for the purchase were raised by a variety of supporters: students from Aquin High School in Cascade, Iowa; students and parishioners in areas where Dubuque Franciscans ministered; and from the Ursuline sisters in Kentucky. Maureen, Darleen and a Latino seminarian joined Fr. Bill Hammer in driving the vehicle to Guatemala from Louisville. The seminarian gave out dollar bills between two holy cards when stopped along the way. It must have served as an effective bribe because the police did not detain them.

Offertory procession dancer

A Vine Transplanted – Guatemala

The jeep was used mostly for long distances, not for travel to most *aldeas* because of lack of roads or their poor condition. The jeep was frequently utilized to drive people to *Huehuetenango*. One time, for example, the sisters were driving a mother with a very sick child to the hospital in *Huehuetenango*. Unfortunately, the child died en route.

Woven throughout the lives and the work of the sisters were two constants: continuous discovery and appreciation of Mayan culture, and the effects of the ongoing civil war. The indigenous people valued processions and seldom missed an occasion for one. Statues dressed in brilliantly-colored native clothing would be carried through the streets. Marimba was the instrument ubiquitously present for both religious and social occasions, and the *son* was the typical dance, simple enough to allow anyone of any age to participate. Flowers, candles, and pine needles were used profusely in ceremonies and celebrations of all kinds.

Darleen describes Christmas in *San Miguel* (letter):

> *"New Year's Eve pm we had a Christmas play with the kids which was a lot of fun. ...The angels' dance was especially cute; they threw flowers and danced with maracas, candles, drums and tambourines. Midnight Mass was almost anti-climactic!"*

Similarly, she describes All Souls' Day in another letter:

> *All the people (except those in the cantinas, which is not a few) are praying a rosary for each deceased – on their knees, in the cemetery, while six marimbas play different tunes, and innumerable cassettes are playing so the dead can dance and be happy. They also put food on the graves, so the dead can eat. Firecrackers are going off constantly and the bells toll every hour.*

Maureen mentions hearing of another custom and not understanding the meaning of it (letter):

> *Yesterday the people told us about a custom where your spirit leaves for twenty days in February and goes to Santa Eulalia (a nearby town). The people eat no sugar during that time, only atol and tamales de frijol (porridge and bean tamales). The customs are fascinating. I would love to find someone who could explain what they mean.*

A Vine Transplanted – Guatemala

The war environment was palpable but very difficult to assess. In a place as remote and isolated as *San Miguel Acatán* it was hard to obtain accurate information about what was happening militarily and politically on either the national or local level. Communications were faulty and sporadic. Much of what the sisters observed seemed to be a mere tip of the iceberg. Yet they had little access to information that would provide a broader perspective. They experienced regular military roundups that forced men between the ages of 18 and 25 into military service. A disproportionately high number of forced recruits were indigenous. Truckloads of military appeared in *San Miguel Acatán* around the time of the town's *fiesta*, the soldiers openly harassing Dianna with flirtatious comments and actions. One way the military would typically wield its power was to oblige *San Miguel*'s men to go out and comb the neighboring hills for *guerrillas*. The sisters mention other experiences in a letter to the community:

> *At Christmas time the comandantes (military commanders) put on a curfew at the time when the traditional posadas [20] were to be celebrated. The Church was charged a fine for ignoring the curfew and holding the posadas. During Lent the military followed us to some of the aldeas and called all the men to a meeting, interrupting our retreat.*

In the first three months of 1988 over 450 people were assassinated in Guatemala and more than 60 disappeared. During March of that year, two military deserters were caught in the area of *San Miguel Acatán*, one shot and the other tortured. Darleen describes other events that took place in the area (letter):

> *Last week we had another guerrilla scare. They blew whistles to round up all the men one night because someone spotted guerrillas in a few of our aldeas, some say buying, others say robbing food.... Some supposedly were caught in Santa Eulalia and were hung alive (not killed) on crosses as torture and a lesson to the people. How much is truth?...It could all be to discourage the refugees in Mexico from returning or put the skids on any Central American peace plan. Who knows?...All I know is after living through the massacres these Migueleños (people of San Miguel Acatán) get panicky and scare me as they run out of town with their clubs and machetes.*

Premature Uprooting:

> *...I tell you, unless a grain of wheat falls into the earth and dies, it remains just a single grain; but if it dies, it bears much fruit.*
> *(John 12:24 NRSV)* [21]

A Vine Transplanted – Guatemala

The complexities of life in an indigenous culture during a civil war were matched by unanticipated complications in the sisters' personal lives. Maureen suffered from amoebas and the resulting dysentery fairly common among missioners in the developing world. However, she was also unable to tolerate the needed medication and developed severe gastritis. As a result she experienced weakness and drastic weight loss, eventually dropping to thirty pounds below the recommended weight for her height. In the spring of 1989, after almost two years in Guatemala, she reluctantly decided to return to the U.S. Maureen moved to San Antonio, Texas, and began a job with *Camino a la Paz* (Path to Peace) Peace and Justice Center, a project of the Inter-congregational Leadership Group of women religious in the city.

In early 1989 Dianna received her first written death threat. Initially she didn't take it very seriously, knowing how common such a thing was in Guatemala. The sisters were more concerned when Dianna received a second threat. When she received a third threat the sisters consulted the acting bishop of *Huehuetenango* about a recommended course of action. He encouraged them not to be overly concerned, but recommended that Dianna leave the country for a few months. He expected that with a little time and distance the situation would resolve itself.

Dianna and Darleen made plans to travel together to the U.S. in July. Both used the time to rest and visit family and friends. The leadership team of Dianna's congregation was concerned but respected her right to make her own decision about staying in Guatemala. Dianna and Darleen returned to Guatemala in mid-September, 1989. Their return flight was routed through Miami where, mysteriously, Dianna's connecting flight to Guatemala had been canceled with no explanation. Darleen and Dianna thought it was odd, but rebooked a flight together and flew to Guatemala City. Darleen recalls deplaning in Guatemala and sensing an ominous sort of darkness. Events soon to follow confirmed her intuition.

One month after returning to *San Miguel Acatán* Dianna received another death threat, which was very disconcerting to Dianna, Darleen and Mimi. Why Dianna was singled out was a mystery. It was also a growing concern and Dianna was frightened. Darleen had seen an advertisement of a month-long Scripture course/renewal program in English in the city of *Antigua*. It was to take place in a walled-in convent with other English-speaking foreigners and seemed a safe place that could afford the time and space for Dianna to think and pray about whether to stay in Guatemala or leave. Before going to the course in *Antigua*, Dianna and Darleen spent a few days in Guatemala City at a guest house for missionaries when another threat was slipped through the mail slot there. They decided to go back to *Huehuetenango* and speak again with the bishop, even if it meant arriving late for the course in *Antigua*. They first went back to *San Miguel Acatán* to update Mimi and to ask her to accompany them to talk with the bishop. While briefly in *San Miguel Acatán*, Dianna received another death threat there, just four days after the last one she had received in Guatemala City. Clearly someone was following her.

The acting bishop of *Huehuetenango* advised Dianna to leave the country. If she chose not to go, the bishop counseled her to make the death threats public, reasoning that the publicity might offer some measure of protection. Dianna was hesitant about publicity lest her parents discover she was in danger. She needed time to think and pray.

Upon their arrival at the retreat house in *Antigua*, Darleen and Dianna requested to share a room on the rear side of the building for Dianna's safety. During their days there Mimi received word of her father's death and quickly made arrangements to return to the U.S. for his wake and funeral. Franciscan Sister Shirley Waldschmitt was in *Antigua* studying Spanish at the time and Carol Besch came from El Salvador to spend time with her. Shirley and Carol met Darleen and Dianna for a meal and could hear Dianna's fear as she related recent happenings. They were extremely concerned.

The night of November 1, 1989, Darleen and Dianna went to a movie with a group from the program they were attending. Dianna told Darleen that she felt someone following her. That night the two prayed together using Jeremiah 37:11 and Dianna made a decision to stay in Guatemala.

On the morning of November 2, 1989, Darleen got up and went to breakfast and class. Dianna told her she wanted to pray first and come later. Dianna went outside to pray in the garden of the retreat house. During that time she was abducted by two armed men, forced onto a bus into Guatemala City and taken to a clandestine prison where she was held, gang raped, and brutally tortured. This brief narrative cannot begin to do justice to Dianna's ensuing history, recounted in her own book, *The Blindfold's Eye*.[22] Her personal testimony of courage, gradual healing, and unwavering commitment to

A Vine Transplanted – Guatemala

the Guatemalan people whose fate she shared, merits a thorough reading. This account will relate briefly how the Franciscan/Ursuline mission in Guatemala evolved in the wake of such a horrific event.

Meanwhile, when it was break time and Dianna still had not come to class, the students began to look for her and found her shawl and watch in the bushes. While Darleen went to the police in *Antigua* to file a missing person's report, others in the group notified people in Guatemala City, among them the archbishop, who publicly denounced Dianna's kidnapping. The news was on that evening's TV news and in all of Guatemala's major newspapers the following morning. Maryknoll's solidarity network activated quick response in the U.S., pressuring the Guatemalan government to act and the U.S. Embassy in Guatemala to intervene. Dianna's torturers were made aware of the publicity by an American who entered the place of her torture, informed them, and told them to leave her alone. The torturers referred to him as their boss and obeyed. He told Dianna that he was going to take her to a friend at the U.S. Embassy who would help her leave the country.

She got into a jeep with him but didn't believe that he was taking her to safety. She left the place of her torture without a blindfold and would be able to identify the location of the clandestine prison as well as the face of this American involved with her torturers. She assumed she was being transported to a place where she would be killed. When the vehicle stopped for a red light she threw open the passenger door, jumped out and ran as far and as fast as she could. She escaped. When she leaned against the doorpost of a house to catch her breath, a small indigenous woman invited her inside, saying she had seen her face on the evening news and wanted to help her. Dianna used the phone to call *Antigua* to report her whereabouts. The Maryknoll priests at the course suggested that she take a taxi to the Maryknoll center house in Guatemala City as a place of safety.

Darleen had gone to Guatemala City to make calls to the U.S. to notify the Ursuline and Franciscan communities of what had happened. She asked Maryknoll missioners for advice about what else she might do to find Dianna. They suggested going to the Chief of Police and made an appointment for the next morning, even though one Maryknoll priest told her he had seen people walk into that office and not walk out. Darleen was waiting to see an official at the Police Academy when she got a phone call from Maryknoll telling her that Dianna was with them at the centerhouse. Darleen recalls: *"I felt such*

126

relief and joy and rushed to see her. Then I looked into her eyes and felt profound sorrow. Shortly afterwards a Maryknoll missioner told us that the police were outside the door and that we needed to seek refuge and safety with the Papal Nuncio."[23]
The Maryknoll men called the papal nuncio who sent a diplomatic vehicle to pick up Dianna and Darleen and take them to the Vatican Embassy where the nuncio could provide Dianna with asylum and help her safely leave Guatemala.

Mimi and a Spanish-speaking member of the Ursuline Sisters' leadership team, Sister Fran, were en route to Guatemala City as soon as they could book a flight. Pat Farrell was in Guatemala, serving as an interpreter for a delegation of Franciscan men and women, intending to visit Dianna and Darleen in *Antigua* after completing this task. Before she was able to do so, news came out of Dianna's kidnapping. Pat found Darleen and Dianna at the nuncio's house, the day after Dianna had arrived and offered assistance.

The papal nuncio could not have been more attentive or more protective of his guests. When Mimi and Fran arrived, the three sisters from *San Miguel Acatán*, reunited again, remained in the Vatican Embassy while Sisters Fran and Pat took care of the necessary external business: informing the archbishop of Dianna's experience, arranging flights to the U.S., etc. It was evident that Dianna needed to leave Guatemala for her own safety. During their time in the Vatican Embassy, Darleen and Mimi made the decision to leave also, realizing after much advice and conversation that their ongoing presence in Guatemala could, by association, put other people in danger. They had hoped to accompany the people of *San Miguel Acatán* for many more years, as they had assured the people they would. Their leaving Guatemala, with no opportunity for explanation or farewells, caused them great sadness.

Sr. Fran accompanied Dianna to her home in Albuquerque while Darleen and Mimi flew to Louisville to deal with the media who would be anticipating Dianna's arrival. After some time for rest and regrouping, Dianna, Mimi and Darleen came together at the Ursuline Sisters' motherhouse in Maple Mount, Kentucky. Darleen and Mimi accompanied Dianna closely during that time. She did not want to be alone. The three spent long hours in conversation about what would be helpful for Dianna and what they could do next. There was also much discernment with the leadership teams of both congregations who were, naturally, very concerned about the three sisters,

A Vine Transplanted – Guatemala

as well as about Maureen Leach who was undoubtedly quite impacted by the news of Dianna's kidnapping and torture.

For reasons of safety, the three sisters' return to Guatemala was out of the question. They eventually chose to pursue a new ministry setting which seemed to them most similar to *San Miguel Acatán*. They contacted Bishop *Samuel Ruíz* in *Chiapas*, Mexico, whose diocese was filled with Guatemalan refugees, many of them from the diocese of *Huehuetenango*. The state of *Chiapas* in Mexico shares a border with the Guatemalan state of *Huehuetenango*. The population of *Chiapas* is predominantly indigenous. The bishop was very welcoming of the sisters and compassionate about what they had recently been through. He invited them to live and work at their own pace in a small, rural parish near the town of *Cometán*.

By the end of January 1990, the sisters were relocated in Mexico, beginning missionary work with Guatemalan refugees. On a clear day they could see in the distance the mountain of *San Miguel Acatán* and felt somewhat at home. It did not take much time for them to see, however, that Dianna was becoming increasingly withdrawn and in need of professional help to process the trauma she had experienced. After just three or four months Dianna returned to Kentucky and was hospitalized for treatment. Mimi and Darleen remained in *Chiapas* for a time.

The three sisters had left most of their belongings in the house in *San Miguel Acatán* and never had the opportunity to return. They asked two friends, Franciscan Sr. Elaine Gehling and Fr. Bill Hammer, a priest from the Louisville diocese, to travel to *San Miguel Acatán* to bring their clothes, household utensils and jeep to their new home in *Chiapas*. The two friends gathered up everything and closed the house. The bishop of *Huehuetenango* asked to keep the jeep and gave them money for it that the sisters could use for their work in *Chiapas*. He then had someone drive Sr. Elaine and Fr. Bill to *Chiapas*.

Darleen liked *Chiapas* and wanted to continue to live and work there. Mimi, however, lost interest after Dianna left. Her real desire was to return to Chile. She left *Chiapas*, went to Kentucky and accompanied Dianna for a substantial amount of time during her treatment process. Mimi did ultimately return to Chile and in 2015 was still in *Chillán*. Darleen stayed alone in *Chiapas* for several months, hoping that another Dubuque Franciscan might join her.

A Vine Transplanted – Guatemala

When it seemed that no one would be coming to be with her in *Chiapas*, she also returned to the U.S. She lived and worked with Elaine Gehling in a predominantly Spanish-speaking parish in Des Moines, Iowa, and enrolled in a clinical pastoral education program at a Des Moines hospital.

No one could have imagined this type of ending to the mission in Guatemala. Darleen, Mimi, Maureen and Dianna shared in the suffering of the Guatemalan people, each in a unique and personal way. Surely it produced a measure of the fruitfulness promised to the seed that falls into the ground and dies. In their own words, the Franciscans express what their time in Guatemala meant to them.

Maureen Leach

When I visited Central America for ministry discernment, halfway up the road to San Miguel my heart told me that this was home. When I met the people, my heart told me that this was where I belonged.

I went to Guatemala thinking I would stay for many years. Yet, people said they would not get close to the sisters saying we would just leave like the other missioners. I wanted to declare that I would stay, but I held my tongue. When I left Guatemala, I remembered what people had said, and I felt like Peter who had denied Christ three times. It was hard to forgive myself.

The Mayan language touched my spirituality deeply. Kanjobal has no abstract terms to hide behind. Having to be direct and concrete when I spoke helped me come closer to God and to the people. The word for "friend" was "watxanima" which meant "good person". The word for "sin" literally meant "big pain in the center of my being". So the reading "whose sins you shall forgive..." translated, "If you let go of the big pain in the center of your being, God will let go of it too." The Magnificat began, "I will speak the good word of my God with my entire being." The greeting that people gave was literally, "Good is the center of your being?" And the response was, "Good, the thanks be to God. And You?" "Human rights" was translated as "kalon ket" which means "we speak together." There were many ways to say "be careful" or "don't fall on the way." When I left Guatemala, I was invited to preach in Kanjobal at the Liturgy. Though I was only there two years, the land, the language, and the people will be forever etched in my heart.

A Vine Transplanted – Guatemala

Darleen Chmielewski

I recall my last days in Guatemala as ones of the most profound sorrow and anguish, followed by sheer joy and relief when I was reunited with Dianna, only to be followed by a long woeful journey of accompanying Dianna. Guatemala is where I lost my mission cross, which seemed to me a loss of my missionary call to Latin America because I was thwarted in my attempts to return. Instead I turned to the Potter in faith and hope to be molded anew.

El Salvador (19 years of congregational presence, 1986-2005)

Archbishop Oscar Romero, Homily, April 1, 1979:

To each one of us Christ is saying:
If you want your life and mission to be fruitful like mine, do as I.
Be converted into a seed that lets itself be buried.
Let yourself be killed.
Do not be afraid.
Those who shun suffering will remain alone ....
But if you give your life out of love for others, as I give mine for all,
You will reap a great harvest.
You will have the deepest satisfactions.
Do not fear death or threats; The Lord goes with you. [24]

The seed of the Gospel had long been planted in El Salvador before our sisters arrived. When Spanish missioners came in the early 1500s, they found indigenous groups of primarily *Lenca* and *Pipil* peoples. They were smaller communities on the edge of the great Mayan Empire concentrated in Guatemala and southeast Mexico. The Christian message became blended with already-existing spiritual inclinations and native traditions, forming El Salvador's unique manifestation of faith. As in other parts of the New World, the evangelization process was tainted with imperialism, conquest, and violence, leading eventually to a society of dominators and dominated. Inequalities were evident primarily in land ownership and the corresponding lack of it.

Land was particularly limited in El Salvador, the smallest and most densely populated country in Latin America. Land, and therefore wealth, came to be concentrated in the hands of thirteen extended families. Those most excluded from resources were indigenous groups. In the 1920s *Farabundo Martí*, in coordination with leaders of similar movements in Central America, helped organize native people to demand access to land. The resulting uprising was quelled by the massacre of an estimated 30,000 *campesinos* in 1932. Native dress and language quickly disappeared in the wake of that violence. Indigenous people feared being identified as such.

A Vine Transplanted – El Salvador

Conditions of domination and economic disparity continued unabated. The worldwide atmosphere of change in the 1960s-70s was reflected in El Salvador's renewed organizing for social transformation. It was met again with disproportionate repression, erupting in full-blown armed conflict by 1980.

In 1986, the year our sisters arrived in El Salvador, the civil war was still raging, funded by a million and a half dollars a day of U.S. military aid. Two notable assassinations had occurred in 1980: Archbishop Romero on March 24 and the four U.S. church women on December 2. Thirteen Salvadoran priests and one woman religious had also been killed and there was widespread persecution of the Catholic Church. Many catechists, particularly those in rural areas, were martyred and those who escaped were suspected of being *guerrilla* sympathizers. Under the guidance of U.S. military advisors, the Salvadoran military had been applying the "scorched earth" tactics used by the U.S. in Vietnam, attempting to eliminate from *guerrilla*-controlled areas the civilian population that served as their support system. Aerial bombings and incursions of combat troops destroyed entire villages. There had been hundreds of massacres, the largest being that of *El Mozote* where an estimated 1,000 civilians were murdered. Salvadorans fled as they were able: some to the U.S. or other countries, some to burgeoning refugee camps just across the border in Honduras, others to homes of relatives elsewhere in El Salvador, and still others to *"refugios"* — camps organized primarily by church groups for internally displaced persons. Twenty percent of the population of the country was displaced due to the violence.

A large percent of the military was forcibly recruited. Young men were routinely picked up, put in the backs of trucks, and taken to military bases in places far from where they were seized, to make it difficult for family members to find them. Paramilitary groups, "death squads," operated with impunity, terrorizing the civilian population. Trust of anyone was in short supply and an environment of fear was palpable.

Maryknoll priests and sisters had been asked by Archbishop *Rivera y Damas* to leave the country for a time, following the death of the four churchwomen and some publicity that could have linked Maryknoll with the *guerrilla* movement. In early 1986, Maryknoll Fr. Ron Hennessey, brother of three Dubuque Franciscans, was among the first to return to San Salvador.

A Vine Transplanted – El Salvador

Uprooting and Transplanting: Beginning Life in El Salvador

Sisters Pat Farrell and Kay Koppes were in communication with Fr. Ron as soon as they knew they would be going to El Salvador. Ron, newly on the ground again in El Salvador, advised them regarding papers to take with them to facilitate getting residency after their arrival. So, their preparations began. Kay Koppes continued working at a clinic in Waterloo to finish her contract there while Pat worked in the Mount St. Francis kitchen until Kay was ready to go. Sr. Susan Seitz wrote to the archbishop of San Salvador communicating the congregation's decision to send sisters. Weeks passed with no response from him. Pat began phoning the chancery in San Salvador with numbers she had from the fact-finding visit there. Curiously, the phone rang and rang at whatever day or hour, again with no response. She tried other phone numbers. No response. Kay completed her work in Waterloo. They continued waiting. No response. Finally they decided to depart without making a connection with the archbishop. Susan Seitz, congregational president, wrote a letter of introduction for them to present to the archbishop and they set out, trusting that Providence would guide their way.

It was late November. They had a flight to Guatemala City and planned to take a bus from there to *San Miguel Acatán* in *Huehuetenango* to spend Thanksgiving with Darleen and Mimi before traveling by bus to El Salvador in time to be there for the anniversary celebration of the four martyred churchwomen on December 2. They underestimated how difficult travel would be to *San Miguel Acatán*. It took two days, over treacherous roads with breathtaking, panoramic mountain views. However, it was a delight to see Mimi and Darleen in their new home. It was also compelling to hear about all they were discovering of the indigenous *Kanjobal* people in their area and the violence and suffering to which they had been subjected.

It took as long to get down the mountains as it did to get up, so Srs. Pat and Kay's travel was delayed and they arrived in El Salvador by bus a day later than anticipated, on December 3, the feast of Mother Xavier. Pat recalls:

> *The border was very militarized. We were welcomed with guns and with Salvadoran soldiers rummaging through our belongings. Once on the Salvadoran side of the border, I was aware of the comfort of Kay's presence next to me on the bus. I stared out the window at the*

A Vine Transplanted – El Salvador

passing fields of sugar cane, wondering what kind of life was awaiting us in El Salvador.

The scene they encountered in San Salvador was one of destruction and rubble. They soon realized that between the time they had first communicated with Ron Hennessey in El Salvador and when they tried to contact the archbishop, an earthquake had occurred in the country, affecting the capital city of San Salvador most acutely. As a result, the communications infrastructure had not been functional.

They took a taxi to a downtown hotel to spend their first night. The next day they were able to make contact with sisters that Pat had met on the fact-finding tour: *"The Pequeña Comunidad."* They stayed the following night with these Salvadoran women who would become friends for the duration of their time in El Salvador. The sisters of *The Pequeña Comunidad* communicated with the Vicar for Pastoral Activity, Fr. *Fabian Amaya,* who arranged for Pat and Kay to stay as long-term guests in pretty minimal accommodations in his parish in *Ilopango.*

The sisters later discovered that the parish was affectionately known in Salvadoran pastoral circles as "the refinery." Newly-arrived foreigners often stayed there for the vicar to assess their suitability for accompanying the people in such volatile times, and to provide them with needed orientation to the Church and the country. For about two weeks Kay and Pat explored San Salvador and waited for an appointment to speak with the archbishop. It was not immediately forthcoming, so Kay proceeded to Guatemala where she would spend five months in language school. For the interim of Kay's absence, the vicar, Fr. *Fabian,* situated Pat in a nearby community of resettled refugees, *Santa María La Esperanza,* on the outskirts of the city. The community was poor, just building homes and rebuilding their lives, but they did have a small church, their first communal construction project. Pat slept in the sacristy on a cot and ate in the home of a different family each day in exchange for providing pastoral accompaniment to the community while there. Though for Pat it was a rather lonely way to begin life in El Salvador, it was an ideal way to learn about the reality of those who had suffered persecution and war. In the privacy of their own makeshift homes, the people of *Santa María La Esperanza* opened their hearts to her and told her their stories.

A Vine Transplanted – El Salvador

As Pat persistently pursued getting an appointment with the archbishop, she learned of some of the politics of the archdiocese in the time of war. Archbishop *Rivera y Damas*, successor to *Romero*, was facilitating talks between government and *guerrilla* leaders in the hope of brokering a peace process. The government was pressuring him to have some control over the influx of international church people coming to provide short-term accompaniment to Salvadorans in conflict zones. The Salvadoran military was unhappy with their presence. They would also be unhappy with our sisters' presence.

It was not surprising that the archbishop would reserve to himself the decision about receiving new religious into the diocese, but Pat had not anticipated the level of caution he would exercise in doing so. She had not expected to be put off and evaluated, though with hindsight she could see the absolute necessity of trusting people only very selectively in a war situation.

It was only after writing a lengthy letter to Archbishop *Rivera y Damas* explaining the circumstances of their fact-finding, discernment, and communication difficulties that the sisters received an appointment with him. Kay came from Guatemala for that important conversation. The archbishop was circumspect, guarded, and astute. A religious himself (Salesian), he asked about the founding and charism of the Dubuque Franciscans. They responded:

> We are Franciscans and our charism is to be with those who are poor. Our congregation was founded in Germany at the time of the Franco-Prussian war and the early sisters cared for orphans and for those wounded in the war. With that, everything changed. He inquired with interest about our foundress and about the sisters who cared for the wounded on the battlefields. Finally he said, "You belong here. Welcome to the archdiocese."

It was the Salvadoran women religious who were most open and welcoming of Pat in her first months alone in the country. They explained what she could expect. If Archbishop *Rivera y Damas* did receive the Franciscans into the archdiocese, he would assign them somewhere far from any of the conflict zones. Earning his trust and that of other key people in the archdiocese would be very important. A good place for building those relationships could be the camp for internally displaced persons run by the archdiocese, *San Jose Calle Real*. Knowing that prior to their conversation with *Rivera y Damas*, Kay and Pat offered to start out working at the camp as soon as Kay returned from language school. He accepted.

Work with Refugees and Internally Displaced Persons: Salvadorans Uprooted and Transplanted

> *I will bring back my people Israel back from exile. They will rebuild the ruined cities and live in them. They will plant vineyards and drink their wine; they will make gardens and eat their fruit. (Amos 9:14) NIV.* [25]

The *San José Calle Real* refuge, located approximately ten kilometers north of San Salvador, was opened in 1985 by the Archdiocese of San Salvador as a shelter for persons displaced by the civil war. The numbers of those in the camp swelled to over 1,000 in January 1986, as a result of the Salvadoran military's "Operation Phoenix", an all-out assault on the *Guazapa* mountain area, the *guerrilla* stronghold closest to San Salvador, within the municipality and parish of *Suchitoto*. The International Red Cross combed the area for civilians who survived the saturation bombing and brought them to the camp in trucks, with only the clothes they were wearing .

Kay and Pat moved to the camp in May. Other international volunteers, coordinated through Jesuit Refugee Service and the archdiocese, were their companions. The housing for Kay and Pat and the other women volunteers was a small, one-room tin structure where six of them slept in bunk beds. The people in the camp were divided into seven living groups, sharing crowded open spaces that afforded very little privacy. Each living group elected a representative to a coordinating committee and had someone who functioned as a health promoter and a pastoral worker and participated in trainings for that role. There was one main cooking area where the women took turns making *tortillas* and preparing meals for the entire camp. The men worked the land surrounding the camp, planting and harvesting corn for the *tortillas*. A rudimentary school was staffed by those who had a little more schooling than the others, regardless of age. For example, an 11-year-old girl with a fifth-grade education was teaching adult literacy. Employees from the archdiocese ran small workshops to teach skills: shoe repair, sewing, and raising rabbits. One room with a few beds was designated as the "hospital" and a smaller adjoining room was used for labor and delivery, attended by midwives. Occasionally a wounded *guerrilla* would be brought over the hills

A Vine Transplanted – El Salvador

in a hammock at night to that "hospital," though the camp was officially designated to be for civilian non-combatants.

Srs. Kay Koppes and Pat Farrell at Calle Real Refugee Camp

Pat and Kay began with minimal instruction from the archdiocese. *"Bring only one change of clothes, since the people have only that much or less. Your main job will be to keep the military out of the camp in order to assure the safety of the people and to accompany the refugees in any way that you are able."* Soon Kay was helping to train health promoters and attending the sick and wounded, occasionally helping to deliver a baby. Pat helped train the pastoral workers, coordinated liturgies and music, formed a choir, and trained guitarists. From them, she learned many of El Salvador's revolutionary songs.

Pat also served as an interpreter for delegations who visited the camp. All the volunteers working in the camp were involved in driving people to San Salvador for medical appointments, and especially for helping the displaced people to get identification papers. Anyone not carrying a personal ID card was considered a *guerrilla* and subject to arrest. The most important role of the volunteers was accompaniment, listening, and being a supportive presence. Pat recalls:

> *By the end of the second or third week I was emotionally saturated with stories of violence, cruelty, massacres and the horrors of war. What the people had suffered was more than I could take in. At the time I didn't yet know about secondary trauma, but now suspect that all of us working at the camp must have suffered from that to some degree.*

A Vine Transplanted – El Salvador

Daily we saw people who had lost an arm or a leg or an eye, or had shrapnel lodged under their skin, or had infected wounds. Almost all the people in the camp had lost family members, or didn't know where they were, or whether they were dead or alive. I witnessed a number of poignant reunions of people coming to the camp and finding a family member who was missing and presumed dead. A Jesuit, Jon Cortina, who came weekly from the war-torn area of Chalatenango to celebrate Eucharist, always brought messages from family members or inquiries from people looking for missing loved ones. The theologian Jon Sobrino celebrated the Holy Week liturgies. For the Holy Saturday litany of the saints he invited people to name the martyrs of their families and their communities. Their response was interminable, yet clearly sacred. Even the children and dogs were suddenly quiet, sensing the emotion and the importance of the moment.

In spite of what they had endured, the faith, solidarity, courage, determination, and resilience of so many people in the camp deeply impressed me. At one point I remember regretfully thinking to myself, "If this is what suffering produces, bring on suffering!" I was also very troubled by the violence of armed conflict on both sides. Having so recently participated in the training and implementation of non-violent resistance in the Chilean anti-torture movement, I kept asking people in the camp if a solution other than taking up arms could have worked in El Salvador. The universal answer I received was that I couldn't possibly understand without living through what they had experienced, particularly the disproportionate repression used against their grassroots mobilizations to demand basic rights. Still, the violence was always disturbing to me.

While Kay and Pat were in *Calle Real,* a new movement had begun in El Salvador. It consisted of refugees and displaced persons organizing to return to the homes they had fled, though in areas still experiencing violence. The first repopulation occurred in *Las Flores, Chalatenango,* and the second in *El Barillo,* a community in the parish of *Suchitoto.* It was a risky undertaking. There was no assurance of protection from violent military repression or repeated massacres. Groups organizing to return did so only under certain conditions: that a sizeable group would go together, that there would be international accompaniment for their protection, and that they would be assured of enough food to last a year until they could once again plant and harvest their crops and be self-sustaining. It created a lot of expectancy and conversation in the camp.

A Vine Transplanted – El Salvador

Similarly, at the large refugee camps in Honduras, the UN High Commission on Refugees (UNHCR) was helping Salvadorans organize a massive return to their country. The Salvadoran government was opposed, not wanting people whom they considered a support system for the *guerrillas* to return. But the people were undeterred and UNHCR exerted international pressure. On October 12, 1987, a group of 4,300 refugees was poised at the border, prepared to repatriate four destroyed rural areas in El Salvador. There had been a call for international volunteers to meet the refugees at the border, to accompany them and to stay with them as long as possible for their protection. Kay and Pat volunteered. Despite government warnings not to support the returning refugees, the two were at the border during the three days of negotiation and protest before the caravan of trucks and busloads of people were allowed to enter the country. Then they boarded separate busses and rode with the people towards *Guarjila* in *Chalatenango*. Pat's memory of it:

> We all got off the busses and walked the last stretch into the area where the people would resettle. There was no longer a distinguishable road to follow. We walked toward....nothing! I will never forget the stark realization of just what it meant for the people to repatriate. What they were returning to was their beloved land, but only that, and covered now with shoulder-high grass. To settle down to sleep that first night, the men chopped a clearing in the grass with their machetes. In the nearby environs were the assorted remains of what had been adobe houses before the military's large-scale bombing of civilian areas. This was really starting over from scratch with just a very few belongings – some clothes, perhaps a chicken or two in a wooden cage, a machete. Very stark, to my first-world eyes. But the mood of the people was jubilant. Perhaps the most moving moment was the arrival of a large group of people who had come walking several hours from Las Flores, the first repopulation community in the country and the only other group of civilians living in the war zone of Chalatenango. They came singing, with guitars and tortillas and heartfelt solidarity. It was hard to say who was happier to see whom. It was the first of many such gestures I would see among the repopulating refugees and I was very moved by it. It made me recall the Scripture read at the Eucharist celebrated at the border by Monseñor Rosa Chavez who had come to receive the refugees in the name of the Salvadoran Church:
>
> On this mountain God will prepare for all peoples a banquet of rich food, a banquet of fine wines, of food rich and juicy, of fine strained wines. On this mountain God will remove the mourning veil covering the people and the shroud enwrapping the nations and will destroy

death forever. God will wipe away the tears from every cheek and will take away the people's shame everywhere on earth, for God has said so. That day, it will be said: See, this is our God in whom we hope for salvation; our God is the one in whom we hoped. We exult and we rejoice that our God has saved us, for the hand of our God rests on this mountain. (Based on Is. 25:6-9)

> *To this day I cannot hear that reading without picturing that huge group of refugees gathered in the mountains of Chalatenango, waiting to return to areas of the country still in conflict, hoping with them that these words from Scripture would be true for them in the days to come.* [26]

The next day Pat returned to work at *Calle Real*, but Kay stayed for three weeks, sharing in the refugees' physical hardship and providing a protective international presence. Kay put to good use her skills as a nurse practitioner. She had a gift for just being present to people and spent long hours in conversation with them.

The first two re-populations, and subsequently this first repatriation from Honduras, set off a chain reaction of other groups gathering the courage to return to conflict zones. The *Calle Real* camp was abuzz with talk and planning.

Our own inter-congregational team was also on the move. Sister Peggy O'Neill arrived in June of 1987 and joined Kay and Pat in the camp. Peggy, a Sister of Charity from Convent Station, New Jersey, was a theology professor at Iona College in New York. She had negotiated a year off initially to join the team in El Salvador, and thereafter to teach the fall semester at Iona each year and spend the rest of the year in Central America. She stayed at the camp for a month or two, daily helping with the cooking, allowing her to get to know the women. She then went to *Antigua*, Guatemala, to learn Spanish.

The time at *Calle Real* had given the sisters what they hoped for and more. It afforded the opportunity for personnel of the archdiocese to come to know and trust them, and vice versa. Additionally, it was a good introduction to the complexities of accompanying people with ties to armed sub-groups of the *guerrilla* movement and corresponding resistance groups, both open and clandestine. Trust was an enormous issue. The trusting relationships built with those in the camp were far more critical than the sisters first realized,

A Vine Transplanted – El Salvador

since these displaced persons were the ones the sisters would eventually work with in the parish of *Suchitoto*.

During their time at *Calle Real* the sisters were aware that the archbishop would assign them and that he was under some pressure to keep foreigners out of areas of conflict. They also knew that their presence as international church workers could provide protection for civilians in war zones, which they had hoped to do. So, on their weekly day off from the camp they began to visit and explore areas of urgent need, usually communities of returned refugees. Peggy returned from language school to help consider options. They were drawn to living in the community of repatriated refugees at *Copapayo* in the *Suchitoto* area. Instead, friends in the archdiocese advised them to consider the town and parish of *Suchitoto* where they could attend to *Copapayo* as well as other future repopulation efforts.

Kay, Peggy, and Pat took time away for prayer and discernment about location for ministry. They named three places of priority: *Cuscatancingo* in *San Salvador*, a neighborhood of more than 100,000 with only one priest; *Nombre de Jesús*, an isolated and unattended parish in the war zone of *Chalatenango*; and *Suchitoto,* the parish and municipality in the conflict zone, mostly under *guerrilla* control, nearest *San Salvador*. They requested and were quickly given an appointment with the archbishop to relate the fruits of their discernment, assuring him of their willingness to go wherever they were sent. On the spot, he asked them to go to *Suchitoto*. The sisters agreed to complete the year at *Calle Real* and move to *Suchitoto* in January 1988. After that late November appointment, Pat returned to the U.S. for a visit and to communicate more directly with the congregation about the sisters' experience in El Salvador and their future projections. She was leaving Central America about the time Sister Carol Besch was arriving. Peggy spent Christmas with her elderly parents in New Jersey.

Carol had spent the month of July in the Maryknoll discernment and orientation program for new missioners. In a November 1987 letter she writes:

> *One of the decisions I made during my time in the Maryknoll program was to spend a few months at our motherhouse in Dubuque before leaving for El Salvador. I felt I needed some time to be rooted in our community and especially to get to know some of the older sisters who are now retired and living in Dubuque. I volunteered to work in the*

A Vine Transplanted – El Salvador

kitchen during September, October and part of November. Recently I read a verse on a card which says "After the fruits of summer have been gathered, the quiet pause of autumn renews our lives with gratitude". The fruits and vegetables of our abundant gardens and orchards have now been stored for the winter... At the same time, my heart has stored up the goodness, support, and warmth of my sisters that I have come to know and love during these weeks. God's goodness has certainly been abundant.

Carol arrived in Guatemala City on November 30, and was met by the four sisters from *San Miguel Acatán*, Maureen, Darleen, Mimi and Dianna. The following day Kay arrived from El Salvador. Maureen Leach stayed with her a few days to orient her to Guatemala City after which she began her intensive Spanish immersion in *Antigua*, Guatemala, where Ursuline Sister Dianna Ortiz was also studying.

On December 19, Carol took a break from language school and traveled by bus to El Salvador to spend Christmas and New Year's with Kay in the camp at *Calle Real*. She found the rituals and celebrations meaningful and motivating and returned to Guatemala with new energy to continue learning the language. Shortly after she left, the sisters in El Salvador reassembled after their travels, left the camp, and moved into the house in San Salvador provided for volunteers by Jesuit Refugee Services to prepare for their move to *Suchitoto*. During the days that followed, two unexpected things happened.

First, the military began to harass the camp at *Calle Real*. The sisters had confronted soldiers twice before when they tried to enter the camp, and the soldiers had left. This time the situation was more serious. A February 1988 *Latin American Mission Letter* from the sisters in El Salvador describes it:

> *Soldiers with machine guns and binoculars set up checkpoints on the fringes. In spite of the agreement that the military would not enter without express permission of Archbishop Rivera y Damas, armed personnel later searched all the buildings and confiscated personal documents. When they tried to take certain people prisoner, the refugees surrounded them, demanding, "Take us all or take none!"*

The military left without the prisoners, demanding, however, that the Church hand them over by a certain date or the soldiers would return. Still later, firing came sporadically into the camp from all sides, with men, women, and children trying to escape the bullets. Gunfire damage was done to eight of the ten buildings, but only one person was wounded – a young man shot in the abdomen as he lay on a 'hospital' bed in the camp. When he returned to the camp from the hospital in San Salvador, twelve soldiers came and tried to take him, though a volunteer managed to hold them off until human rights workers from the archdiocese arrived and intervened. Tension prevailed for some time afterwards at the camp, adding to the refugees' desire to return and resettle their abandoned villages.

Second, Kay, Pat, and Peggy proceeded to move to *Suchitoto*, setting out in a borrowed pickup with their belongings, letter in hand from the archbishop assigning them to the parish there. However, at the first military check point, some miles from *Suchitoto*, they were promptly turned back. The soldiers said it was not the archbishop but the military who gave the orders in that zone. The sisters returned to the capital city, reported the event to Archbishop *Rivera y Damas*, waited and thought about what to do next.

Both unexpected events were continuing sagas. The military surrounded the camp for an extended time, while refugees' plans to resettle elsewhere took more concrete shape. The sisters also continued their effort to move to *Suchitoto*. In February they made a second attempt, going on a local bus and taking nothing that would suggest they were going there to stay. They were taken off the bus and sent back. Again they reported the situation to Archbishop *Rivera y Damas* who told them he was gathering a number of issues to bring to a negotiation session with the high command of the Salvadoran military, including his right to name pastoral personnel to combat zones. Since accepting the sisters into the archdiocese, his support of them had been unwavering. Finally, in March he phoned them to announce that he had secured permission from the military for them to work in the *Suchitoto* area. They would need to get written clearance from the national military headquarters and from the First Brigade, which had local military oversight of the area. Each permission would have to be renewed every six weeks.

Planted in New Soil: Life in Suchitoto During the War

Documents in hand, Pat, Kay, and Peggy arrived in *Suchitoto* on March 12, 1988, passing through the two military checkpoints that would become a routine part of their lives for years. They rented half an adobe house (for $25 a month!), with the owners living in the other half. There were available church properties in *Suchitoto* but they had been abandoned and were in unlivable condition. The house they chose had one critically decisive feature: a telephone. There were only a handful of phones in *Suchitoto*. The owner of the sisters' house worked for the phone company, so their house was among the few. Peggy O'Neill had recently been in the U.S. because her father was seriously ill. After their first night sleeping in *Suchitoto,* the sisters were awakened with a call saying that her father had died. Kay and Pat accompanied Peggy right back to San Salvador where she got a flight home. The two sisters stayed in the capital city until Peggy's return on March 21.

Meanwhile, Carol Besch was completing language studies and anticipating her move to El Salvador. She wrote in a March 1988 letter:

> *I am eager to get to El Salvador and begin to share in the lives of the Salvadoran people. This is not an easy time for the people. For me it is encouraging that the leadership of the Church stands with the people in their struggle. Both of the bishops of San Salvador, Rivera y Damas y Rosa Chavez continue to speak out against the atrocities committed against their people. Recently I read in the papers that Rosa Chavez denounced the reappearance of the death squads in El Salvador. During the first week of February there were 26 reported assassinations by the death squads. All this happens in a country that the U.S. supports as a 'democracy.'*

Since Carol's March 21 move to El Salvador coincided with the day on which Peggy O'Neill returned from her father's funeral, providentially, the four sisters were finally an assembled group and could travel together to *Suchitoto*. The journey took 1 ½ hours by bus from the capital and the road was lined with bombed-out houses, abandoned since the peak violence of 1979-80. In *Suchitoto* buildings were pock-marked from bullets, echoing a former vitality now shriveled. It looked like a ghost town. Here the four would begin life together, finally sleeping for the first night in their new home, sharing two bedrooms, reserving the third for a prayer space.

A Vine Transplanted – El Salvador

Bullet-riddled house in Suchitoto

During their second night in *Suchitoto*, *guerrilla* forces came into town and there was combat on the street in front of their house. The four huddled together in an inside room during the shooting, wondering what they were getting into! A week later there was a similar attack, but by then people had told them that bullets were less likely to pass through adobe than cinderblock, so they were not as frightened and just stayed away from doors and windows when the fighting began. Another frequent nocturnal disturbance was the firing of nearby cannons that would shake dirt from the tile roof onto their beds. A park two blocks away had cannons installed there, permanently pointed at *Guazapa*, the mountain in the *Suchitoto* area controlled by the *guerrillas*. After a few weeks the sisters were sleeping through the sound of the cannons and settling into life in *Suchitoto*.

The beginning days held many learnings. The movement of returning refugees was picking up speed and growing in complexity. The government and military had opposed early efforts. The second national repopulation community, *El Barillo*, and one of the first repatriation communities from Honduras, *Copapayo*, were part of the *Suchitoto* parish. They could attest to threats and repression. But the returning refugees were undeterred and enjoyed the support of international solidarity groups. They were undaunted, disciplined, and organized. The movement would not be reversible. The tactics of the government changed under the guidance of U.S. military advisors. Counter-insurgency efforts were designed to win the minds and hearts of the civilian population. Attempts at government-sponsored repopulations in conflict zones deliberately promoted more individualistic resettlement, minimized local organization and leadership, and espoused pro-military propaganda. Two such communities were newly established in the *Suchitoto* area when the sisters arrived, *Aguacayo* and *Ichanquezo*. During the war years, neither grew much nor was ever very successful, despite being the only rural communities with electricity. There were two other smaller, self-organized repopulations in the zone. By early 1988, *Montepeque* and *Estanzuelas*, and several others were in planning stages. The repopulation movement was clearly not a homogeneous reality.

Wall with names of those killed in the Copapayo massacre

As archdiocesan personnel had predicted, this zone was one of the epicenters of repopulation. With the exception of the town of *Suchitoto* and two nearby villages, the entire surrounding area had been bombed and the rural villages destroyed. There had been at least ten massacres of differing sizes in the parish. The two largest were of more than 200 people each.

Once a population of 35,000, the municipality of *Suchitoto* had decreased to fewer than 5,000 in 1988. Thousands of the original residents had escaped. Most of those now living in *Suchitoto* had fled there from nearby villages. People living at the edge of town would move into abandoned houses near the center to sleep each night, avoiding the skirmishes that happened on *Suchitoto's* periphery when the *guerrillas* attempted to wrest control from the 300-400 soldiers permanently stationed there. The town was strategic, with the surrounding area predominantly under *guerrilla* control.

It quickly became evident where the sisters were welcome and where they were not. *El Barillo* and *Copapayo* were thrilled to have them nearby, feeling protected and supported by their presence as international and church

A Vine Transplanted – El Salvador

persons. In Suchitoto, they were met with fear and suspicion, reflecting the overall suspicion of neighbors for each other. No one hinted at allegiances with the military, *guerrillas*, or death squads, though all of that existed in *Suchitoto*. Even those who did not want to be associated with any side did not let that be known.

The sisters knew they were walking into a delicate environment, so before moving to *Suchitoto* they sought out the Dominican sisters who had abandoned their school there in 1980 because of threats. The Dominicans had given them the name of their former janitor as a person of trust who could orient them. When the newly arrived U.S. sisters approached him, he quickly turned and walked away, unwilling to engage in conversation.

As a non-threatening initial project in *Suchitoto*, Pat began to form a youth choir. An invitation went out and several young people came for the first gathering. The second meeting was significantly smaller and one of the youth told the sisters that three military in plain clothes had come the first time to eavesdrop on the effort, which likely discouraged others from coming again. Similarly, a *Suchitoto* woman immediately befriended the sisters and came frequently to the house, bringing fruit and other gifts, and sometimes picking up a broom to sweep the patio. She asked to be hired to cook and clean. The sisters declined. Eventually the sisters' landlord told them that she was well known in town as a poor woman paid as an informant. She was feared and credited with the deaths of a number of people whose names she had given to the military.

The decision to focus time and energy in *Copapayo* and *El Barillo* was easy. The sisters went every week, always staying overnight, sometimes for several days at a time. *El Barillo* was a two-hour walk. *Copapayo*, however, was not accessible by land. The only road in that direction was partly destroyed, partly mined. Nonetheless, it was possible to get there by motorboat from the edge of the lake just below *Suchitoto*. It was *Copapayo*'s only access to the outside world.

Those visits were as supportive for the sisters as for the communities. The four women learned to take their cues from the people about what was appropriate and safe. They were advised never to walk alone, so went in pairs or with the people. They were never to step off a road or well-beaten path. There was always the danger of landmines. It was unsafe to go out after nightfall. It was equally unsafe for anyone from the repopulated communities to attempt to walk home from *Suchitoto* after dark. The sisters' home became an alternative. In the entry area just within their house there were often people spread out for the night on the floor, and there was frequently an extra plate or two added to the supper table. A poster of Archbishop Romero hung on the wall of the house's entry area, and it was common to see someone standing in prayer before that image. Franciscan associate John Donaghy writes in an unpublished manuscript:

> *Valentín…noted that the situation the people faced in those days was extremely difficult. There was this immense comandancia, the headquarters of the military in Suchitoto, a real threat to the people. But, better than that, there was the sisters' house, the comandancia de Jesucristo, (Jesus Christ's command post!)*

To accompany the Salvadoran people at the level of their faith was a privileged point of entry into the tumultuous world of *Suchitoto* in the 1980s. The Catholic Church in El Salvador was very important to the Salvadorans and clearly bore the mark of Archbishop Oscar Romero. The sisters' first return trip to San Salvador was with a busload of people from the repopulated communities going to the annual march to commemorate the 8th anniversary of his death. Their first letter from *Suchitoto* says:

> *The people's enduring love for their bishop-martyr was celebrated in the marches of the Christian Communities, workers' organizations, university students and Mothers of the Disappeared converging on the cathedral for a manifestation and a Mass.….The Salvadoran people draw continued strength from the witness of Romero… It is a real sign of hope…to see the courage and resiliency of this people. The voice of the prophet continues to be heard…. This statement was made one month before his assassination: 'As a pastor, I am obliged by divine mandate to give my life for those I love – for all Salvadorans, even for those who may be going to kill me. If the threats come to be fulfilled, from this moment I offer my blood to God for the redemption and for the resurrection of El Salvador. Let my death, if it is accepted by God, be for the liberation of my people and as a witness of hope in the future. A bishop will die, but the Church of God, which is the people, will never perish.'*

A Vine Transplanted – El Salvador

Archbishop Oscar Romero

The spirit of Archbishop *Romero* lived on in the Church in many ways. His successor, Archbishop *Rivera y Damas*, continued *Romero's* tradition of holding a press conference after the Sunday liturgy at the cathedral. It provided an update of the week's human rights situation. *Tutela Legal*, the Church's human rights organization, documented testimonies from all sides of the conflict, earning the reputation of reliability and truthfulness. Most reported abuses, nonetheless, were attributed to the government and military. The Social Secretariat of the archdiocese channeled an enormous amount of the humanitarian aid coming into the country for those in conflict zones. The sisters in *Suchitoto*, known as "the Suchi Sisters," served as on-the-ground contacts for identifying needs, designing logistical coordination, and distributing aid. The papal nuncio was also attentive to the plight of the repopulated refugees. An April 1988 letter from the sisters reads:

> *While we were in Copapayo and El Barillo, the papal nuncio attempted to visit those two communities, stopping first at our house in Suchitoto. However, at the military check point before El Barillo, he was refused entrance. He indignantly drove straight to the lake and got a boat for Copapayo. Pat and Peggy were among those welcoming him there. They heard both his supportive words to the refugees and his avowals to complain directly to [President] Duarte about his treatment by the military.*

Archbishop *Rivera y Damas* was very interested in the vulnerable people repopulating war zones and readily received the sisters to get first-hand news from them. One time their wait to see him was particularly long. He

A Vine Transplanted – El Salvador

apologized, saying that he had just received one of frequent visits from the U.S. Embassy, giving him their viewpoint on the situation in the country. *"They want to influence my thinking,"* he said. *"But I need to come to Suchitoto and hear for myself what the people are really experiencing."* The sisters proceeded to plan his coming to *Suchitoto*, his first pastoral visit to the parish.

> *People from surrounding villages came walking to greet his arrival from as much as four hours away, carrying banners and waving little white flags. After a liturgy, he listened to representatives of each village explain their needs, taking lots of notes and questioning them with interest. Then he seemed as happy to go as we were to take him to the repopulation community of El Barillo. In the jeep on the way he reminisced about the last time he had driven down that road – when he served as mediator for guerrillas and government to negotiate the release of President Duarte's kidnapped daughter. Arriving at El Barillo, crowds of people met him on the road and he got out [of] the jeep to walk the last half mile or so in to the village with them. Again, he listened. One after another the people told him their stories, asking him to be their voice in denouncing the mistreatment they've suffered at the hands of the military. (Pat, letter of July 17, 1989)*

Daily accompaniment of the people was provided by the local Church, the pastor, and the four U.S. sisters. In an unpublished manuscript, Pat writes:

> *Most of our early work was that of simply accompanying the people. We slept in their homes, ate at their tables, played with the children. We mourned and cried with them, especially over news of loved ones killed in the war. We celebrated with them, sometimes with formal liturgical events, sometimes with rituals of our own making. Often we danced with them, in the dust, or in the rain and mud, at times till dawn. We accompanied them to offices of human rights groups to denounce the atrocities going on around us. We prayed with them and tried together to make sense of the horrors going on around us. We also helped manage the international solidarity aid channeled through the archdiocese in the form of food, medicine, provisional housing material, low interest loans for seed and fertilizer, etc. We all did pastoral work, surfacing and preparing the new leaders brave enough to assume responsibility after former catechists and delegates of the Word had been murdered.* [27]

In another 1988 letter, Carol speaks more concretely of accompanying people at critical times:

A Vine Transplanted – El Salvador

Last Wednesday we were greeted early in the morning by a group of women who came to report the capture of a man and woman from El Barillo. The man was a friend, a member of the "directiva" in El Barillo, a young, light hearted, courageous man, father of several children. He is a man we respect and admire for his leadership and goodness. We began the search for these two people, visiting the different military bases here in Suchitoto. We were finally told that they had been captured and taken to San Salvador. It was a relief to get this news. When the people are killed outright, the military usually denies knowing anything about them. The disconcerting information was that they had been captured by the "Policia de Hacienda", a group well-known for its torture tactics.

While we were searching for these two people we found out that there had been a [land]mine explosion in Estanzuelas, one of the villages of our parish. ...This time a 7 year old boy and his 18 year old brother were searching for fruit when the little boy stepped on a mine. Little David was killed instantly when the shrapnel hit him in the temple. His brother was severely injured in the foot. We arrived in the home before either the father or mother had returned. The mother had recently given birth to a new baby who was too sick to return to the village and the father had just gotten a new job in San Salvador. When we arrived the neighbors had already placed the little boy's body on a table and covered it with flowers. The boy's face was covered with a towel. When the father came home, he walked directly to the body of his son, took the towel away and looked into the face of his dead little boy. I don't know when I have experienced such intense sadness and pain. At times the senselessness of this war and the loss of innocent people's lives are more than one can bear. ...The two people from El Barillo were released on Friday. The man had been severely tortured.

On another occasion Peggy left the Sunday liturgy in *Suchitoto* early to check on something and a man from *Copapayo* broke away from the military who were holding him and came running after her. She embraced him and then stood between him and the soldiers. She kept saying *"I know this man. His wife is a catechist. I have stayed in his house. What has he done? Wherever you're taking him, I'm going with him."* She got in the car first, and they all went to the military base. After an hour or so they released him, saying that something on his ID card had been erased. Peggy walked with him down to the lake and waited until he got the boat to *Copapayo*. The following day the pastor and all the sisters were called in to the military base. The commander spoke only to the pastor about the chain of command in the military and his understanding that there are also chains of command in the Church. He said, "Please control your nuns and do not allow them to interfere with arrests." Peggy mentioned to him that a young military man was at the Way of the Cross that week, drunk and brandishing his gun. Someone could have gotten hurt. She asked him to please control his soldiers as well.

There were many instances when the sisters accompanied people to look for captured or missing family members, to denounce human rights abuses, and to seek the release of people being held and tortured. The daily walking with them was less dramatic but did entail some hardship. There was no electricity or potable water in the villages, giving the sisters frequent intestinal parasites. There was no means of transportation other than walking long distances, or flagging down an occasional passing truck for a ride. But being received into the lives of the Salvadoran people was a singular joy. Carol describes:

> The ten years I spent in El Salvador without a doubt were some of my happiest years in ministry....We were taken in and made one with a people not our own. It is true that experiencing the same dread of bombing raids and flying bullets forged bonds very quickly with the people. ... It was always a humbling experience to be unconditionally accepted by the people, but it was a freeing experience, also. The Salvadoran people have a contagious spirit of celebration and love for life. Maybe the close contact with death made life all the more precious, or maybe it is just in their makeup to celebrate life....

> I especially remember moments when I was filled with this conviction that happiness lies in relationships and not in material things. I had just spent a very enjoyable evening with a family. Story-telling and laughter abounded as we sat outdoors under the stars. At the end of the evening, we entered the one-room house to retire for the night. I remember mentally counting how many of us there were in this little room measuring no more than 12 by 12 feet. There were 14 of us. I was ashamed to be occupying one bed by myself. The other beds were shared and several of the children slept on plastic sheets on the dirt floor. The house itself was made of bamboo slats filled in with mud, and a tin roof. There was neither electricity nor running water. ...There was a time when I might have imagined that people living in those conditions could not be happy; but now I knew a different reality. Knowing that I could actually live with very few material comforts and still be quite happy gave me a real freedom. [28]

A Vine Transplanted – El Salvador

Srs. Janet May and Anne Sedgwick, visiting Sisters in Suchitoto

Another source of joy for the sisters lay in the people who supported them, particularly women from both congregations. Two Sisters of Charity, Srs. Mary Canavan and Grace Reape, came during Holy Week of 1987, and were followed by several others from that congregation in due time. Over the years, more than fifty Franciscans came to El Salvador.

The first to come to *Suchitoto* was Sister Sharon Sullivan. The sisters had enthusiastically prepared for her visit, getting all the necessary permissions from the military for her to visit repopulated communities.

Sharon flew into Guatemala City first, was met by Maureen and Darleen, and spent a day exploring the city with them. Carol had traveled from El Salvador to meet her and accompany her by bus to *Suchitoto*. In El Salvador, Sharon visited just one repopulated village, *Montepeque*, when she began to have severe back pain. It worsened dramatically and when Sharon herself expressed concern about the possibility of a recurring staph infection, the sisters secured stronger pain medication and consulted with U.S. doctor friends in the country who suggested getting her back to her own doctor in the States as soon as possible. She was disappointed to cut the trip short and left declaring that she would be back. Saying goodbye to her at the airport, the sisters never imagined that they would never again see her alive. They were shocked to receive the phone call two days later saying that she was dying and then the news of her death the following day.

Sister Sharon Sullivan visiting Sisters in El Salvador (1988)

Kay, who was visiting in the States at the time, attended Sharon's wake and funeral and brought back a video for the others to see. Archbishop *Rivera y Damas* was very concerned when he heard of Sharon's death, and took the time to watch the video. He was also interested in seeing how the congregation celebrated such events liturgically. The neighbors in *Suchitoto* who had seen Sharon painfully climb into the back of the pickup where she lay en route to the airport were also very concerned. They asked if the sisters were going to have the traditional prayers of the dead for her in their home. They did. Carol describes it in a letter:

> *Last evening we fixed our front room with a Salvadoran cross,...a picture of Sharon, flowers and candles. The neighbors gathered and we shared with them Sharon's desire to be in solidarity with the poor---the poor of Mississippi and the poor of Central America. ...Sharon's spirit was present and alive in our midst as we celebrated her new life with our neighbors...Sharon's visit, so full of promise and pain, has been for us a blessing and a pledge of her continuing faithfulness.*

A Vine Transplanted – El Salvador

In addition to the support of their own congregations, the "Suchi sisters" were sustained in important ways by the Salvadorans. One of *Suchitoto's* repopulated women had commented *"The sisters came and took away our fear."* However, the sisters continually experienced the reverse. It was the faith and courage of the Salvadoran people that took away their fears. A monthly meeting of religious, Salvadorans and internationals, working in pastoral settings provided orientation, encouragement, and friendship. Kay, Carol, Pat, and Peggy rarely missed a meeting and found them very helpful. A second support group was of English-speaking friends, mostly from the U.S., who met to pray together and to exchange information about happenings in different areas of the country. Many lived in repopulated communities in conflict zones with experiences similar to those in *Suchitoto.* A third group, initiated by Pat and Dominican Jim Barnett (from what was at the time St. Rose Priory in Dubuque), gathered international aid workers for analysis of the reality in the country. Given the tension and ambiguities of the war, each gathering was valuable.

Sisters receiving a gift of a chicken

It was harder to connect with the sisters in Guatemala because of the distance, but both groups in El Salvador and Guatemala took advantage of every logistically reasonable opportunity to do so. The sisters in El Salvador always flew in and out of Guatemala City when going to the States and tried to connect with one or more of their companions from *San Miguel Acatán.* There was one total gathering in *Suchitoto* of the sisters from both countries

A Vine Transplanted – El Salvador

when Franciscan Sr. Camilla and Ursuline Sr. Fran were both visiting Central America.

Sisters from Guatemala and El Salvador with congregational leaders

The most immediate ongoing support for the sisters in *Suchitoto* was, of course, their own local community. In a 1996 unpublished manuscript, Pat writes:

> *When I think of the group of us, I picture two places in the house – the kitchen table and the chapel. The table is where we most seemed to find each other, not only at meal time. The exchange that happened there varied from the sublime to the ridiculous. At differing times it was thoughtful, raucous, affectionate, tense, affirming, humorous, relaxed, confrontational, profound. Always there was popcorn. The chapel was the only space in the house to be alone, so it was a refuge of sorts for each of us. It's where we also gathered in the morning to silently pray alone in one another's presence and then to share and pray together. I can picture where each of us typically sat and still feel the power of being silently present to each one, to the prayer of each one. It was*

A Vine Transplanted – El Salvador

intimate and strengthening in the face of the many struggles we faced. Individually and collectively we kept running into the best and the worst of ourselves. The struggles with language, culture, relationships and war had us often insecure and vulnerable. At the same time, the intensity of the situation we were living called forth all the faith, ingenuity, maturity and generosity we could muster.

Sisters Pat Farrell and Kay Koppes at Christmas time

We could never have done individually in the Suchitoto zone what we were able to do as a group. We were in an area of vast need and great geographical distances and five of us, for one thing, were just able to cover a whole lot more territory than any one of us could have. Our presence as a group made us able to be present to the people in a more decentralized way – out with the folks. Our being able to specialize in differing areas of pastoral work made it possible to be a more holistic support to the people. Also, we were in a situation of such tension and complexity that four heads could more easily piece together what we were hearing and seeing around us. We had to learn everything from the people, and each of us had a set of relationships from which to draw. Group discernment, without thinking in those terms or calling it that, helped keep us on track in a situation in which it was clearly important to stand for and stand against certain things. We did a lot of creative planning together and elaborated materials that we thought responded to the continually changing reality the people were living. We played off one another's strengths. We also triggered one another's vulnerabilities. Some of the fear and stress of the war around us we took out on one another. The dynamic among us was not always easy. It was, however, rich and real. [29]

Together the sisters were finding their way. As their language skills and confidence progressed, they shared the task of aid distribution channeled through the archdiocese's Social Secretariat: food, medicine, housing materials, seed and fertilizer. The challenge was to get materials through the two military check points on the road to Suchitoto. The sisters were sometimes called to meet supplies coming to Suchitoto at the check point to help negotiate their passage. The military wanted to prevent anything coming into the area that could make its way up the mountain to support the *guerrilla*s. The plastic tubing brought in for projects of potable water could be made into pipe bombs. Food could nourish the FMLN army. Medicine was most suspicious for its potential to heal wounded combatants. Most questionable of all would be any kind of anesthesia, particularly coveted in the mountains where it was very difficult to perform needed amputations for wounded *guerrillas* without it. Medical supplies were carefully scrutinized before being allowed into the area.

Once Kay had organized the transport of medical supplies from the archdiocese. She had been told that there was anesthesia included. She was asked to hide it as best she could. Two of the other sisters were with her in the pickup carrying the load and all were nervous that if it were found they would be labeled as *guerrilla* sympathizers and captured by the military. They began praying as they turned north to take the road into *Suchitoto*. It was the rainy season, and as they approached the first check point there was such an extraordinarily heavy downpour that they were just waved through. No soldier wanted to brave the heavy rains. It was the only time in all their years in *Suchitoto* that they were ever waved through the checkpoint!

Carol writes (October 1988 letter):

> *About a month ago the director of El Barillo went to San Salvador to purchase 400 baby chickens to be grown by all the families in one community. When the truck arrived at the military checkpoints they were told they did not have the necessary permission to let the chickens pass. So the 400 chickens had to be left there while the men went for the military permission. Finally they were told that the chickens could pass but the vehicle could not. So the community, adults and children, walked two hours to Suchitoto and returned with the chickens tucked*

A Vine Transplanted – El Salvador

under their arms. As they recount the story, they tell how a simple little errand that might have taken a couple of men two hours in a pickup took the effort and time of the whole community and four days of negotiating. They were happy they only lost six chickens in the midst of all this hassle!!

Most important of all was to ensure the safe passage of the Salvadoran people through the military checkpoints! Groups of displaced people continued to organize and repopulate vacated lands in the municipality and parish of *Suchitoto*. When the sisters arrived in 1988, there were six repopulated communities. In 2015 there were more than eighty and for most of them the sisters in *Suchitoto* constituted the international accompaniment considered essential to the safety of those returning. To give the flavor of just one, the repopulation of *Pepeishtenango* is recounted by Pat in a letter:

I walked with a crowd of people going to accompany the returning refugees....Gradually the road was more overgrown... Clearly the area had been abandoned for years. The first clue that we were approaching Pepeishtenango was the white flag protruding from a distant tree top – a message of neutrality and a plea for peace to passing helicopters and bombers. Second clue was the chop-chop of machetes whacking away at trees, as they were clearing, building.

We want peace with justice in El Salvador." A banner marked the entrance to a festive sort of chaos. People meeting and greeting, tortillas being slapped into shape to feed the crowds, children "helping" here and there: it was all a contagion of emotion. Mixed emotion. So many memories. "See this piece of what used to be a wall? This is the house where I grew up. And over here is where I used to sneak off with Juan before we were married. And this cave-like formation of rock is where we'd run for shelter from the bombs. And see the old church over there? Just a lot of rubble now, but it was such a beautiful church. There are three bodies buried there at the entrance. We buried them just before we all fled. I'll never forget how they looked when we found them... We knew then it was time to leave.

Then followed the celebration of the Eucharist. It was a real thanksgiving, ending with the song 'When the poor believe in the poor, then we'll be able to sing freedom.... Afterwards came a series of pep talks from...visiting popular organizations, offering lots of encouragement, support and solidarity. ... By nightfall every family had a shelter: a frame of branches with a sturdy piece of plastic over it. The visiting gringos would be given special attention. We got the "Sheraton": a Coleman camping tent, assembled with difficulty as we deciphered the English instructions by flashlight, just in time before it started to pour.

Even with the rain, the refugees were determined to celebrate this homecoming with a dance. We muddied up one area so badly we had to move to another. But spirits were high and the people continued dancing, wet, muddy, and delighted. Personally not so sure this was "fun", I retreated to the "Sheraton." Finding, however, drips from the ceiling and leaks in the floor, I rejoined the dance, literally until dawn.

Since the day of repopulation, the numbers in Pepeishtenango have more than doubled and house building is well under way. There have been a few combats uncomfortably near, but with no harm to the new community. Pepeishtenango has won back the space that is theirs. Another victory for the Salvadoran people.

"Peligro Minas" (Danger Land Mines)

In addition to accompanying the growing number of repopulations, the sisters gradually concentrated on individual areas of responsibility. Kay worked with the Social Secretariat of the archdiocese to train health promoters, hoping to have in each repopulated community a dispensary and a person able to tend to basic health concerns. Both the numbers and expertise of health promoters increased steadily. She coordinated with and supported a number of international solidarity efforts focusing on health: giving further training to local midwives, participating in vaccination

A Vine Transplanted – El Salvador

campaigns, fitting amputees with prosthetic limbs, promoting potable water and latrine projects to improve hygiene, helping get individuals with the most critical health needs to the U.S. for medical attention, etc. She was frequently sought out as the contact person for health concerns.

Kay also wrote a grant proposal for funds to rehab the parish center, needed as a training location where people from distances could spend the night. She sent it to the Dubuque Franciscan leadership team, requesting their help to find a funding organization. The congregation itself chose to provide the needed money and Kay meticulously managed the building project, overseeing the workers and their progress. Weekly she traveled by bus to a town that had a bank in order to withdraw money and pay each laborer. The rehabbed parish center was highly used and proved to be indispensable for all kinds of leadership training.

The Social Secretariat promoted micro-lending programs and one of the most successful in the *Suchitoto* area was the one Kay managed with women from the market. Her frequent meetings, support, and detailed oversight of the funds made it work and endeared her to the women. The other sisters would tease her about her "market ministry" when she would go out in the morning to get bread for breakfast and return an hour later. She never rushed her contact with people, and of all the sisters, she was, perhaps, the most temperamentally suited to the Salvadoran culture. Always generous with her time, she was very attentive, compassionate, and present to people.

Carol focused on the training of catechists, on supporting efforts to reorganize some semblance of a rural school system, and on preparing teachers for those schools. In an environment where church workers were often the first to be captured, tortured, or killed, the people willing to be trained and serve in that capacity were truly heroic. In less than a year after the sisters arrived in *Suchitoto*, there were already fifty catechists who had attended a week-long training.

Franciscan Associate John Donaghy tells of Carol's work of catechist formation:

> *The development of the local Church demanded the training of catechists in the local communities, a task that Sister Carol undertook with great skill and sensitivity to the needs of the people. Carol helped*

A Vine Transplanted – El Salvador

catechists develop a basic understanding of their faith and she trained them in ways to use a popular, participative methodology in their teaching.

These efforts faced many obstacles. Some of the catechists were very young and some could barely read. They were all very poor and had to bring their own meals to the training sessions. In the countryside they would meet wherever they could, in people's houses, in the ruins of the Church, under trees, in communal buildings, often fashioned from buildings devastated by the war.

Carol held regular training sessions, sometimes in Suchitoto, sometimes in the communities where she would bring together people from that particular geographical area of the parish…. There was a major effort to get parents involved. The catechists in each community were responsible for leading a monthly meeting of the parents of the children, which included materials for the catechetical formation of the parents. These were not merely meetings to hear about what their children were doing; they were attempts to get the parents to understand their faith more fully.

Carol also gave experienced catechists major roles in the training programs. For example, in 1992, experienced catechists accompanied and trained new catechists during the months when Carol was out of the country. [30]

Provisional classroom to replace a school that was bombed

A Vine Transplanted – El Salvador

To this day, many of the same catechists faithfully continue their work after years of organization, creative methods and continuous encouragement from Carol.

Carol was involved with promoting basic education in the repopulation communities where there were no schools or where they had been destroyed by the bombings. The archdiocese developed a program of support for "popular teachers"---that is, volunteers from their respective communities willing to gather the children to provide basic education. Carol recruited, trained, and supported those teachers and eventually helped find funds to pay them a minimal stipend. Her supportive attention to each of them gave courage to some who didn't think themselves capable of the role and reinforcement to others overwhelmed with so many additional tasks. Rina, for instance, the "principal" of the school in *La Mora,* was a bright, energetic fourteen-year-old. She began as a popular teacher at age twelve with a classroom of 40 first graders. The director of the school in *El Barillo, Guadalupe,* was the mother of nine children and a grandmother and also taught fourth grade. Carol speaks of her history in a letter:

> *Lupe's teaching days go back several years. In the early 1980s the people from her village often spent days and weeks hiding from the Salvadoran military... During these days of hiding, Lupe would gather the children for informal classes. They wrote numbers and letters with sticks in the dirt. For the children's safety, the classes were held close to 'tatus' – underground caves dug out for shelter from bombing attacks.*

Young child near a "tatu" – bomb shelter

A Vine Transplanted – El Salvador

Carol was the support for these teachers who, along with many others she prepared, are still teaching classes.

Pat formed a youth choir and later a children's choir in *Suchitoto* and worked with them at weekly liturgies. She gave guitar lessons both in town as well as in the rural communities and helped repopulations purchase or make instruments. The goal was to have a choir and groups of musicians in each village. Pat and the other sisters coordinated attendance at music workshops by *Equipo Maiz* both in *San Salvador* and in *Suchitoto*. Later a core group of the best local musicians helped her replicate the workshops for larger groups in *Suchitoto*.

Working with local fishermen, Pat helped set up an agro-fishing cooperative and secured funding for collectively-owned boats and nets. The co-op was legalized with 100 members, but for a number of reasons it was relatively short-lived.

Together Pat and Peggy focused on working with women. They began with special parish-wide rituals for events like Mother's Day and the International Day of the Women. Specific consciousness-raising work was established in the areas of sex education and domestic violence. John Donaghy again writes:

> The role of women is a major problem in El Salvador, especially in a culture suffused with machismo. A major and very successful effort of Pat and Peggy has been in assisting in the formation of a women's movement in Suchitoto.
>
> Their work began with simple sex education. They had found that some women were only vaguely aware of the connection between intercourse and pregnancy. To address this lack of basic knowledge they arranged for some gender and sexuality workshops for women which were facilitated by Equipo Maiz. Yet as the work progressed resistance arose among the men. In a clear case of projection, some men complained that if women know their menstrual cycles and the times when they could become pregnant, the women would be able to have affairs and not get pregnant! The sisters also provided opportunities for women to meet together and to pray using rituals full of symbols that reflected women's experiences. [31]

A Vine Transplanted – El Salvador

March in San Salvador: Women for Dignity and Life

After the signing of the peace accords in El Salvador the work with women grew significantly and will be described in more detail later in this book.

Peggy's rhythm of teaching theology the fall semester in New York and spending the remainder of the year in El Salvador was beneficial on several levels. Her teaching was informed by the war in El Salvador and she was able to do theological reflection on that reality in preparing for her classes. This reflection benefited the sisters in *Suchitoto* who were busy responding to emergencies and had less opportunity to reflect on what they were living. When in El Salvador, Peggy worked with Pat on women's issues. Peggy's background in feminist theology and ritual shaped and enriched their work.

One of Peggy's central responsibilities was working with agricultural projects. She worked in the form of low-interest loans for seed and fertilizer. A local agronomist assisted her in providing technical support and training to improve productivity and care of the land. The sisters enjoyed the obvious reversal of expectations in having a woman from the New York area overseeing agricultural projects while the women from Iowa focused on other things!

Peggy used her theology background teaching for five years in the inter-congregational novitiate program sponsored by CONFRES, the Conference of Religious of El Salvador, and in other programs for the formation of pastoral leaders in parishes.

A Vine Transplanted – El Salvador

As the number of repopulation communities multiplied, the sisters and pastor subdivided the parish into geographical zones, with a sister in charge of each. She would visit regularly and gather pastoral workers, both in individual communities as well as in the zone for support and planning. Five Jesuit scholastics joined the parish team on weekends, each regularly visiting at least one rural community.

Every Lent the sisters prepared reflection materials responding to El Salvador's current situation. This resource was sprinkled with the creative use of symbol and ritual. Rural pastoral teams received training for using it. The sisters conducted Lenten missions in the villages, staying three or four days in each community, gathering groups at night, and visiting the homes by day. The result of some of the missions was the formation of a few Base Christian Communities that met for a time, though there was insufficient follow-up for them to continue long term. Carol says of those Lenten experiences (letter) *"For me this time was very special.... It was good to have the time to listen to their stories, share their beans and rice, bathe in the river with them in the morning and sleep with the whole family in their one-room adobe house in the evening."*

The military was not happy with the sisters' presence in the repopulation communities. Local commanders began to require them to sign in and out at the *Suchitoto* military base to monitor their comings and goings in rural areas. When the sisters went to renew military permission to be in *Suchitoto* they were told they could no longer visit any rural community. They had to limit their presence and work to the town of *Suchitoto*. They were very distressed about this and sought advice from the archdiocese. In order to avoid confrontation with the military, it was suggested that they restrict their work to Suchitoto for awhile They began to conduct a pastoral census in town, with each sister accompanied by someone from the neighborhood where she was working. The soldiers began following them to the houses and stood in the doorways to hear conversations. People were intimidated and wouldn't express much. The sisters were called to the military base and told they could no longer do a census in *Suchitoto*. They decided to just visit homes, not making any reference to a census. One day when Kay and Carol were alone in *Suchitoto*, a soldier came to the house with a written order saying that all the sisters had to be completely out of *Suchitoto* within 48 hours. They phoned archbishop *Rivera y Damas* who was furious. His ability as bishop to have pastoral workers in combat zones was at stake. He told

A Vine Transplanted – El Salvador

Carol and Kay that he would take care of it. In a matter of hours the soldier returned and asked for the written order back. From that time on, the sisters continued their work without being blocked by the local military.

This was not the end of suspicions about them and they continued to face dangers. Those who worked in conflict zones were suspected of links with the *guerrillas*, or at the very least of being sympathetic toward them. The sisters were often accused of being communists, *guerrillas*, or subversives. John Donaghy writes: *"The story is told that a priest who was talking with Archbishop Rivera y Damas about possibly working in Suchitoto expressed his concern that the sisters were guerrillas. The archbishop stood up and pounded his fist on the desk: "They are not guerrillas."* [32] In fact, the sisters worked hard at transcending ideological categories and not being identified with any given group. *Guazapa* (the *guerrilla*-controlled mountain area in the *Suchitoto* parish) was the place where the umbrella organization of five separate, geographically-based armed groups came together to form the FMLN (*Farabundo Martí de Liberación Nacional* – The *Farabundo Martí* National Liberation Front). The repopulated communities had strong loyalties to one or the other of those sub-groupings, with certain rivalries among them as a result. The sisters made every effort to relate to all communities and organizations equally.

They also shared with the people the dangers of living in a war zone. Each of the sisters found herself, at differing times, in the midst of life-threatening situations. Walking from village to village, they would frequently be warned by the *guerrillas* to go by another path, or to turn back, because of combat either in progress on the road ahead or likely to take place soon. Sometimes a warning was not possible and they found themselves in situations of cross fire, needing to run or look for a place to take cover. Occasionally they encountered dead bodies on the road. The military were always irritated when finding the sisters in the zone, whereas the people of the communities sought them out at times of a military incursion in the area, knowing their presence to be a deterrent and a protection. After the publicity about human rights abuses in El Salvador following the murder of the four U.S. church women, another dead U.S. sister would endanger continued military aid and could be quite problematic for the Salvadoran military. Nonetheless, the parish sacristan told the sisters after the war ended that he had been pressured into being an informant. He gave as little information about them as he could but had discovered that one of the commanders in *Suchitoto* had a plan to kill them and the priest. That would have been a serious tactical error, and when a higher authority discovered that commander's intentions he removed him from responsibilities in *Suchitoto*.

By autumn of 1989, military aid from the U.S. was being seriously questioned due to growing opposition from the general American public, especially Central American solidarity groups. Congress was asking whether the war in El Salvador was close to being won. The Salvadoran military's response was that the *guerrillas* were pretty well defeated and were no longer even a significant number. That was hardly the case. The *guerrillas* began moving troops into the capital to stage an all-out offensive there, making themselves visible and their force felt in the hope of forcing the government to the negotiating table.

The preparations were observable in the repopulation communities. Groups of *guerrillas* were on the move at night, walking little by little towards the capital. When staying in the communities, the sisters saw them in greater numbers. Some were saying goodbye to family members and the sisters were asked to take a picture of several of them, so the family would have at least one photo if they did not return alive.

The November offensive was a bloodbath. The military responded to *guerrilla* attacks and their presence in poor neighborhoods by bombing those areas. An estimated 2,000 people were killed, mostly civilians. Six Jesuits and two women, their housekeeper and her daughter, were murdered on November 16. Despite the government's claim of no persecution of the Church, at least fifty church properties were raided and ransacked. Some 54 Salvadoran church workers were captured by the military and over forty foreign church and humanitarian agency workers were forced to leave the country. Some received death threats and left voluntarily while others were captured by the military and deported. The sisters' support group of other foreign missioners was almost halved.

Suchitoto was outside the zone of this offensive, and it was difficult for the sisters to get accurate information about what was happening, aside from cryptic phone calls from friends in the capital who strongly suspected that their phones were tapped. Carol and Kay were alone. Peggy was teaching in the States and Pat had gone home for a visit, finding herself caught up in the situation of Dianna Ortiz's kidnapping and torture. Both Pat and Peggy took advantage of speaking in the U.S. about what was happening in El Salvador. Carol writes of her experience (December 1989 letter):

> *During the worst of this time we had only two sources of information – the official military radio station and the clandestine radio station of the rebels. Needless to say, neither source was impartial. ... We are grateful that we could remain in Suchitoto during this time. Because we are in a "state of siege" many of our normal activities and meetings have been suspended... After the first week of the conflict we were told by the military that if we continued to visit the villages we would be taken to the First Brigade in San Salvador (and we knew that meant we would probably not be able to return). During the first few weeks we had a 6 pm to 6 am curfew. People had to be in their homes and anyone out after this time would be shot on sight. ... The people from the villages come to our house when there have been captures or attacks and we do what we can to help.*

Two of the *Suchitoto* villages were attacked. In *Copapayo* the houses were identified by flares dropped by the air force, followed by machine gunning from the air. Carol continues,

> *Miraculously, the community was prepared. The week before each family had dug a trench beside their "champitas" (small homes) and the flares gave everyone enough time to seek the safety of their trenches. No one was killed or injured though several houses were hit during the attack.*

The next morning there was another attack during which the community's boats, its only means of transportation, were machine gunned from helicopters. In an attack on the community of Montepeque, two people were killed and two injured from aerial shooting, while others spent hours hidden under beds or wherever they could find shelter. Carol again comments:

> *I want to stress that these were direct attacks on civilian populations. There are not armed communities and there were no armed combatants in the communities at the time of the attacks. In their frustration, the military has decided to retaliate against communities they suspect of supporting the guerrillas.*

In the midst of the chaos of those days, a woman from one of the repopulation communities managed to get to *Suchitoto*. She told Kay and

A Vine Transplanted – El Salvador

Carol that if they had to leave they should, telling them *"Don't think that you're abandoning us. We know that you're leaving us in God's hands."*

Gradually some semblance of normalcy returned to daily life in both the capitol and in *Suchitoto*. However, a qualitative shift had occurred in the trajectory of the war. There was growing insistence from both national and international voices on a cease fire and negotiated end to the war.

Growth of the Community

That was the environment Sister Nancy Meyerhofer (age 42) encountered when she came to El Salvador in August of 1990. She traveled all the way from the States by land, chauffeured by Passionist priest Arthur Carrillo (a friend from her time in San Antonio) and his sister. Nancy was a very welcome addition to the community. It was to everyone's advantage, particularly her own, that she came as an experienced missioner, fluent in Spanish and tempered by the violence and unrest in Chile. Her previous pastoral experience, especially her work with youth and mental health, would prove to be invaluable. Before focusing her work in El Salvador she began exploring the area and meeting people. She received an early baptism by fire when she and Kay were caught in cross fire.

Sr. Nancy Meyerhofer and Orlando Menjivar in the village of San Antonio

A Vine Transplanted – El Salvador

Nancy began helping with music and eventually took over the youth choir in *Suchitoto*, where she became acquainted with youth who would become group leaders. No one was doing full-time youth work in *Suchitoto* when she came and she saw the great need. The first youth group she formed, Cristos *Jóvenes* (Christs Youth), became a seedbed of leadership for spawning other groups. Nancy put a great deal of emphasis on leadership formation of youth throughout her time in El Salvador. She developed a variety of venues and formats for forming and developing leaders, both in *Suchitoto* and in the rural communities. By the end of her first year, she was working with seven youth groups. John Donaghy describes her work:

> One of her goals was to break down the fears and divisions between the youth in the city and the countryside. To do this she would often bring youth from town with her when she went out to the rural communities. Overnight training sessions (capacitaciones) in Suchitoto brought together youth from all parts of the parish. Nancy saw the need for group monitors in each community and for developing leadership among the youth. But young people, not adults, had to be the leaders of youth groups....

> At the height of her youth work there were 30 groups and 55 leaders in the parish. After the war ended, with more things for youth to do, fewer were involved in church youth groups. But even in 1994 there was a youth encounter...in the department of Cuscatlan. Over 300 young people came from the parish of Suchitoto. [33]

Nancy obtained funds in the U.S. for scholarships for the most promising youth leaders to pursue university studies. One who was an English major even spent a semester at Iowa State University. Three became Associates of the Dubuque Franciscans.

Transition to Peace

Nancy's beginnings in El Salvador in 1990 allowed her to witness the process that would eventually lead to the end of the war. A series of dialogue and negotiation sessions began, bringing together government, military and *guerrilla* leaders. The second session yielded an agreement on basic points of respect for human rights. The third session attempted to reach agreement on a process for demilitarization of the country, ending in a stalemate on that issue. There was halting progress, as both sides persisted in the dialogues, in a national environment of both tension and expectation.

171

A Vine Transplanted – El Salvador

Finally, government and *guerrilla* leaders came to a tentative peace agreement when they met in New York during the closing hours of 1991 and as Perez de Cuellar was concluding his time as Secretary General of the UN. El Salvador's 12 years of civil war had come to an end! The official signing of the peace accords took place in *Chapultepec*, Mexico on January 16, 1992. The same day there was an ecumenical prayer service in the central plaza in San Salvador. The sisters were present to witness that historic moment, to pray for the 75,000 Salvadorans killed in the war, and to weep with the gathered crowd---tears of joy for peace as well as tears of sorrow for those who did not live to see that long-awaited day.

Men knocking down a bunker in Suchitoto.
Dismantling the mechanisms of war

It wasn't until February 1, that the actual cease-fire went into effect. The sisters awoke in *Suchitoto* that morning to the sight of men with sledge hammers knocking down the bunkers on street corners, literally dismantling the mechanisms of war.

They traveled to San Salvador for another massive celebration in the central plaza. Even en route to the capital they sensed a different tone. When they arrived at the military check point where they had been stopped and searched for years, the soldiers were taking down their post, already in the process of leaving. When they got as far as the Pan-American Highway they met truckloads of people coming from poor communities in the eastern part of the country waving FMLN flags. Previously people would have been shot for such a display. Those visual signs of peace were very moving.

A Vine Transplanted – El Salvador

The central plaza in San Salvador was teeming with people. The cathedral, facing the square, displayed one huge banner with the face of *Romero*, saying *"Mons. Romero you have arisen in your people!"* It reflected the murdered archbishop's words: *"I have often been threatened with death. Nevertheless, as a Christian I do not believe in death without resurrection. If they kill me I shall arise in the Salvadoran people."*

It is impossible to describe the jubilance of that gathering. People were hugging those standing around them, both friends and strangers. Cheers erupted when the *guerrilla* leaders who had lived clandestinely in the mountains for years, appeared in public. It was a sign of both resurrection and initial reconciliation to see officials of both the military and FMLN standing together on one public platform, addressing the same assembled crowd of Salvadorans. It was unforgettable, and certainly inspired hope for healing the divisions of war!

The celebration of the signing of the peace accords

A Vine Transplanted – El Salvador

Pastoral Work in the Post War Environment

Carol (1992 letter) describes how the effects were felt in *Suchitoto*:

> *I can't tell you how much difference the cease fire makes in our work. Before, we never knew when we left the house in the morning if we would encounter cross fire, machine gunning from helicopters or military checkpoints. When we planned meetings here in Suchitoto, we never knew how many of the communities would arrive. These days it is great to set out walking in the early morning for a distant village, confident that we can enjoy the beauty of the countryside and arrive at our destination without problems.*

Popular Education teachers

Carol's work with schools and teachers intensified. The needs were extreme. During the war, 786 schools had closed, 771 of them in rural areas. Over one million school age children were not in school and the illiteracy rate of those over age ten was higher than 50%. There were an estimated 10,000 unemployed certified teachers in the country, but the national budget for teachers' salaries had dropped dramatically as the military budget more than quadrupled. Now, gratefully, there were major developments in the area of education, partly due to post-war reconstruction money designated to support education and to build schools in war-torn areas. The government began to assign a few certified teachers to work in them. The archdiocese sponsored ongoing education for the "popular teachers". A long-term goal was to help them eventually complete high school and even college and be certified, government-salaried teachers in their own villages.

Sr. Carol recognized for supporting Popular Education teachers

A letter Carol wrote in 1994 chronicles the situation at that time:

> *This year our parish has 53 popular teachers who are working in 14 different villages... Each month these popular teachers receive four days of training from a diocesan team of professionals. Some of our teachers from the first four schools have now received five years of formation and are doing a great job.*

Carol found funding for them to receive a small stipend for their work and provided continuous personal support. Their appreciation of her was shown by one of the rural schools naming its new building after her. The archdiocese presented her with an award for her steadfastness and dedication.

Similarly, Kay's presence in *Suchitoto* was a key factor in coordinating the stepped-up programing for health issues promoted by the Social Secretariat of the archdiocese. Money became available to build more facilities. Two rehabilitation centers were established and equipped in *Copapayo* and in a less-destroyed section of the old hospital in *Suchitoto* that had been damaged by bombings. Kay's ongoing support of the health promoters was very important at a time when they, like the popular teachers, were taking advantage of the opportunity to pursue nursing studies, even as they continued working in their communities as health promoters. Kay spent a great deal of her time connecting people in need with newly-available services, particularly in terms of prosthetic devices for amputees. The many relationships she had built through her companionship of presence had made her particularly aware of peoples' needs.

Pat had enlisted people from several rural communities to attend a series of trainings with her to become popular mental health promoters. The Jesuit University (*UCA*) in San Salvador was interested in the participation of former combatants, in the hope that they could be a link to the emerging post-traumatic stress needs surfacing among many of their companions. Several from *Suchitoto* attended and found the sessions very helpful. Their implementation of the work afterwards, however, did not materialize as hoped. They were facing other more immediate demands of re-insertion into family and civilian life, not the least of which was finding a way to make a living. Pat supported the few who did continue and also brought psychologists from the university to *Suchitoto* to assess some of the most acute mental health needs. She accompanied a number of people to the country's only psychiatric hospital and followed up with them.

In Peggy's post-war work with agricultural projects, she found herself interfacing more with the popular organizations in the area that were linked to FMLN sub-groupings. Though Peggy still coordinated projects available through the archdiocese, a proliferation of agricultural organizations began, each writing grant proposals and trying to capture available monies for their own grassroots groups of returned refugees. Most funding approved for agricultural and a host of other projects, included training and skill building to assure good implementation. The parish center, *Centro Romero*, restored with funds from the Dubuque Franciscans, was a beehive of activity in those days, hosting a multitude of training workshops.

Among the many challenges in the early post-war environment was the competition for the time and attention of individuals and communities. People were pulled in many directions at once. Just when Salvadorans all over the country most needed to rest and regroup, they had to be attentive to

A Vine Transplanted – El Salvador

whether the peace accords were being implemented and to mobilize efforts that would pressure the government to do so. Demonstrations, usually in San Salvador, depended on participation from the repopulation communities, their loyalty and commitment to change was assumed by national leadership to be strong. Meanwhile, there was reconstruction money to build houses, latrines, water projects, but the people had to supply the labor, without the help of construction machinery and in sweltering tropical heat. If they were to take advantage of project monies, they had to attend training sessions and assume leadership and responsibility for implementation. It was impossible to do everything. Much of the money was badly used, a number of projects failed, and corruption was rampant in the distribution of funds. Nonetheless, the people now had land, a house, and the basics they did not have before the war. It was a great victory, though an exhausting and costly one.

The moment was psychologically difficult. People could finally let down their guard and mourn the dead, as well as other losses from the war. Grief and hope, resiliency and vulnerability were intermingled. Former *guerrillas* returned to families where women had assumed all of the responsibility in their absence. Many wives were not ready to be sidelined again by *machista* attitudes that didn't recognize their newfound capacities. Former combatants from both sides had to find work or take advantage of the scholarships offered to former members of the *guerrillas* and military. Though many floundered in the process, success stories abounded, evident in the sustained service ex-combatants offered in their communities. Post-traumatic stress reactions slowly began to surface, manifested often in alcoholism, drug addiction and domestic violence.

As reconstruction money poured into the country and the four sub-groupings of the FMLN operative in the *Suchitoto* parish began scrambling to develop projects for their respective grassroots constituencies, competition among the communities increased. The sisters in *Suchitoto* recognized their potential to bring people together in ways that transcended political loyalties. If any one of the local organizations would convene a meeting, only their respective communities would come. If the parish invited, all would come. They discerned how to best utilize that advantage to serve as agents of unity and reconciliation.

One initiative of Peggy and Pat that proved to be very successful was the creation of a coalition of women's organizations, the *Concertación*

A Vine Transplanted – El Salvador

de Mujeres de Suchitoto (The Coalition of Women of Suchitoto). The sisters had already built relationships with the women, identified and formed leaders and done consciousness-raising around gender issues. Now, a variety of new organizations were springing up both nationally and locally, capturing available funds for women's projects. One of the main hopes of the new coalition was to use potential funding as a source of unity rather than division. The *Concertación de Mujeres de Suchitoto* would identify and prioritize needs together and look for funds for collective projects.

The Coalition of Women of Suchitoto

The first priority was to address the discrimination against women in certain provisions of the peace accords. Ex-combatants were offered either land to farm or a scholarship to study. However, women ex-combatants (about 25% of the FMLN) were not included if they were married to or living with another ex-combatant. In spite of the indignation of the women, their protests were unsuccessful.

The second priority was to address domestic violence. The Committee for the Defense of Women was established. The committee quickly mobilized when a woman's former husband returned to kidnap their child. She suspected that he had taken the child to his own mother's house, such a distance away, that the former wife could not travel there. A group from the newly formed committee piled in a pickup with Pat and Peggy, traveled to the mother-in-law's house, declared that they would not leave without the child, and returned successfully. The women felt empowered, and the Committee for the Defense of Women was launched with determination. The organization is still strong as of this writing, providing legal advice, accompaniment and education. One of their members works in the police station, available to assist women in situations of domestic violence or sexual assault. The committee, now a legal non-profit organization, has devoted itself to education of both men and women in rural communities on issues of violence against women and the instances of violence have decreased significantly.

A third priority was women's literacy. While illiteracy in general in El Salvador was over 50%, it was disproportionately higher in rural areas and even more so among women. A program was developed using feminist literacy materials from Nicaragua based on *Paulo Freire*'s method which combined reading skills with a process of raising awareness of gender issues. Some of the men became alarmed and objected, in some cases not allowing their wives to attend classes. The work continued, somewhat adapted, for eight years. Many women benefited from the program until the funding was discontinued.

Everyone benefited from the more peaceful post-war environment, and in such a climate the sisters' pastoral work flourished. Reconciliation became the focus of Lenten missions. In that spirit, Nancy's work with youth was all the more meaningful in its goal of building bridges between youth from *Suchitoto* where there had been more support for the military and from the villages that had been under *guerrilla* control. As the number of groups and trained youth leaders increased, so did the camaraderie that crossed ideological differences.

An unanticipated and very moving moment of reconciliation took place when Carol prepared dinner for six *Suchitoto* catechists in appreciation for their hard work. One of the women was the wife of the right wing party's mayor of *Suchitoto* who had resigned after a death threat from the FMLN. Others were from villages and moved to *Suchitoto* when the military's massacres began. Carol recounts in a letter:

A Vine Transplanted – El Salvador

These women have worked closely with each other for four years but have felt it necessary to hide their personal pain. I'm not sure what caused Juana to open up that night, but once she began her story she was like a floodgate that had been opened. I watched the shocked faces of the other women and thanked God for the courage she had to share. Back in 1981 she received word that her son had been killed by the death squads and that his body was scattered all over a local soccer field. She left the house with a wicker basket in her hands and a heart filled with fear and pain. When she arrived at the soccer field, the dogs had already begun to eat parts of her son's body. He had been tortured and sliced up into small parts. She told how she found one of his lips and then the other. She placed them together and put them into the basket. Slowly gathering all the parts, she collected what had not been eaten. Her tears flowed freely. There was silence at the table when she finished. There are no words. As Scripture says of Rachel, "Her tears cannot be silenced because her children are no more."

Reconciliation came as grace in such moments of sharing the human sorrow found on both sides of the civil war. But, on the whole, it did not come easily anywhere. The Catholic Church of El Salvador was no exception. Different sectors of the Church reflected the whole spectrum of political tendencies and allegiances. The archdiocese of San Salvador had a legacy of progressive bishops after Vatican II and *Medellín*: Archbishops *Chavez y Gonzalez, Oscar Romero,* and *Rivera y Damas.* The other members of the Salvadoran hierarchy had not supported Archbishop *Romero* and had, in fact, denounced him to Rome for his outspoken defense of human rights which they interpreted as naïve alliance with the *guerrilla* movement. In the latter part of 1994 Archbishop *Rivera y Damas* died unexpectedly of a heart attack. Archbishop *Saenz La Calle,* a member of the Opus Dei community, was named in his place.

Transition: Other Uprooting and Transplanting

The sisters did not respond enthusiastically to the new episcopal appointment. *Rivera y Damas* had supported them unreservedly and had consistently appointed pastors to *Suchitoto* whom he considered adept at working on a team. Shortly after being consecrated archbishop of *San Salvador, Saenz La Calle* appointed a new pastor to *Suchitoto.* The new priest made his authority felt and soon began to re-centralize parish management, reversing much of the work the sisters had done to place direction for pastoral work in the hands of local leaders.

A Vine Transplanted – El Salvador

Sisters. Peggy, SC, Carol, Pat,Kay, and Nancy

The turn of events in the parish contributed to decisions that were, to some degree, already in the making concerning future directions for several of the sisters. Peggy had been sought out to help establish a three-year Masters' program for pastoral workers in the diocese of Venice, Florida. She agreed to be part of the traveling team teaching theology in parish locations, with a schedule designed for working lay persons. She left in the summer of 1995, committing herself to help set up the program and to see it through for three years until the first cohort would graduate. Her plan was to then return to *Suchitoto* full time. Kay, who had gone to the U.S. in the summer of 1994 for a sabbatical with every intention of returning to El Salvador, decided to stay in the U.S. and accepted a job, beginning in the summer of 1995, at a health clinic in Washington, DC that served primarily Salvadoran and other Spanish-speaking immigrants. That same summer of 1995 Pat began a job in *San Salvador* as Executive Secretary for the Conference of Religious of El Salvador (*CONFRES*), wanting to help strengthen the organized influence of religious at that particular juncture in the Salvadoran church. She returned to *Suchitoto* on weekends to lend some pastoral support in villages. Nancy and Carol remained together in *Suchitoto* until late November of 1995 when Carol returned to the U.S. to begin a sabbatical program in January of 1996. By June of 1996 Pat had decided to return to the States to begin an MSW program at Loyola University in Chicago.

A Vine Transplanted – El Salvador

Shortly after Pat left, in August of 1996, Carol returned to work in *Suchitoto*. She chose to focus her work more exclusively in the area of education, spending less time in parish work. Many developments were happening in the schools and with teachers at the time, and her supportive presence was very helpful. In the summer of 1997 she decided, for personal and family reasons, to return permanently to the U.S. Her pastoral work in El Salvador was a good preparation for the work she did in Iowa on her return, serving many rural parishes with Latino immigrants.

Nancy was alone then, except during summers when Peggy returned. She was determined to remain faithful to supporting the youth leaders and their work during this time of transition. The pastor did not make it easy; one of his initiatives was to set up his own parallel youth program. Nancy guided the youth through their own conflicts and difficulties with the changes taking place in the parish and continued supporting the youth choir. With time the youth leaders had begun to marry and start families and Nancy enjoyed accompanying them in that, as well, forming couples' groups. However, she was beginning to sense that her presence was less necessary.

A new door opened for Nancy which seemed providential. She had met Pat Cane, the founder of *Capacitar*, at a workshop in San Salvador sponsored by the Conference for Religious. *Capacitar* is a popular education program that teaches holistic self-healing practices, many of them particularly helpful for trauma. It uses a train-the-trainer model designed to prepare people who can replicate workshops in order to broadly disseminate the work in areas where access to psychotherapy is neither possible nor culturally familiar. She asked Nancy to be part of the team that would promote the work of *Capacitar* in El Salvador.

As Nancy and a newly formed *Capacitar* team began doing workshops, the demand for them grew and Nancy devoted herself more full-time to this work, while continuing to work with the youth choir. Though the Capacitar team was available to work nationally, many of the early workshops were in the *Suchitoto* area, where the need for healing from trauma was great. Over time, the idea emerged to form a holistic wellness center in *Suchitoto*, a treatment facility to supplement the *Capacitar* workshops and to address war-trauma needs in the area. With the help of the Ministry Fund of the Dubuque Franciscans, Nancy's additional grant-writing and fund-raising,

A Vine Transplanted – El Salvador

and the support of *Capacitar's* international administrative team to channel grant requests, the wellness center rented a space, hired two professional Salvadoran psychologists, and was able to pay team members to do body work there. Those trained in the body-based practices so useful for the healing of trauma were themselves returned refugees. The center served many people with acute needs, most of whom were suffering from some degree of war-related trauma. Those who came were offered three modalities of treatment which, when used in combination, seemed to hasten healing: individual psychotherapy, energy-based body work, and Bach flower essences, an energy-based herbal remedy. The center clearly met a need not otherwise being addressed.

In the summer of 1998 Peggy completed her commitment in Florida and returned to El Salvador full time, living with Nancy in *Suchitoto*. Peggy continued to accompany people in repopulated communities with special attention given to the community of *El Sitio*. The people built her a small adobe house where she often stayed for extended times, developing numerous projects in that community. Soon after her return to El Salvador, Peggy began working with CRISPAZ, Christians for Peace in El Salvador, a U.S.-based solidarity group with long-term volunteers serving in a variety of locations in El Salvador. She was on their board and worked with the volunteers, giving orientation, spiritual accompaniment, and theological input. Her professional preparation in theology was a scarce resource in Central America and led her to accept two other teaching positions. The first was with the *Casa de Solidaridad* (House of Solidarity) program sponsored by the Jesuit university in San Salvador (*UCA---Universidad Centro-Americana* – Central American University). The program receives students from any U.S. Jesuit university for a semester in El Salvador. Peggy has been teaching liberation theology in the program almost since it began. Additionally, she taught liberation theology in Augsburg College's Global Education Program which offered students from any U.S. college a semester in Central America.

While Nancy's work with *Capacitar* continued to develop, so did other requests for her services. Religious congregations in need of formation resources looked to her for both spiritual as well as psychological accompaniment of mostly younger members. The Franciscan Spirituality Center in Guatemala asked her to help with TAU programs in El Salvador, Guatemala and Nicaragua. The TAU program was a month-long intensive experience for Franciscan religious. The first two weeks focused on

183

A Vine Transplanted – El Salvador

psychological input and the second two weeks were an individually-directed retreat. She often continued doing individual companioning afterwards with those she had accompanied in the TAU experience. In both El Salvador and Guatemala she initiated a formation process with Franciscan Associates, who continue to be active.

In January of 2001 Pat returned to El Salvador. During her four years in Chicago she had completed a Masters' degree in social work, with an internship at the Kovler Center for Survivors of Torture, where Dianna Ortiz had received treatment. After graduating she worked for two years in a community-based mental health program for Spanish-speaking clients and was licensed as a social worker before returning to El Salvador. She joined the *Capacitar* team in *Suchitoto*, helping with workshops and doing therapy several days a week at the wellness center. She provided therapy one day a week at the women's center in *Suchitoto*, another day at a rural health clinic in the community of *La Mora*. With time, *Capacitar* opened a satellite wellness center, open two days a week, in the neighborhood of *San Bartolo* in *San Salvador*. Pat's work there was to provide therapy primarily for religious, while a Salvadoran psychologist worked another day with the general public. Such services in El Salvador were typically available only to the wealthy. *Capacitar*, asking only for whatever donation was possible, was able to provide service to low-income people.

In July of 2002 Nancy turned over the leadership of *Capacitar* to the team that was in place, and returned to the U.S. for formal, degreed study in counseling and spiritual direction. She enrolled in an MA program in counseling at the University of San Diego and completed a two-year program in spiritual direction at the same time. She worked 20 hours a week as a chaplain at a sweat shop in *Tijuana*, Mexico, a CPE (Clinical Pastoral Education) placement. The combination of study and work was a three-year process.

Amidst so many comings and goings, the configuration of the sister presence in *Suchitoto* had been in flux for several years. Similarly, El Salvador was also undergoing continual change. At the beginning of the new millennium, the environment in El Salvador was very different from earlier post-war years. International sources of reconstruction money stopped flowing, redirected to other troubled spots around the globe. International aid came in the form of loans, conditioned by criteria for development set

A Vine Transplanted – El Salvador

by the International Monetary Fund and the World Bank, with considerable U.S. influence.

Accordingly, the Salvadoran government began to privatize all public services, shifting higher costs to citizens and directing greater profits to corporate businesses. The process was carried out with unheeded grassroots protest, until the government attempted to privatize the few public health services that had been in place. Doctors and nurses who served in *Rosales*, the large public hospital in *San Salvador*, balked, knowing that the impoverished population they served would have no access to health care if it were privatized. Hundreds of thousands of Salvadorans joined them in protests known as the "white marches." Health care workers dressed in their clinical whites and other participants also wore white. The government eventually halted the privatization of public health services, at least temporarily.

Support for agriculture noticeably waned, while the number of sweatshops in the country proliferated. The rural labor force shifted in large numbers toward urban factories. Most workers were well aware of being exploited by long hours, low salaries and prohibitions on union organizing, but they lacked other employment options. The Salvadoran government, beholden to the United States after so many years of military aid, agreed to CAFTA, the Central American Free Trade Agreement, which benefited U.S. trade to a far greater degree than its Central American counterparts. The cost of imported seed and fertilizers skyrocketed while farmers were paid less for their crops. As a result, rural communities were planting less and less and beginning to see migration to the United States as their only viable option.

Meanwhile, in the capitol, U.S. franchises were springing up everywhere and San Salvador began to look more and more like a city in the United States, while economic desperation was growing for the majority of Salvadorans. Youth, who had migrated to Los Angeles and gotten involved in gangs there, began to be deported to El Salvador and reproduced the gang culture in their home country. For diverse reasons, young people in El Salvador were susceptible to recruitment by gangs and the resulting violence has produced more homicides than during El Salvador's civil war. As a consequence, there has been a massive exodus to the United States.

A Vine Transplanted – El Salvador

Pat and Peggy, from their lives in *Suchitoto*, observed all of this with concern, even as they continued to appreciate the amazingly resilient spirit of so many of the people who surrounded them. In 2004 they became acquainted with a couple who had recently moved to *Suchitoto*. The man was originally from *Suchitoto* and had fled to Canada during the war. He and his wife were artists and were looking for a way to use art to benefit El Salvador. Peggy and Pat had been talking at length about what they could do to promote a culture of peace in the increasingly violent social milieu after the war. Together, the four of them developed the idea of beginning a center to promote a culture of peace through the arts.

The site of the project is directly across the street from the sisters' house. Central American Dominican sisters had a school there since 1914 which they abandoned after death threats in 1980. The property, an entire city block, had been abandoned for 25 years and badly needed to be restored. Through vigorous fund-raising efforts over the years, including support from the Dubuque Franciscan Ministry Fund, the property was purchased from the sisters. Restoration is ongoing as money is available and the programming is a continuous work in progress.

The center includes a multi-media community-based museum, the only one of its kind in the country. It houses a permanent collection of interviews, relating personal experiences before, during and after the war. Other thematic displays change regularly. A variety of classes are offered such as computer skills, art, music, dance, theatre, collaborative games, non-violent parenting, and others. Unique to the center is the group of young harpists, who receive ongoing preparation by a Canadian volunteer and are invited to perform in a variety of venues. Pat writes:

> *The official inauguration of the center was a day I will never forget. It took place on January 16, 2005, the anniversary of the signing of the peace accords, with more than 400 people present. Some of the Dominican sisters who left in 1980 came in a homecoming that was emotional both for them and for people from Suchitoto. We had a lovely ritual in which we used 1,000 paper cranes made by the Japanese-American artist, married to the man from Suchitoto, who was one of the co-creators with us of the project. People in attendance chose one, held it, and poured into it their prayers for peace. The paper cranes were then collected and half were received by the Japanese ambassador to El Salvador to send to the peace park in Hiroshima, and half were received by the Dominican sisters to send them to their sisters in Iraq*

A Vine Transplanted – El Salvador

whose hospital had recently been bombed. The paper cranes carried the desires for peace from one people who had known war to another.

Pat helped initiate the project in 2004-05 and then decided to return to the States, hoping to be part of establishing an intentional community focused on contemplative prayer. Moving to Omaha with Sisters Kay Forkenbrock and Marian Klostermann, that dream became a reality. Working as a bilingual therapist for Catholic Charities, she negotiated annual time away from her job to return and 195do "Alternatives to Violence" workshops at the center. The couple that began the project with the two sisters moved to Costa Rica. Peggy remained, and has been the consistent presence in the ten-year period of the development of the Center of Art for Peace. In a 2014 interview, Peggy says of the project:

Sr. Peggy at the Center of Art for Peace

When I look back at our years in El Salvador, it has, of course, all been a marvelous privilege. It seems to me that each new thing we began was the right thing at the right time, something that was needed at the moment, produced by the context. That's how I see the Center of Art for Peace. It emerged, with fluidity and connectivity. We were here at the time when the great need was material and social rebuilding after the war, when people were in need of schools, houses, even busses for transportation. But this Center of Art for Peace now aims to rebuild and nurture peoples' spirits, to rebuild hope. The world around us is so broken. There is need for a healing space, and the center is actually very quieting to those who enter. I think it touches people's pain with tenderness. We want to help people tap into beauty, into

A Vine Transplanted – El Salvador

*imagination, and to find a personal peace that can help build the social
peace that is so needed. We are now in the midst of a different kind of
war. Young people are surrounded by clouds of fear that are paralyzing.
The opportunities we provide here help them deal with their fears and
find hope. We offer options and skills that, hopefully, prevent violence
and teach collaboration and trust.*

Each of the women who served as part of the inter-congregational team
in El Salvador both left her mark and was forever marked by the people of
El Salvador. This section concludes with their own words.

Carol Besch

*It is difficult to capture my experience of El Salvador in a few words. I am
grateful for the congregational decision during chapter to establish a Border Crossing
group. It was through the support and discernment of this group that I was able to
make real a long time desire to work in Latin America. While I was in my last days of
language school in Guatemala, another student returned from a visit in El Salvador.
She was present at the refugee camp (where Pat and Kay had been working) during a
military attack. She was quite traumatized by the whole experience. As she recounted
the experience, her fear spread through my body. I remember saying to God, "If I am
filled with fear, I will not stay. I will use the Spanish I have learned to minister with
people in the U.S."*

*It was the people who taught me courage and inner strength, generosity and
endless hope. We listened again and again to the losses they had suffered, dear ones
massacred, their homes destroyed, years spent in refugee camps, and still they trusted
in God and believed that a new day would come. I was humbled by the people's
trust in us, knowing that it was our country that financed their war. How could
they welcome us so wholeheartedly into their lives? One dear friend, Lucia, was
reminiscing after the peace accords were signed: "Maybe if the war hadn't happened,
we might have never known you Sisters. I can't imagine our lives without your
presence and friendship." To this day the friendships continue and I cannot imagine
my own life without the witness of these strong folks, living and dead.*

Pat Farrell

*I am very grateful for my years in El Salvador. It was a gift to share life so
closely with the people, to be taken into their homes and their hearts, and to be
trusted beyond any merit of that. The deep emotional bonds formed through shared*

A Vine Transplanted – El Salvador

vulnerability and suffering still remain. It has made me even more grateful for the congregation, without which I would not have had the freedom and support to be in a critical place at a critical time for such an extended period. I know that our presence there made a difference, and we all share in that.

I carry an intensity of contrasting emotions and images from those days: pain and beauty, violence and tenderness, transformation, resiliency and terror. It was a real experience of paschal mystery to participate in the Salvadoran people's struggle for liberation. I learned that courage is contagious and that there is no need to fear complex situations. Strength is given as we need it. In Oscar Romero and the many martyrs I know vividly the power of lives lived in faithfulness. Biblical texts of exile and homecoming will always evoke in me images of returning refugees. My experience lays claim on my energies to do all in my power to prevent war and torture and to commit to ongoing conversion to non-violence.

Nancy Meyerhofer

To have lived in El Salvador was, again, very meaningful. Surprisingly, I never felt much fear; in that, Chile was an excellent preparation. Much of what I learned pastorally in Arica I was able to apply in Suchitoto---especially in regard to starting up the youth pastoral and later on working in the area of mental health. It was in Suchitoto that I had my first---and I hope---last experience of learning to handle conflict with hierarchy. Said conflict lasted a bit over four years and helped me know areas of myself such as an unsuspected wisdom. Again, the people taught me much: about faith and fidelity, about suffering and survival, resiliency and new beginnings. The example of Archbishop Romero was also very significant, as was that of so many anonymous martyrs. Lastly, the people called from me the service of spiritual direction and counseling, so much so that when I left Salvador in July of 2002, I enrolled in the University of San Diego to deepen my capacity to accompany in those areas. Again, I am so grateful for all that I lived and learned in El Salvador.

A Vine Transplanted – El Salvador

Chronology of Franciscan Sisters' Service in El Salvador

1986   December 3, Sisters Kay Koppes and Pat Farrell arrive in El Salvador

1987   January, Pat Farrell lives and works temporarily in *La Esperanza;* Kay Koppes goes to language school

May, Kay Koppes returns from language school and moves with Pat Farrell to the displaced persons' camp, *San José Calle Real*

June, Sister Peggy O'Neill, SC arrives and joins the others in *San José Calle Real*

1988   March 21, Sister Carol Besch arrives in El Salvador and the four sisters move to *Suchitoto*

1989   November 2, Sister Dianna Ortiz, OSU is kidnapped in Guatemala

November 11, The *guerrilla* offensive begins in San Salvador

November 16, Six Jesuits and two women employees are killed

1990   August, Sister Nancy Meyerhofer arrives in El Salvador and lives in *Suchitoto*

1992   January 16, The peace accords are signed, ending El Salvador's twelve years of civil war

1994   Summer, Kay Koppes returns to the U.S. for a sabbatical

1995   Summer, Peggy O'Neill begins a three-year commitment in Florida

Pat Farrell begins a year of service with the Conference for Religious of El Salvador

Kay Koppes decides to stay in the U.S. and begins working in a clinic in Washington, DC

Late November, Carol Besch returns to the U.S. to begin a sabbatical in January of 1996

1996   June, Pat Farrell leaves El Salvador and begins an MSW program in Chicago in the fall

August, Carol Besch returns to *Suchitoto*

A Vine Transplanted – El Salvador

1997   Summer, Carol Besch returns to the U.S. permanently

1998   Peggy O'Neill returns to El Salvador full time

2001   January, Pat Farrell returns to El Salvador and lives in *Suchitoto*

In 2001 Kay Koppes moved to Mount St. Francis in Dubuque and was diagnosed with early on-set Alzheimer's. She died in 2009.

2002   Nancy Meyerhofer leaves El Salvador to study counseling and spiritual direction in San Diego

2005   July 14, Pat Farrell returns to the U.S.

2015   Peggy O'Neill still lives in *Suchitoto,* working at Center of Art for Peace

Mexico: In Partnership with the Archdiocese of Chicago
(5 years: 1989-1994)

There is something about taking a plow and breaking new ground.
It gives you energy.   –Ken Kesez

Sister Carol Ann Berte was part of the original group that began the mission of the Archdiocese of Chicago in Mexico. What follows here is a brief account of her experience. Her own words, in a detailed diary, tell the story much more adequately. It is available in the Mount St. Francis library in Dubuque.

Sr. Carol Ann Berte, Fr. Flaherty, and Carlota with a family

Carol Ann ministered for five years in a poor, rural, indigenous area of Mexico, relatively near both Mexico City to the north and Acapulco to the west. She formed a pastoral team with four others: two priests and a layman from Chicago, and Sister Jeri Cashman, a Sinsinawa Dominican. They lived in Quechultenango in the state of Guerrero, first in a wooden shed with a dirt floor, and later in the roomy cement house constructed for the team. Her diary relates the joys, hardships, cultural richness, and great privilege of life as a missioner among a people materially impoverished and spiritually rich.

The team regularly carried out recorridos (travels) to a series of villages, one after another, staying in peoples' homes. The hardships had a great deal to do with the limited accessibility of the remote mountain villages. Travel was by any combination of pickup, motorcycle, walking, horseback or mule. Most common was travel by mule, frequently for a stretch of five hours or more at a time. A sure-footed mule afforded some sense of security over steep mountain paths near precipices, and allowed the riders to take in the gorgeous mountain scenery without having to keep their eyes on the road ahead. Not surprisingly, other hardships awaited the team when arriving in a village: saddle sores; bites from fleas, bed bugs, and an occasional scorpion; bathing and washing clothes in the river; little access to clean drinking water, resulting in stomach cramps, diarrhea, intestinal parasites; meager food; sleeping on cement or dirt floors in sleeping bags.

The joys of this rugged mission life center around the lovely and inspiring interactions with people. In Carol Ann's words, a description of arriving at a village:

> When we arrived at the village we were greeted with garlands of marigolds and bouquets of flowers which we then placed at the altar of the Church. A barefoot, elderly woman clung to me as we walked the stony path to the Church. Her husband was recently deceased … The faith of the people is incredible as are their problems: scarcity of food, lack of health care and sanitation. I felt so small next to this giant of faith and I prayed for strength as I was overwhelmed at my powerlessness to verbally communicate or to render medical care. What I did was to walk with her and to bless the numerous children who were following us. [34]

A Vine Transplanted – Mexico

Sr. Carol Ann, Carlota and Ted with a
family in village of Cocoyul

There was a singular, if bittersweet, sense of privilege in being taken by the people to visit the homes of those most in need of comfort: the physically and mentally handicapped, the bedridden chronically ill, the dying, the mentally ill, the grieving. Carol Ann comments: *"To enter these homes, which for the most part are so poor, is so touching… These are the ones for whom Jesus had a special love and concern. I loved to visit these homes and did so regularly."*

Other privileged pastoral moments Carol Ann mentions in her diary: preparing a Baptism at which the child was named after her; holding a very ill elderly woman who died in her arms; transporting a pregnant woman to the hospital only to have her give birth in the front seat of pickup; blessing a young couple at their wedding only to be blessed in turn by them; walking in procession to the cemetery and presiding at burials beautiful in their stark simplicity. Carol Ann's diary describes the cemetery scene:

> *This is always such a moving experience for me. Everything is so simple in its expression, the procession as it swells, flowers, candles, a band playing horribly, mescal (alcohol),the men carrying the casket, the rocky path, bare feet, the extreme heat, the confusion as to how to lower the casket, the final prayers, the relatives waiting and the shoveling of the dirt at the very end. A last farewell is said but it all seems so beautiful and simple.*

The team received a multitude of visitors primarily from Chicago, among them Cardinal Bernadin and Bishop Wilton Gregory. Their guests were thrilled at the magnificent natural beauty of this mountainous area and supported them in their essential pastoral tasks of sacramental preparation, formation of Base Christian Communities, training of catechists and other pastoral agents, and providing Eucharist in the most isolated of areas. Missioners and guests alike were fascinated with the customs, those most typical in all of Mexico, and those unique to the indigenous peoples of the parish.

They saw native dances with dancers dressed in a variety of costumes, wearing masks carved of wood and painted in brilliant colors, resembling things like fish, the Moors, tigers, goats, and mafia bosses. For their parish's patronal feast, *Santiago Apóstol* (James the Apostle), the team witnessed the Ocoxuchitl dance, honoring a sweet-smelling herb of the same name. Dancers would swish the herbal plant in their hands as they danced around the statue of their patron. When visiting the Tlapaneco Indigenous people, local men would lead prayers in their native tongue, and an interpreter would translate the priest's homily. They participated in the *Fiesta de Plantas Medicinales*, the festival of medicinal plants, and the sunrise dance with people in their native clothing bowing to the four cardinal directions. In Tolixtlawaca they enjoyed watching a rain dance done between the Alligator and the Fish

This was not a people or a culture familiar to Carol Ann. But she entered into this world to such a degree that leaving was not easy, either for her or for the people. Her diary relates this farewell scene:

> *I went to visit the elderly and shut-ins so that I could have a chance to say good-bye to them as I would soon be leaving the village and*

A Vine Transplanted – Mexico

returning to the States. Lady Conchita, who lived alone in a very small hut and had hardened and swollen feet, took the small golden ring from her finger and put it on my finger. I tried to dissuade her but she insisted that I take it. She took my face between her wrinkled hands and gave me a kiss.

Through Carol Ann Berte the Sisters of St. Francis were a compassionate presence in a remote part of Mexico. She tells in her own words what the experience meant to her.

Carol Ann Berte

After a month of discernment at the Redemptorist Retreat Center with lay people and religious, five of us were asked to be part of the missionary team: Fathers Gary Graff and Father Paul Flaherty, two priests from the Archdiocese of Chicago; Sister Jeri Cashman, a Dominican Sister from Sinsinawa, Wisconsin; Ted Johnson, a layman from Chicago; and myself. I was 52 years old. I attended a Spanish language school for six months to prepare myself for my ministry.

My village was called Quechultenango, located in the state of Guerrero, 75 miles south of Mexico City. The major social problems of the area were poverty, limited health care and drug trafficking. Our ministry consisted of pastoral work though I was called on frequently for health-care issues.

Our team ministered to 23 villages scattered throughout the Sierra Madre del Sur Mountains. Celebrating Eucharist and the Sacraments was an important part of our ministry but perhaps what was equally important, was our being with the people, sharing their food, listening to their pain, accepting lodging in their homes, being present at the funerals, and walking with them. To live and to be surrounded by mountains and to travel in them almost daily brought to mind the Psalm [121] that says, "I lift up my eyes to the mountains."

My five years in Mexico were invaluable as they made me aware of the struggles of the indigenous farmers and their families, the plight of the poor in the absence of health care and the limited education of so many. The people were very welcoming and never apologized for their poverty. Living among the people helped me to appreciate another culture and it made me aware of eating a simple diet: beans, squash, tortillas, and at times boiled chicken or goat. This experience has seared me for life.

A Vine Transplanted – Mexico

Sr. Carol Ann Berte with children in Mexico

Amaranta's kindergarten graduation

Sr. Carol Ann visiting Sisters in El Salvador

Sarah's Daughters: Transplanting the Franciscan Charism

Yesterday is gone and its tale told.
Today new seeds are growing. --Rumi

In preparation for the 2004 General Chapter of the Dubuque Franciscans, area groups [35] were invited to submit ideas for the future which would be considered by the entire congregation as part of the Chapter process. One group's vision was to give birth to a new expression of Franciscan life, not necessarily following the familiar structure of religious life, but genuinely embodying the Franciscan charism. The initiative would be to invite persons from impoverished areas, particularly those of other cultures, nationally or internationally, to form a faith community for service within their own social context. The role of the Dubuque Franciscans would be to nurture this emerging community with the vision of the Franciscan charism, spiritual guidance, moral support, and possibly with financial backing. The intention would be to accompany the developing community as needed until it could be a fully functioning independent entity that would be self-directed.

The theme of the 2004 Chapter, "And Sarah laughed", referenced the Scripture story of Sarah and Abraham. In their advanced age God invited them to newness, assuring them of offspring more numerous than the stars in the sky or the sands on the seashore. Though Sarah initially laughed at such an implausible promise, she believed and was not disappointed. This biblical narrative invited the congregation, with its diminishing human resources, to trust God's inexhaustible providence to provide a future beyond predictable scenarios. Framed by this leitmotif, the Chapter body reflected on the area group's vision of a new expression of Franciscan life. The name "Sarah's Daughters" surfaced to describe the women who could be called to transplant the Franciscan charism into their own culture.

Conversation about the proposed vision was lively and divergent. Varying opinions clustered around whether to birth "Sarah's Daughters" as eventually independent from the congregation or as a new branch of the Franciscan community. The Chapter body leaned decidedly in the direction of a connected group. The final version of the Chapter-approved statement reads: *"That the Sisters of St. Francis move toward the founding of at least one branch of the congregation among people who are economically poor. A new branch*

A Vine Transplanted – Transplanting the Franciscan Charism

will shape the living of the Franciscan charism within the local cultural setting." [36] Responsibility for development of the project was given to the Leadership Team to guide with the involvement of a committee.

The unfolding work of the Sarah's Daughters Committee bore striking resemblance to that of the "Border Crossing" group of twenty years earlier. Discernment of the location and culture of the project took on an international focus, but with one marked difference from previous international missions. A founding intention of Sarah's Daughters initiatives would be to welcome local people to formal association or vowed membership in the congregation. To participate, sisters needed to be open to being part of a formation community.

The committee established criteria for choosing a country and for selecting sisters. After much research and discussion three locations were prioritized: Honduras, St. Lucia in the Caribbean, and the state of *Chiapas* in Mexico. In August of 2005, a fact-finding delegation of sisters traveled to explore the three options. Sister Kathleen Grace served as the Leadership Team's liaison, while Sisters Nancy Meyerhofer, Pat Farrell, and Frances Nosbisch made the trip with interest in participating in the project.

The sisters received a warm invitation from the bishops of St. Lucia and the diocese of *Santa Rosa de Copán* in Honduras. The bishop of the diocese of *San Cristobal de las Casas* in *Chiapas* was receiving only cloistered congregations into the diocese at the time, though it would be possible for the sisters to work in *Chiapas* without official affiliation with the Catholic Church. The choice of the other two locations seemed obvious. Sarah's Daughters Committee saw wisdom in choosing one Spanish-speaking and one English-speaking location, if there were sisters available to form two teams. St. Lucia was clearly the English-speaking choice. Nancy Meyerhofer had a strong preference for Honduras, and set out on the fact-finding trip with suitcase packed to stay in that country. She remained in Honduras, hoping that other Franciscans would eventually join her. This historical narrative will continue to relate the beginnings of the mission in Honduras, with the hope that in the future a similar history will be written of the project in St. Lucia.

Honduras (10 years, 2005-2015, and continuing presence)

Help us to be ever faithful gardeners of the spirit,
who know that without darkness nothing comes to birth,
and without light nothing flowers. –May Sarton

Sister Nancy Meyerhofer (age 57) arrived in Honduras with the Sarah's Daughters' fact finding team in late August of 2005. The group visited the diocese of *Santa Rosa de Copán*, which Nancy had identified prior to the trip as a primary area of interest. Bishop *Luis Alfonso Santos,* a Salesian religious, welcomed the sisters to work in the diocese, showed them parishes and projects, and spoke of the great needs in that area. The sisters then went by bus to *Choloma*, a community just outside of *San Pedro Sula*, where they were guests in the home of the Medical Missionaries of Mary. While there, they began to reflect on the entire trip and begin to summarize their findings. On August 30 the rest of the team returned to the U.S. and Nancy traveled to *Santa Rosa de Copán* where she took up temporary residence for four months with the *Hermanas Franciscanas de la Purisima* (Franciscan Sisters of the Most Pure One).

In this initial period of exploration, Nancy took time to get to know the situation and discern where to put down roots. She had periodic meetings with the bishop, traveled with him to see a number of parishes and locations, and met many priests and religious. She learned that the diocese of *Santa Rosa* is very large, encompassing five states (*Copán, Lempira, Santa Barbara, Ocotepeque and Intibucá*) and covering a large expanse of the rural, mountainous terrain which is home to more than a million Hondurans. Nancy was impressed with the diocese's plan to form both Base Christian Communities and pastoral leaders in every town and village. Priests, sisters and lay leaders regularly met together to do pastoral planning and follow-up and to assess needed response to justice issues. She noted a great deal of grassroots participation in the Church as well as the effective use of radio for formation programs, given the travel difficulties in a mountainous area.

Nancy chose *Lempira*, the only state in Honduras with no religious women or men and one of the poorest parts of the country. Bishop *Santos* was pleased, and asked that she live in *Gracias*, the capital of *Lempira*. Nancy was the first religious to minister in *Gracias*. She was happy to learn that the parish of *Gracias,* even before her arrival, was one of the few and probably the first in the diocese to have women lectors, Eucharistic ministers, and women leading Communion services. She was about to expand on the space in the parish that had been opened to women.

On December 23, 2005 Nancy found a house to rent, the ground floor of a two-story home whose owner, *Juanita Reyes*, lived upstairs. She and *Juanita* developed a sustained friendship. *Juanita* finalized her formation and became a Franciscan Associate in 2015. In the last days of 2005 Pat Farrell visited and she and Nancy moved some furnishings into what would be Nancy's new home in *Gracias.*

Sr. Nancy Meyerhofer surrounded by neighborhood children

On January 2, 2006, Bishop *Santos* came with his pickup to move Nancy and her remaining furnishings to the house in *Gracias*. He took a personal interest in her and was grateful that she hoped to gather other sisters, both from the U.S. and Honduras, to join her to serve in an area of the diocese so in need of religious. He provided bed frames to go with the mattresses she had. He also accompanied her to meet with *Padre Manuel Gutierrez,* the pastor of *San Marcos* Parish in *Gracias,* in order to officially affirm her role as Pastoral Associate of the parish. He phoned her that night to make sure she was settled and not too lonely her first night in a new house. Bishop *Santos* was consistently solicitous and supportive of Nancy and her work in *Gracias.*

Nancy dedicated 2006 to getting to know the parish of *Gracias,* encompassing three municipalities (towns) and 80 villages, making a total

A Vine Transplanted – Honduras

parish population of about 65,000 inhabitants. Of that, 24,000 people lived in the town of *Gracias.* The name of *Gracias* came from early Spanish explorers who searched among the mountains for a place flat enough to establish a town. When they found such a place they exclaimed *"Gracias a Dios!"* the original name of the town, which was later shortened to *Gracias.*

By the end of her first year Nancy had visited 73 villages and had stayed overnight in most of them. She describes her visits to the villages in a letter, written in early 2007:

> This I found to be a tremendous learning experience: to share bed and board, to hear their stories, to witness the poverty and the struggles for a better life as well as their hunger for closer accompaniment and more formation experiences by church representatives. I experienced tremendous acceptance by the parishioners and remain grateful for this.

Nancy was becoming familiar with the Honduran reality and preparing the soil for ministry that was just beginning.

New Soil: Honduran Context

The reality of Honduras is complex. The physical landscape of the country is beautiful! Most of Honduras is mountainous and heavily forested, with lovely beaches on the northern Caribbean coast and some of the world's finest coral reef ringing the Bay Islands. The climate at higher elevations is pleasant. The scenic countryside contrasts with a hard life of rural poverty. Honduras is the second poorest country in the Western hemisphere, second only to Haiti. The southwest sector of Honduras, where the diocese of *Santa Rosa de Copán* is located, borders Guatemala and El Salvador and is one of the poorest areas of the country. An estimated 71% of Hondurans live below the poverty line and 41% live in extreme poverty. The average annual per capita income is less than $1,500. The causes of such destitution are myriad: injustice, fraud, corruption, poor distribution of limited resources, lack of education and job opportunities. The economic hardship of the country influences all aspects of life. Hygiene, health care, and nutrition are deficient. Many rural areas are without potable water and electricity. It is common for babies to die from intestinal parasites or malnutrition. Only 40% of Hondurans complete a 6th grade education, and there is a high rate of illiteracy, particularly in rural areas.

A Vine Transplanted – Honduras

In a 2006 pastoral letter, the bishops of Honduras commented that the disillusionment of the Honduran people could lead to worsening violence unless the root causes of the problems are addressed. Nancy quotes the bishops in her 2006 letter:

> *In our daily experience we encounter the laments and longings of the poor for justice, work, food, education, and health. When we travel in the barrios (neighborhoods), villages, and mountains, we see over and over this situation of poverty and development of our people encountering seemingly insurmountable obstacles such as: inequality in the generation and distribution of wealth; low quality and insufficient availability of education; deficient health services; irrational exploitation and illicitly taking advantage of natural resources; generalized corruption; forgetting the common good, the dignity of the human person justice, truth, liberty, solidarity and subsidiarity.*

Honduras has experienced pronounced international influence since the 19th century when U.S. fruit-growing companies were given substantial tracts of land and tax exemptions to develop banana plantations and export industries. Several U.S. military incursions into Honduras helped protect the interests of the fruit companies. The term "banana republic" was created by the writer O. Henry to describe Honduras.

During the Central American civil wars of the 1980s the U.S. military set up a large air strip and military base in Honduras from which to operate its counter-insurgency efforts in the region. Honduras borders Nicaragua, El Salvador and Guatemala, a geo-politically strategic location for the U.S. military at the time. The influx of large numbers of U.S. troops in the 1980s greatly contributed to Honduras' AIDS problem.

Since the 1980s the poverty experienced by the majority of Hondurans has grown more desperate. Economic exploitation of Honduras shifted emphasis from banana exports to sweat shops, concentrated in the northern city of San Pedro Sula and employing about 30% of the country's work force. Honduras accrued one of the highest foreign debts in Latin America, partially pardoned in 2005. The Central American Free Trade Agreement (CAFTA) disproportionately favors U.S. trade interests over those of Honduras. Corruption is rampant on all government levels. In 1998 Hurricane Mitch caused massive and widespread destruction, killing 5,000 and seriously injuring another 12,000. In 2015 the country is still recovering.

A Vine Transplanted – Honduras

Because of a severe problem with gangs and drugs, the government has declared it illegal to belong to a gang. Youth suspected of gang activity can be arbitrarily arrested with little respect for civil liberties. There is a veritable war on youth who are threatened by gang members as well as by law enforcement agents. In 2015 Honduras had the highest homicide rate in the world. A complex mix of poverty, violence, and organized crime has been driving undocumented migration, including that of unaccompanied minors, to the U.S. in numbers that only seem to increase annually. About one third of the GNP of the country comes from Hondurans in the United States sending money back to family members. There is also a growing ecological awareness, seen in the efforts to protect forests and water sources from devastation and poisoning by mining companies.

Imbedded in this national context, the world Nancy was discovering in *Gracias* was less characterized by the drug and gang violence of larger urban areas and more filled with the myriad hardships of the structural violence of extreme rural poverty. In discerning how to be Church in such an environment, she encountered the faith and resiliency of the people whose lives were already becoming intertwined with her own.

Tending the Growth: Early Pastoral Work in Gracias

As Nancy began her work, she quickly took advantage of the pastoral resource of *Radio Caleb*, the radio station of the parish in *Gracias*. Already by January 16, 2006, she broadcast her first weekly radio program, "Life Lived in Equilibrium". The program shares wisdom from both counseling and spiritual direction sources and has been quite popular. The radio station is funded by a sister parish in the U.S. and most employees are young people from the parish, some living in rooms on the parish grounds. Nancy learned that the radio's frequency goes beyond the confines of the parish as she began to receive feedback from other towns beyond *Gracias*, and even from a neighboring state.

Also beyond *Gracias*, Nancy responded to a request from the Medical Missionaries of Mary in *Choloma*, just outside *San Pedro Sula*, to work with their health promoters. She used the *Capacitar* methods she had taught in El Salvador to give them additional skills to work with AIDS victims and their families.

A Vine Transplanted – Honduras

By February she began to form youth groups in the *Gracias* parish and met weekly with two groups during 2006. That year, she met and began regular conversations with *Erika Calderon,* a young woman who expressed an interest in religious life. Through *Erika* and other parishioners Nancy learned more about the kind of violence that took place in the environs of *Gracias.* She writes in a 2006 letter:

> *A woman who is a Eucharistic minister told me the other day she was talking with the new mayor. He said he had gone up on Celaque Mountain with soldiers as they were told that people were using electric saws to cut timber (not permitted). This was in effect true, and the culprits opened fire on them when discovered. They also tried to poison the water source for Gracias when they were prevented from further harvesting of the trees. The military caught them in time and prevented the poisoning.*

Another parishioner who was teaching in the village of *Quelacasque,* about a two-hour walk up the mountain to get to the school each day, told Nancy of another incident. One morning on her way she encountered the body of a young man who had been macheted to death, with cuts on his throat and face, and an ear missing. It was traumatizing for her. Nancy became her sounding board to talk about such a troubling experience.

Nancy visited the prison in *Gracias* weekly, first focusing her attention on visiting and counseling the women, then providing English classes open to men as well. At the request of the pastor she began a year-long training program for Eucharistic Ministers for the countryside with eighteen men and women participating. The pastor of *Gracias* who was not in good health and discerning whether to leave the priesthood gave Nancy a lot of responsibility. She became his representative in the rural villages, often called on to do Celebrations of the Word and bring the Eucharist, at times to some of the remote areas rarely visited (perhaps twice in ten years).

The travel was not easy. Nancy found some of the roads to be impassable during the rainy season and so steep as to be scary even in the dry months. Just a few days after visiting in one of the villages a father and his twelve-year-old son died trying to cross a river near their home. She concluded that it would be necessary to visit the most remote villages on horseback since not even four-wheel-drive vehicles managed the treacherous travel in the rainy season.

A Vine Transplanted – Honduras

In February she began to do baptisms and by the end of April had baptized 96 children in various parts of the parish. Though the bishop knew and gave tacit consent, her baptizing ended due to complaints from a neighboring pastor that she was giving scandal by doing so. Nancy's pastor resigned from the parish and left the priesthood a few months after she arrived, and the priest who had found her baptizing scandalous was named interim pastor for the remainder of the year.

Sr. Nancy - baby presentation ritual

The greatest challenges to rural pastoral work were communication and travel. There was no easy way to organize visits to distant villages or to communicate unexpected changes. Nancy sometimes used the parish truck when available or found someone with a four-wheel-drive vehicle to transport her. Sometimes she took a bus for part of the way. At other times she walked with a guide, or traveled on horseback or by mule.

Sr. Nancy Meyerhofer at a baptism

A Vine Transplanted – Honduras

In 2007 Nancy began a confirmation preparation program in *Gracias* with a group of 70. Later in the year she worked with the pastor and a retired priest to assist with Confirmation retreats and confessions in all eight zones of the parish. Nancy gave a series of reflections while the priests celebrated the Sacrament of Reconciliation. There had been no Confirmations in the parish for several years and the group confirmed that year numbered about 1,000. Since then Nancy and the two priests have been doing an annual marathon of Confirmation retreats in each rural zone during October.

Confirmations, Gracias, Lempira, Honduras

In 2007 Nancy started to do counseling in the parish office with parishioners as well as with several young women religious who traveled several hours by bus from the state of Santa Barbara. The ministry of counseling women religious grew with some caming from great distances, such as the state of Olancho. They always stayed overnight. Nancy also traveled to Guatemala to help give a one-month renewal program called the TAU for the Franciscan Spirituality Center, and developed the pattern of giving a yearly retreat for the Dubuque Franciscan Associates in Guatemala.

From the beginning of her time in *Gracias* Nancy supported the "evangelizers" who helped to promote and maintain the Base Christian Communities. There were over 350 evangelizers, organized into nine geographical sectors. One sector alone had 80 communities. Nancy eventually became involved with the parish Kerigma retreat team, a lay group that provides a transformational retreat experience to those who have gone through preparatory stages for forming Base Christian Communities. Nancy relates:

> *"Other formation experiences which became regular events each year were the music workshop to teach singing the psalms to various choirs in the parish, a retreat with the Eucharistic ministers (about 40) of the parish, and a yearly retreat with members of Base Communities who had already lived the Kerigma retreat. With members of the youth choir of Gracias I also gave music workshops in all the rural zones."*[37]

Support

During Nancy's first three years in Honduras she was the only Dubuque Franciscan. Though there were times of loneliness, she formed solid relationships with the people around her that were both pastorally beneficial as well as personally supportive. Her first Christmas in *Gracias* she received several invitations to parishioners' homes and had lunch with women in the prison. Just after Christmas several visitors came from El Salvador, young men who had been youth leaders and part of the youth choir when she ministered there from 1990 to 2002.

On December 31, 2006, Nancy received word of a new pastor appointed to Gracias: *Padre Luis Alonzo Gonzalez* (affectionately known as *Padre Loncho* or *Lonchito).* He is a gentle, open and collaborative man whom Nancy readily recognized as a supportive partner. His hard work and dedication to the people did not go unnoticed in *Gracias*, evidenced by the growing number of people participating in liturgies and parish activities. *Padre Loncho* and Nancy became a strong mutual support to one another.

Padre "Loncho" at confirmation

A Vine Transplanted – Honduras

Congregational support for Nancy was present in a variety of ways. In January of 2006, Sister Shirley Waldschmitt visited. Shirley had difficulty walking, attributing it to back pain from a fall, as yet unaware of the ALS that would claim her life. She enthusiastically explored the world of *Gracias* with Nancy and found ways to offer financial support upon her return to the United States Other visitors in 2006 were Sister Sarah Kohles, present in Honduras with a team from Le Mars, Iowa, doing a water project; John Donaghy who was discerning a re-location to Honduras after years of campus ministry at Iowa State University; and Sister Maureen Leach, whose visit in April of 2006 was the first of her annual supportive trips to *Gracias*.

Maureen structured ministry in the U.S. to allow her to spend extended time each year in Honduras. During Nancy's first years in *Gracias*, Maureen accompanied her in pastoral activities, participating wherever possible. She co-presented with Nancy for the weekly radio program. She visited homes, listened to the peoples' stories, participated in the choirs, helped give workshops to choirs, and took part in meetings of the Base Christian Communities. She also accompanied Nancy on overnight visits to the villages. In the prison clinic Maureen taught the health promoters acupressure points for headaches and began to give massages to the women and to help with English classes. She was Nancy's emissary in the U.S., looking for funds for various needs, giving presentations about Honduras, generally connecting needs in Honduras with resources in the U.S. She also served as witness to the work Nancy was doing, making it known to others. For example, Maureen was present at a surprise party the youth group and evangelizers had for Nancy and communicated afterwards this birthday tribute given to Nancy:

> *For us, the spiritual and social work you do in our parish is a blessing from God. When you came we were in a difficult time of transition in our parish... You came just at the opportune time to encourage us to continue on. We don't know what we would have done without you. You have played an important role in breaking down the divisions in our parish. We have never experienced a person like you before. You help us to see things in new ways. We admire your dedication, energy, and above all your commitment. You have gained our admiration and respect. We consider you as family. We love you a lot.*

A Vine Transplanted – Honduras

Srs. Maureen and Nancy at a village for a choir retreat

Maureen was helpful to the mission in Honduras by lending some of her computer skills, developing power point presentations, and assisting with communications. In the following text she speaks of Nancy's classes with children in the neighborhood:

> *Gracias for the children. They come with the pretext of learning English, but deep down I think it is attention they crave. Five of the children lost their father to a heart attack that month, and another five were the cousins whose household doubled in size because of the death in the family. This generosity gives family values a whole new meaning. Nancy tells the children to come at 5:00, but at 3:00 they are standing outside the door calling. "Sister Nancy, is it 5:00 yet?" This ritual may repeat four or five times before 5:00 finally comes. They come rushing in, bundles of enthusiasm, not at all shy about asking for affirmation.*

In 2007 Sister Anna Marie Manternach came to *Gracias* and offered a course to 65 catechists of the parish, helping Nancy initiate the family-centered model of faith formation that had been so effective in Chile. The pastor, *Padre Loncho,* later discovered that the program had already been introduced, approved and adapted to the Honduran reality by the diocesan catechetical office. Anna Marie had effectively jump-started it in the parish. Sister Mona Wingert came for two weeks and taught Nancy's English classes in the prison. Animated by the experience, she hoped to return. Sisters Rita Goedken and Nancy Miller visited Nancy while they were in the country as part of the Dubuque Franciscans' first Sister Water Mission Team.

A Vine Transplanted – Honduras

Sr. Nancy Meyerhofer, with visitors Srs. Nancy Miller and Rita Goedken

More long-term, supportive presence came when John Donaghy moved to the nearby city of *Santa Rosa de Copán* in June, eventually becoming the first Dubuque Franciscan Associate in Honduras. He and Nancy were a steady encouragement to one another in difficult moments and always gathered to celebrate birthdays, holidays, and significant events. In July of 2007 Sister Brenda Whetstone came to *Gracias* for a month, to explore the possibility of full-time ministry in Honduras. She and Nancy visited several villages and Brenda met many people. On Brenda's last full day the two were walking home from a village and were robbed by two armed, masked men who gleaned a total of about eight U.S. dollars from them. The bulk of it was collection money from the Celebration of the Word Nancy had just led. The pastor mentioned the robbery on the radio program and for weeks people from *Gracias* came and apologized to Nancy for the behavior of their fellow citizens. The robbery must not have been unduly disturbing to Brenda because the following year, after her final vows, she came to Central America and spent the last months of 2008 in an intensive language immersion program in *Copán Ruinas*, Honduras. Brenda (age 47) returned to the U.S. for Christmas and moved to *Gracias* on March 25, 2009

A Vine Transplanted – Honduras

Growth of the Franciscan Community in Gracias

I said to the almond tree, "Friend, speak to me of God,"
and the almond tree blossomed. --Nikos Kazantzakis

Just as Brenda was settling in and becoming acquainted with life in Honduras, *Erika Calderon* decided to take steps toward entrance into the Dubuque Franciscans. She informed her parents and found them supportive. Nancy was in conversation with other young women in the youth groups, who with varying levels of seriousness, expressed interest in religious life. It appeared that the vision of Sarah's Daughters, to found a new branch of the congregation in an economically poor area, was likely to become a reality. Through ongoing conversations with the Franciscan Leadership Team the decision was made to purchase land in the *Gracias* area where a house suitable for a formation community could be built. With the help of the pastor, *Padre Loncho*, Nancy found and purchased land in an area outside *Gracias* that was just beginning to be developed. There were not many houses nearby and a stream close enough to provide the steady, soothing sound of running water. It seemed an ideal location.

Brenda, in the meantime, was finding her way into ministry. She volunteered twice a week in the prison clinic. A few of the inmates served as health promoters, paramedics of sorts, and a doctor came several times a week to work with them. Brenda and the inmates did health assessments, dispensed medications, and treated those things within the scope of their competency. A 2009 letter to the community describes: "Few are coming lately because there are no medicines available in the whole country for public hospitals and clinics. If one has money, of course, it is another story. There are private hospitals and pharmacies which are well stocked, but most of the people we work with don't have that kind of access." Brenda put a fair amount of energy into securing, mostly in the U.S., the medicine and other resources needed for the clinic to continue to treat the prisoners.

A Vine Transplanted – Honduras

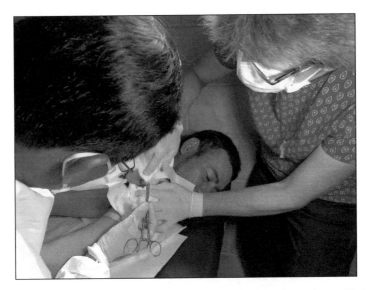

Sr. Brenda removing a bullet from a patient in the prison clinic

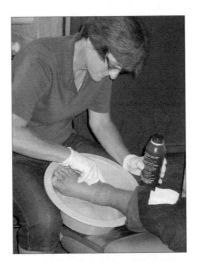

Sr. Brenda treating a patient

Brenda assisted Nancy with youth groups for several years and was a lively presence and support. Her real love, however, was visiting and taking communion to the elderly and shut-ins of the parish, a neglected population. She spent extended time in each home, listening, building relationships, and responding to simple health needs. She found the home visits a helpful means of developing her language skills as well. It was also difficult that those she got to know died, yet the list of people in need of visits continued to grow. The elderly loved Brenda, and their families were equally grateful for her visits. Much of Brenda's time was spent walking from one home to another, sometimes over a considerable distance. She and Nancy decided to purchase a small motorcycle, a Vespa, which decreased travel time, allowing her to spend more time with the people.

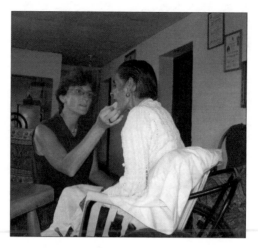

Sr. Brenda serving as Eucharistic minister

In January of 2010 *Erika Calderon* began a live-in experience with Nancy and Brenda. The occasion was celebrated with a simple prayer service and ritual of giving *Erika* keys to the house. Her parents were present and Pat Farrell represented the larger Franciscan community in affirming the first formal step she was taking towards entrance.

Erika Calderon with her parents and the Sisters

A Vine Transplanted – Honduras

Erika shared a room with Brenda. In August the sisters took into their home a young woman in crisis who had nowhere to go. She stayed until graduating from high school in late November. The crowded conditions in the house reinforced the sisters' sense of urgency to begin projected construction on a house. They had been in the process of raising funds for the project and already had start-up money. On November 8, supplemented by an interest-free loan from the congregation, they began construction of the home they would name Casa Betania.

A Changing Context

During 2009 political turmoil was brewing in Honduras. The president, *Manuel (Mel) Zelaya*, had begun, as other Honduran presidents, functioning to maintain the interests of the wealthy who for years had ruled Honduras hidden behind the scenes of formal power. During his presidency *Zelaya* came to realize that until the basic needs of the disenfranchised majority were addressed there would be no solution to the entrenched poverty of Honduras. He initiated changes that raised political ire. One of them was to propose a non-binding national referendum to poll citizens' willingness to hold a national assembly to consider constitutional changes. The attempt to do so placed him in a stand-off with the Supreme Court and military who opposed the plebiscite. Early on the morning of June 28, President *Zelaya* was taken from his home by the military, held temporarily at a U.S. airbase in Honduras, then flown to Costa Rica. That afternoon *Roberto Micheletti* was sworn in as the new interim president.

Members of the U.N. condemned the event as a *coup d'état* and no country recognized the interim government. A time of much chaos and division resulted. *Zelaya* managed to enter Honduras and the neutral territory of the Brazilian Embassy, addressing his followers from the roof. Enthusiasm for *Zelaya*'s return was met with repression and a decree the following day that suspended human rights. Brenda and Nancy write in a 2009 letter to the community:

> *Politically Honduras seems to be at a stalemate. Neither side will budge, and if things continue this way, we may simply live [in] a situation of "hold on till elections in November," trying to keep the violence and division at a minimum. The news is censored, the major newspapers, radios and TV stations being in the hands of those who financed the coup. Our bishop continues to speak out criticizing excesses*

on both sides. We recommend that you read John Donaghy's blog for up-to-date information. As for Gracias, we are an oasis of tranquility normally. Do continue your prayers for this troubled people.

The presidential election was held as scheduled on November 29, and *Porfrio (Pepe) Lobo* was elected. The legitimacy of the election was disputed, given the climate of intimidation and repression, but the newly elected president took office, albeit with tenuous support. A sizeable resistance movement emerged, its leaders suffering predictable persecution. Eventually the movement became a political party, *LIBRE* (free).

Soon after President *Zelaya* was removed, Bishop *Santos* of the Diocese of *Santa Rosa de Copán* spoke out publicly condemning the coup. The rest of the Honduran hierarchy, following the lead of Cardinal *Rodriguez Madariaga* of *Tegucigalpa*, took an opposite position, denying that what occurred was a "coup" and supporting the interim government. Interestingly, the December meeting of Honduran Episcopal Conference was scheduled to be held in *Gracias* for the first time. The differing opinions of recent political unrest surely made for an interesting exchange among the bishops.

The turmoil that began in 2009 did not resolve easily. It did, however, precipitate a qualitative shift in the power dynamics of Honduran politics, which gave rise to a grassroots movement not seen in the recent history of the country. Nancy writes in March 2011:

> *Starting with the coup on June 28, 2009, when the constitutionally elected president was ousted and sent into exile, there has been much social unrest. The de facto president, Roberto Micheletti, apparently robbed much of the national treasury in his five months of office and his successor, Pepe Lobo, used the teachers' pension fund for his own ends as well. He also intends to privatize education in this poor country, or so it seems. The teachers are a strong union and have gone actively on the offensive in a series of strikes. Socially, a Resistance Movement was born shortly after President Zelaya was ousted and the teachers are a significant part of it, as well as campesinos and many poor people. Here in Gracias we are into the third week of no classes, and I know of others areas of the country where it has been even longer. A number of newspaper reporters who tried to tell the truth about what is happening have been killed and a number of protestors have also died. There would seem to be no easy solution to the stalemate: Lobo says he won't talk to the teachers until they go back to the classroom and the teachers feel*

A Vine Transplanted – Honduras

they have no option but to strike. Tomorrow the Resistance has called for a national general strike.

During years of confusing and distorted information about happenings in Honduras, John Donaghy's online blog has been an important resource for English-speaking solidarity efforts around the world. It is a significant part of his ministry.

Continued Growth of the Franciscan Community

During 2011 and 2012 the Franciscan community planted in Honduras grew several new shoots. After a year of living with Brenda and Nancy, *Erika Calderon* requested entrance into candidacy with the Dubuque Franciscans. Sisters Nancy Schreck and Pat Farrell, also in Honduras as part of a Sister Water Mission Team, were present for the simple ceremony. They subsequently helped the local community plan for Erika's formation. Brenda and John Donaghy participated in the water project while Nancy Meyerhofer and Erika interacted with the Sister Water team as schedules allowed.

Erika signing the official book of entrance into candidacy

A Vine Transplanted – Honduras

Nancy's March letter speaks of the new challenges:

> *Brenda and I are walking a new road (being formation personnel) and learning as we go. Erika is a lovely person with a great sense of humor. We hope she will continue to journey with us and that other young women will do the same. The other first-time project on our horizon is the construction of Casa Betania (Bethany House), our future home here in Honduras. In general things are going along very well, and the building is over half-finished. This has been a huge learning curve for us, and we have the greatest respect for the labor-intensive work that is construction in a Third-World country. From July on, we will have room not only for other young women in formation but guests and retreatants as well.*

Two consecutive U.S. teams from Common Venture, the Franciscan volunteer program, helped with the construction of *Casa Betania*. In May Sister Kathleen Grace visited, and in June three Franciscan Associates from Guatemala arrived and were the sisters' first guests in the not-quite-completed *Casa Betania*. The completed building was officially handed over to the sisters on July 16. After a vigorous cleaning, it was ready to move in on July 24.

Construction of Casa Betania

A Vine Transplanted – Honduras

Casa Betania was built for several intended uses: a home for the sisters, a formation house, a place to receive guests, and a retreat center for individuals or small groups. Within the first month of occupancy the building was used for all those purposes. Nancy directed two young women religious in a discernment retreat before vows. A young Honduran woman studying medicine in Cuba spent a week with the sisters in her discernment of a vocation to religious life. Four visitors from a sister parish in Virginia came for a week. There was room for everyone!

On September 5 Betty Grissom moved into *Casa Betania* as a long-term Common Venture volunteer, committed for two years. Betty had already worked for five years in Honduras as a volunteer in another program. In *Gracias* she taught English classes in the prison and helped in a variety of pastoral activities in the parish. After two years as a volunteer she decided to stay in Honduras, built her own house across the road from *Casa Betania* and began the formation process to become a Franciscan Associate.

In November Nancy and Brenda visited St. Lucia where Sisters Mary Lee Cox and Frances Nosbisch had also initiated a Sarah's Daughters venture. The congregational Leadership Team had recommended that each Sarah's Daughters group visit the other, to provide mutual support and to exchange experiences and ideas. The following year Frances and Mary Lee visited Honduras. Maureen Leach met them at the airport and served as their interpreter on the trip.

Before year's end, on December 30, 2011, *Erika* was received into the congregation as a novice. In the same ceremony, John Donaghy celebrated his commitment as an associate, and Betty Grissom ritualized the beginning of her formation in the associate program. The combined celebration was a reflection of the congregation's recent approach to formation through the Charism Team, providing shared initial formation in the Franciscan charism, after which those who are formed discern a particular modality of Franciscan life. The ceremony took place in the parish church with a reception afterwards for family and friends.

A Vine Transplanted – Honduras

Ceremony of association for Betty Grissom and John Donaghy and reception into novitiate for Sr. Erika Calderon

In January of 2012, Sister Janet May brought a group of students from Briar Cliff University to help with a water installation project in the village of *San Jose Quelacasque* in the *Gracias* parish. Janet thought it was the most powerful experience of any service group she had led because the students shared the conditions of the people: sleeping on thin mattresses on the floor, the lack of running water, etc. It was also one more fruitful connection among Dubuque Franciscans.

Another such collaboration was the visit of Srs. Dorothy Schwendinger and Carol Besch who came to *Gracias* in February to do formation work with *Erika*. By the end of the month Sister Carol Hawkins (age 68) arrived, having left her work in San Antonio, Texas, to join the sisters in *Gracias*. Her first ministry was to accompany *Erika* during her time with the inter-congregational novitiate experience in *Lima*, Peru.

A Vine Transplanted – Honduras

Srs. Carol and Erika en route to Erika's novitiate in Peru

Carol had a very quick turnaround in *Gracias*. Just three days after arriving, she and *Erika* left for *Lima*. In *Lima* the two lived in a large formation community with Franciscan sisters from Spain who had sisters living in *Santa Rosa de Copán*. During their time in *Lima* they became acquainted with *Susana Sigueñas* who expressed interest in religious life with the Dubuque Franciscans. Nancy Meyerhofer visited them in *Lima* once during the year.

In June of 2012, *Lícida Membreño*, a woman the sisters in *Gracias* had known for several years, expressed interest in entering the congregation. She had helped do the landscaping in the inner garden of *Casa Betania* and was frequently a guest in the house. In July she requested acceptance into the candidacy program and was received in a ceremony in the house on October 31. The participation of Maureen Leach and Pat Farrell made more present the larger Franciscan community. Sister Mary Beth Goldsmith also visited in December.

A Vine Transplanted – Honduras

Sr. Pat Farrell giving "the light" to Lícida Membreño

As the Franciscan community in *Gracias* grew, so did the ministries of the community. Needs in the prison changed dramatically when the inmates from *Santa Barbara* whose prison burned were relocated to the already overcrowded prison of *Gracias*. They arrived with nothing but the clothes on their backs and had to sleep on the bare floor. The prison's shortage of medicine was felt more acutely. Most serious was the exacerbated water shortage due to the increased prison population. It complicated bathing, sewage elimination, food preparation, prison life in general. Drinking water was in critically short supply. Not surprisingly, violence among prisoners escalated. The sisters worked with leaders of the neighborhood surrounding the prison to help organize a water project that would benefit both the neighborhood and the prison. Funds were approved from the Franciscan Sister Water Project and prisoners helped supply the labor to install the infrastructure of pipes and a holding tank. The difference in the prison environment was immediately evident when the water situation improved. The prisoners carved a lovely plaque with words of gratitude and gave it to Nancy.

A Vine Transplanted – Honduras

Sr. Nancy Meyerhofer doing prison ministry

The Franciscans with volunteers and women in formation continued prison service in the areas of health care, liturgies, English and Scripture classes, gardening, and bodywork.

In addition to visiting and bringing the Eucharist to shut-ins, Brenda together with Betty Grissom developed a ministry with the mobile elderly. Their regular Saturday afternoon gatherings of the group called *Abuelitos* (grandparents) were varied and fun and provided social outlets for many older people who had none. Often food was served to the group.

Sr. Brenda listening to Doña Honoria

A Vine Transplanted – Honduras

When Brenda and Betty noticed that a number of people were not eating their food they realized that they were saving it to take home to family members. Once the people were told they could refill their plates again before leaving, they began to eat more freely. Brenda also provided wellness screenings for early detection of health problems. A number of the elderly who participated commented that they were thrilled that someone had taken them into account. The parish had activities for all other age groups and some of the elderly had considered themselves the forgotten ones.

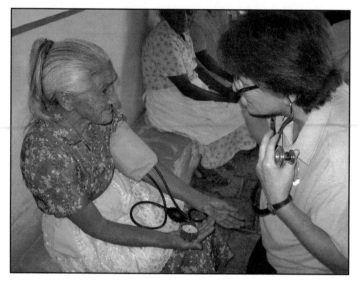

Sr. Brenda Whetstone doing a senior wellness screening

Work with youth was a constant and continued to grow with annual Confirmation preparation in both rural and urban areas. Numbers for the sacrament were so large that pews had to be removed from the church of *Gracias* for the standing-room-only crowds. With Nancy and Brenda's consistent faith formation and leadership training, the youth grew in being articulate about their faith, socially conscious, and in touch particularly with environmental issues and the problem of political corruption. Youth leaders began to take turns preparing and leading an hour-long weekly radio program each Saturday evening, responding to people who called in during the program. They also assisted Nancy on occasion with a television program.

A Vine Transplanted – Honduras

Sr. Nancy filming TV show with member of youth group

Work with youth is predictably an adventure. Nancy's letter describes one example:

> *Last Saturday we had a short paseo (overnight outing) with 26 youth… All went well until about two in the morning …when the top bunk bed fell on the boy in the bottom bunk. The iron frame sliced his scalp open and there was much blood! How to get to the hospital at that hour (we were about three miles out of town at a campsite and no transportation)? Our beloved parish priest rose (literally) to the occasion and drove out to pick up the boy and take him to the hospital. Eight stitches were the result – plus some great stories. We have noticed that the kids have bonded even more after the experience.*

Srs. Nancy, Brenda, and Erika with youth group

A Vine Transplanted – Honduras

Another continuous and ever-growing work of the Franciscan community was to support the formation of Base Christian Communities, a priority in both the diocese and parish. In addition to Nancy's participation in the Kerigma retreats, the sisters visited communities at various stages of formation. A letter from Brenda and Nancy relates:

> We just returned from staying overnight in San Jose, Quelascasque, a village about a two-hour walk from Gracias, the last hour straight up a mountain. We have been visiting there regularly every month for two years. It was gratifying last night to see real growth in the community: this year several youth were confirmed and the New Evangelization process has been started (a way to form communities).

Erika had been the mainstay of the youth choir before leaving to do novitiate in *Lima*. Nancy formed new musicians and singers and kept the choir going in her absence. At the same time, Nancy's work in counseling, spiritual direction, and facilitation for religious congregations in Central America steadily grew. Beginning in 2011, she worked monthly in *Santa Rosa de Copán* with residents of a home for girls orphaned or taken from their homes due to violence or abandonment. She gave courses for novices and formation personnel, retreats for a variety of individuals and groups, facilitated a general chapter and other congregational assemblies, and did counseling and spiritual direction as requested or as crises arose. Most years she spent the month of November in Guatemala helping with the Franciscan TAU, a renewal experience for religious men and women. Her service of counseling and spiritual direction, especially for religious, is in continual and increasing demand.

In August of 2011, a group of concerned citizens in *Gracias* approached the sisters with their dream of starting a rehabilitation center for persons with physical, mental and emotional disabilities. There was no such resource in the area. With broad consultation and participation, the project quickly moved from dream to reality. Promoters of the initiative formed a non-profit organization, got a building donated and rehabilitated it to meet their needs, recruited and trained volunteers, and found start-up funding. On December 5, 2012, CRILE (*Centro de Rehabilitación Integral de Lempira*---The Holistic Rehabilitation Center of Lempira) opened for service. Brenda and Nancy were part of the planning from the beginning, with Brenda taking the lead as Franciscan contact person, attending meetings and seeing the project through. She enlisted the help of Maureen Leach to write the

A Vine Transplanted – Honduras

grant proposal to the Ministry Fund of the Dubuque Franciscans which provided important start-up money. CRILE organized many fundraisers, elicited monthly pledges of support from local people, and committed itself to fiscal transparency. The center offers physical therapy, counseling, special education therapy, occupational therapy, and motor skills therapy, involving and training family members of clients whenever possible A goal of the project is to make services equally available to people of varying political, religious, ethnic and social backgrounds.

Maureen Leach's support of the Honduras mission shifted with the changing needs of the community. She did fund-raising projects for construction costs of the house. Every year, for instance, she participated in an alternative gift market in San Antonio with a display about Honduras and sale of her cards and photos. The sisters in *Gracias* dedicated their chapel to Maureen's mother after she died. They would also send Maureen a wish list and she would find funds for things such as medicines for the prison, money for the needs of the elderly, and scholarship funds. Somehow chocolate always found its way onto the list of things to bring! Maureen worked with her congregational commitment circle, the "Earthlings," to raise money to pay for a water purification system to provide safe drinking water for the house.

With growing ministerial demands, the sisters realized that they needed a vehicle. *Casa Betania* is a 25-minute walk from *Gracias*, which was no problem during the day or in the dry season. But walking home in the dark or in the rain was neither desirable nor safe, so the sisters bought what they thought was a good used car, later selling it to buy a more reliable one.

During 2013 and 2014 the Dubuque Franciscan family in Honduras was again evolving. *Erika* and Carol returned from Peru for the first half of the year. The community decided that it was in a position to do pastoral outreach to the town of *Belen*, a part of the parish that was quite divided and in need of attention. *Belen* had an available, though rustic, adobe rectory and parishioners there did necessary repairs. Nancy would go there from Tuesday afternoons until Friday morning, holding Wednesday Confirmation classes. *Lícida* knew the area well, her home village being in the high mountain region of the *Belen* area. She and *Erika* each accompanied Nancy for overnights and pastoral work. *Erika* taught guitar and *Lícida* helped with home visits and a regular holy hour.

A Vine Transplanted – Honduras

In the meantime, Betty Grissom, a life-time educator, had been spending months tutoring *Erika* and *Lícida* in English. With high-level letters of recommendation and several appointments at the U.S. Embassy, the two were finally given tourist visas to the United States. In June of 2013, *Erika* and *Licida* came to Dubuque for the first time. The sisters at the Franciscan motherhouse had also been preparing for their arrival, learning simple greetings and conversation starters in Spanish. *Erika* and *Lícida* attended the congregation's summer gathering and jubilee celebrations and interacted with many sisters, through gestures, a few words, and a lot of laughter. They spent significant time with the candidates that had entered the congregation's formation program in the U.S. Together the four candidates and Sarah Kohles traveled across country by car to attend an assembly of "Giving Voice," a national organization of young women religious. The trip provided the group of five an opportunity to see beautiful areas of the country and to get to know one another.

New members on the road to Giving Voice

A Vine Transplanted – Honduras

New members at the door of Mount Saint Francis Center

In July, while *Erika* and *Licida* were in Dubuque, lightning struck the house in *Gracias* and did substantial damage. Shortly afterward, in the fall of 2013, *Erika* and Carol returned to Peru for the final part of Erika's second year of novitiate. During the same months *Susana Sigueñas*, the woman the two had gotten to know the previous year in *Lima*, came to *Gracias* for a three-month Common Venture volunteer experience. It was an opportunity for her to become acquainted with other Dubuque Franciscans, their work and lifestyle, and for the sisters to get to know her. She returned to Peru, discerned with her spiritual director and decided to request entrance to the congregation. She was accepted.

By early 2014, the Franciscan house in *Gracias* had become quite a gathering place. Some neighbors would come by to pray in the sisters' chapel, at times leaving flowers or other devotional symbols. Others would bring jugs to fill with clean drinking water from the purified water system in the kitchen. Children were in and out. Several women were coming regularly for formation to become Franciscan Associates. The sisters were using the congregation's "Franciscan Way of Life" materials in Spanish for their meetings with Betty Grissom, *Elena (Nena) Díaz, Suyapa Díaz, Juanita Reyes, and Doris Menjivar*. They completed two years of preparation in December of 2014 and were ready to join John Donaghy as Associates.

A Vine Transplanted – Honduras

Franciscans and Associate at Casa Betania in Gracias

The country's social and political climate at the beginning of 2014 was fluid and somewhat unpredictable. Peace Corps had already pulled its volunteers out of the country because of the escalating violence felt mainly in the two largest cities, *Tegucigalpa* and *San Pedro Sula*. There was a newly-elected president, *Juan Orlando Hernandez*, a native of *Gracias*. He had run against and defeated the candidate of LIBRE, the newly-formed resistance party. That candidate had been a strong contender and the wife of the former president who was removed in the coup. Social unrest followed the election, the legitimacy of which was questioned by many Hondurans, though its outcome was affirmed by international observers. Media attention turned to the thousands of unaccompanied, undocumented minors streaming across the U.S. border fleeing violence in Honduras, Guatemala and El Salvador. All of this was felt even in the tranquil environment of *Gracias*.

With *Erika*'s novitiate complete, she and Carol were again settling in to life in *Gracias*. They entered an environment of mixed emotion at *Casa Betania*. *Lícida* had decided to withdraw from the congregation and moved

A Vine Transplanted – Honduras

out of the house during the last days of January. *Erika* requested to take first vows and had been approved. *Susy Sigueñas* was making preparations to move from Peru to enter candidacy with the congregation in Honduras. Arriving in early February, Sisters Nancy Schreck and Pat Farrell represented the total congregation for the solemnities. *Susy Sigueñas*, delayed by visa complications, arrived the night of February 7, just in time for *Erika*'s first vow ceremony on the 8th.

Sr. Nancy Schreck with Sr. Erika Calderon at her ceremony of first vows

Celebrating Sr. Erika's first vows

Sr. Erika Calderon with her family

A Vine Transplanted – Honduras

Erika pronounced her vows in Spanish and English during a parish liturgy presided by the pastor, *Loncho*, and her priest uncle who recently returned from studies in Rome. Nancy Schreck, congregational president, received her vows and Pat preached. It was the first event of its kind in the parish of *San Marcos* and *Erika's* family was proudly present. It seemed of historical importance to the sisters, aware that this was the first time someone in their community had taken vows outside the U.S. since the Chinese sisters in the 1940s. *Susy* was welcomed into candidacy at the house with a simple prayer service in the house; each person present articulating a blessing.

Susy Sigueñas at prayer service for entrance into candidacy

Susy receiving candle from Sr. Brenda

A Vine Transplanted – Honduras

Nancy and Pat stayed in Honduras for several days, facilitating, processing, and planning with the community. Pat communicated her plans to join the group by 2015. The sisters helped one another to discern ministries, assess needs and mutually affirm one another's gifts. A few plans began to take shape rather immediately. Carol became part of the staff of CRILE as a part-time child and family therapist, while she continued supporting the other pastoral efforts of the community.

Neighbors Doña Pedrina and grandson, Daniel, with Sr. Carol

Maureen Leach had taught *Susy* massage techniques and she began to put them to use at CRILE. *Susy* was soon leading a new youth group as well. To focus more in the area of music, *Erika* took piano lessons and worked with choirs while continuing to work in *Belen*. Brenda began to concretize her long-standing hope of creating a home health care service in *Gracias*. She had seen the critical need for it in her visits to the elderly and shut-ins, and wanted to train Honduran women to provide this service to people in their homes. In dialogue with the congregation, start-up funding was identified and Sister Camilla Hemann came to Honduras to help Brenda with preliminary planning. Later in the year, it was decided that *Erika* would participate in a new program of intensive English for Latin American religious which was offered in San Antonio, Texas, in the fall. She was again able to clear the visa hurdle and participated as an observer at the 2014

A Vine Transplanted – Honduras

General Chapter. She remained in the U.S. for several months of intensive English. On December 14 of 2014 Pat Farrell moved to Honduras to begin life and ministry in *Gracias*. On December 28 *Susana Sigueñas* withdrew from the congregation and returned to Peru.

In 2015 the transplanted Franciscan charism is continuing to take root in Honduras. The mission is unfolding, nourished by the Spirit who first called each of these sisters and associates to entrust their future to the Holy One who is faithful. The U.S. sisters express what the experience has been for them.

Carol Hawkins

After living in the United States a number of years following my years in Chile, my coming to Honduras was to discover anew how the "poor and oppressed" can still teach and transform me.

I joined Nancy and Brenda in Gracias, the Franciscan community of two living in Casa Betania. I would join them in their efforts to provide a place in which to receive and form Honduran women interested in religious life. One of the most enriching and transforming experiences of my religious life was to accompany our first novice, Erika Calderon, to Peru for her novitiate formation. It was a unique blessing and opportunity to participate in this novitiate formation as a preparation for the celebration of my Golden Jubilee the summer of 2013.

I assumed I had an awareness and understanding of the struggles of people who seek a better life and migrate to the United States. Living now on this side of the border I see the immigrant experience in a different light. I am saddened by the negative influence/impact that powerful countries, consumer cultures, and economic systems have on Central American peoples.

Amid the hardships and trauma, the country, culture and faith-filled people of Honduras provided me with another opportunity [to] deepen my relationship with God, with nature, and to value the importance of relationships.

Nancy Meyerhofer

The Honduran experience is totally different from that of Chile or El Salvador, or at least it began that way. Having been alone for more than three years, (meaning

A Vine Transplanted – Honduras

I didn't live with other Franciscans) I came to rely on supportive friendships with the laity more. I also assumed much more pastoral responsibility from the beginning in San Marcos parish, as the pastor was discerning leaving ministerial priesthood and suffered from ill health. The pastor who followed him is an open and compassionate man; we have a mutually respectful relationship. I also take great satisfaction in responding to requests from other religious congregations for retreats, facilitation of assembly or chapter, workshops, etc. At first the Honduran people seemed rather passive, but that was a mistaken impression, as was obvious from the response to the coup d'état in June of 2009. I feel like a wisdom figure here, and that is no doubt due to accumulated experience and my age. But there is always learning happening, especially in the area of formation for new members. All in all, I feel that for now, this is where God wants me to be, and I am fine with that.

Brenda Whetstone

I came to Gracias, Lempira, Honduras in 2009 to begin my life as a foreign missionary. Prior to actually living and working here, I had visited Sister Nancy Meyerhofer, a "well-seasoned" missionary sister from our congregation. I accompanied her to various villages and ministry sites around Gracias. It was quite evident that she was a very capable and competent missionary. I also came to learn that there were MANY needs that still were as yet unmet. Nancy was open and encouraging to the possibility of me joining her in ministry and offering my own gifts and talents to meet the unmet needs in the area.

Honduras is a BEAUTIFUL country! From what I have experienced over the past five years I can honestly say there is no other place at this time in my life that I would rather be. I enjoy working and living with the people of Gracias in the capacity of missionary. Overall, I have found the people I minister to and with to be warm and hospitable, tolerant and accepting of me. I am a stranger in a foreign land, an immigrant of a sort, and I have been welcomed. Daily I am touched by the faith, generosity and goodness of the people.

A Vine Transplanted – Honduras

Chronology of Franciscan Sisters' Service in Honduras

2005   August 28, Franciscan fact-finding team arrives in Honduras

August 30, Sister Nancy Meyerhofer remains, moves to *Santa Rosa de Copán*

2006   January 2, Nancy Meyerhofer moves to *Gracias*

2007   June, John Donaghy arrives in Honduras, lives in *Santa Rosa de Copán*

2008   September, Sister Brenda Whetstone begins language school in *Copán Ruínas*

2009   March 25, Brenda Whetstone moves permanently to *Gracias*

2010   January, *Erika Calderon* begins a live-in experience in *Gracias*

November 8, Construction begins on *Casa Betania*

2011   January 1, *Erika Calderon* enters and begins candidacy in the congregation

July 24, Sisters move into *Casa Betania*

September 5, Betty Grissom begins as a two-year Common Venture volunteer in Gracias

December 30, *Erika Calderon* is received into the novitiate

John Donaghy becomes a Franciscan Associate

Betty Grissom ritualized the beginning of her formation in the associate program.

2012   February, Sister Carol Hawkins comes to Honduras

March through December, Sister *Erika Calderon* participates in first year novitiate in Peru, accompanied by Carol Hawkins

November 1, *Lícida Membreño* enters and begins candidacy in the congregation

2013   August through December, *Erika Calderon* continues novitiate in Peru accompanied by Carol Hawkins

A Vine Transplanted – Honduras

Autumn, *Susana Sigueñas* is in *Gracias* for three months as a Common Venture volunteer

2014   January 31, *Lícida Membreño* withdraws from the congregation

February 8, *Erika Calderon* takes first vows

February 10, *Susana Sigueñas* begins candidacy in the congregation

December 14, Pat Farrell moves to Honduras and lives in Gracias

December 28, *Susana Sigueñas* leaves candidacy in Gracias and returns to Peru

Epilogue

In 2015 the Sisters of St. Francis of Dubuque, Iowa, marked 50 years of presence and mission in Latin America. This history commemorates that milestone. Since that initial writing, the life of our sisters has continued to unfold with important changes. In 2016 Anna Marie Manternach died. Being one of the pioneers of our Franciscan presence in Chile, she lived to see the full spectrum of the congregation's 50 years of Latin-American mission. She was especially supported in both her living and dying by Amelia Thole who shares the same 50-year distinction.

In Honduras, 2015 was a year of community adaptation and visioning, as our congregational presence grew to be a six-person team. Pat Farrell began to find her way into ministry in *Gracias*, even as she continued responding to invitations from US congregations to speak and facilitate. In July Mary Beth Goldsmith came to Honduras to begin learning Spanish and to explore ministry there. Before and during her three months of language school in *Copán Ruinas* she spent some time with the sisters in *Gracias* and recognized in herself a desire to live and minister in Honduras. Before the end of 2015 she had discerned settling into Honduras more long term. In October of 2015 the six Franciscans in Honduras entered into a discernment retreat to do future visioning for the mission. It had long been a hope that the house in *Gracias* would be a center house, gathering place, and formation community with other small groups of sisters living in different areas, closer to the local people and serving a variety of needs in diverse settings. The fruit of the discernment was the decision to open a second house in *La Entrada de Copán* with Nancy, Erika and Mary Beth. Brenda, Pat and Carol would continue in *Gracias*. The six agreed to spend a day together each month for mutual support and to continue to create together the life of the congregation in Honduras.

The move was a new beginning for both Honduran communities. In *Gracias*, the sisters gave priority to follow-up work with associates and vocation ministry, meeting monthly with young women interested in religious life. The larger space of the house and more established contacts in *Gracias* lent themselves to linking with other congregational efforts such as Sister Water projects, Common Venture, and hosting a Briar Cliff mission team. Each of the three sisters further focused her ministry: Carol with

A Vine Transplanted – Epilogue

CRILE, youth, elderly, single mothers and counseling; Pat with the radio, prison, counseling, single mothers and religious congregations; Brenda with prison ministry, massage therapy and a non-profit organization of home health care and other services to the elderly and home bound.

The move to *La Entrada* took place on January 2, 2016. The sisters were accompanied by a caravan of supportive friends and parishioners in cars and pick-ups. *La Entrada* proved to be a strategically good choice for a number of reasons. It is located half way between *Gracias* and the four-hour distance to *San Pedro Sula*, the closest airport, providing a convenient stop-over place. The language school in *Copán Ruinas,* near the Guatemalan border, is a relatively short distance to travel for continued Spanish study for Mary Beth and others. There are two local universities in *La Entrada* and Erika began her studies at one of them in September of 2016. No other religious congregations serve within a large radius around *La Entrada*, though the pastoral needs are great. *La Entrada* is a large commercial center and its population is rather transient and very poor. It is a known corridor for drug trafficking and for "narcos" living in the area. The parish is very large, with over 100,000 inhabitants in three sizeable towns and 120 rural villages. The sisters arrived at a pastorally critical moment, working with two new priests in the wake of scandals from the previous pastor and a very disillusioned group of parishioners. It was a moment to begin again.

Erika, Nancy and Mary Beth live in a rented second-floor apartment in a very poor neighborhood. Though the climate of *La Entrada* is very hot, the neighborhood noisy, and their space confined, they are happy in their new community. Their pastoral beginning has been to work primarily with catechists and youth leaders organized in ten geographical zones. Distances are vast and travel difficult in the very mountainous area of many of the villages. The sisters have provided formation in Scripture, theology, prayer and pastoral methodology. The numbers in attendance have been large and the response enthusiastic. Clearly the sisters' presence meets a great need. Each of the them continues to define more specific areas of service, as together they live into being a new Franciscan presence in *La Entrada de Copán.*

A Vine Transplanted – Epilogue

Vocational gathering at the house in La Entrada

Sisters and Associate Betty Grissom at La Entrada

A Vine Transplanted – Epilogue

Birthday celebration for Erika Calderon and Associate John Donaghy

Celebration in La Entrada of Erika's renewal of vows

Blessing of Sister Erika at Shalom in Iowa (150th anniversary of the congregation)

Picture Index

A Vine Transplanted – Picture Index

A Vine Transplanted – Picture Index

A Vine Transplanted – Picture Index

A Vine Transplanted – Picture Index

A Vine Transplanted – Picture Index

Sisters Named in the Book by First Name

Listed by Last Name in the Proper Name Index

Albert (*See* Anna Marie Manternach, OSF)
Amelia (Ida) Thole, OSF
Anna Marie (Albert) Manternach, OSF
Anne Sedgwick, OSF
Barbara Aires, SC (Srs. of Charity)
Brenda Whetstone, OSF
Camilla Hemann, OSF
Carol Besch, OSF
Carol Hawkins, OSF
Carol Ann Berte, OSF
Carolyn Lehmann, MM (Maryknoll Sisters)
Connie Popsilil, MM (Maryknoll Sisters)
Darleen Chmielewski, OSF
Dianna Ortiz, OSU (Ursuline Srs., Maple Mount, KY)
Dorothy Schwendinger, OSF
Elaine (Bibiana), Gehling OSF
Eleanor Gilmore, SSJP (Srs. of St. Joseph of Peace)
Elizabeth (Mimi) Ballard, OSU (Ursuline Srs., Maple Mount, KY)
Erika Calderon, OSF
Fran Wilhelm, OSU (Ursuline Srs., Maple Mount, KY)
Frances Nosbisch, OSF
Georgia Kilburg, OSF
Gertrude Ann Brown, OSF
Ginny (Virginia) Heldorfer, OSF
Grace Reape, SC (Srs. of Charity)
Ida, (*See* Amelia Thole, OSF)
Ita Ford, MM (Maryknoll Sisters)
Janet May, OSF
Jean Hurley, OSF
Jean Beringer, OSF
Jeri Cashman, OP (Sinsinawa Dominicans)
Kate (Cathy) Katoski, OSF (President starting in 2014)
Kathleen Grace, OSF
Kay Forkenbrock, OSF
Kay Koppes, OSF

A Vine Transplanted – Sisters Named in the Book by First Name

Linda Donavan, MM (Maryknoll Sisters)

Liz Brown, CSJ (Congregation of St. Joseph)

Louisa Beckett, OSU (Ursuline Srs., Maple Mount, KY)

Lucy Larouche, (Daughters of Jesus, Canada)

Margaret Berns, SSJP (Srs. of St. Joseph of Peace)

Margaret Clare Dreckman, OSF, (Major Superior 1972-1980)

Margaret Francis Brockcamp, OSF

Margaret Wick, OSF

Marian Klostermann, OSF

Marie Therese Kalb, OSF

Marilyn Thie, SC (Srs. of Charity)

Mary Canavan, SC (Srs. of Charity)

Mary Lenz, OSF

Mary Beth Goldsmith, OSF

Mary Clare O'Toole, OSF, (President 1988-1992)

Mary Lee Cox, OSF

Mary Luke Tobin, SL (Srs. of Loretto)

Matilda Adams, OSF, (Major Superior 1962-1972)

Maureen Leach, OSF

Maureen Wilwerding, OSF

Mona Wingert, OSF

Monica Hingston, RSM (Religious Sisters of Mercy)

Nancy Meyerhofer, OSF

Nancy Miller, OSF

Nancy Schreck, OSF (President 2008-2014)

Pat Farrell, OSF,

Peg (Shaun) Moran, OSF

Peggy O'Neill, SC (Srs. of Charity)

Rita Goedken, OSF

Rosa Lyons, OSF

Ruth Mary Kann, OSF, (Mother General 1950-1962)

Sally Mitchell, OSF

Sarah Kohles, OSF

Sharon Sullivan, OSF

Shaun (*See* Peg Moran, OSF)

Shirley Waldschmitt, OSF

Stephanie Marie Kazmierzik, MM (Maryknoll Sisters)

Susan Seitz, OSF, (President 1980-1988)

Proper Name Index

A Vine Transplanted – Proper Name Index

A Vine Transplanted – Proper Name Index

A Vine Transplanted – Proper Name Index

A Vine Transplanted – Proper Name Index

A Vine Transplanted – Proper Name Index

Jesuit 3–5, 11, 18, 27, 34, 35, 46, 51, 56, 71, 89, 136, 138, 142, 166, 176, 183

Jesuit Refugee Service 136

JOC - (Juventud Obrera Católica - Young Catholic Workers) 13, 28

Johnson, Ted 196

John the Baptist Sisters 18

K

Kalb, OSF, Sr. Marie Therese 9, 251

Kanjobal, (Mayan Language spoken in San Miguel Acatán) 110, 114, 115, 119–121, 129, 133

Kann, OSF, Mother Ruth Mary (Mother General of the Sisters of St. Francis) 1, 251

Katoski, OSF, Sr. Cathy (Kate) (President of the Sisters of Saint Francis) iv, 250

Kazantzakis, Nikos 212

Kazmierzik, MM (Maryknoll Sisters), Stephanie 11, 251

Kennedy, Jr., President John F. (USA) 4

Kentucky 35, 72, 75, 104, 121, 127, 128

Kerigma Retreat 207, 208, 226

Kesez, Ken 192

Kilburg, OSF, Sr. Georgia 26, 250

Klostermann, OSF, Sr. Marian 187, 251

Kohles, OSF, Sr. Sarah 209, 228, 229, 251

Koppes, OSF, Sr. Kay v, vii, 106, 133–144, 154, 155, 157, 158, 160, 161, 166–170, 175, 176, 181, 187, 188, 190, 191, 250

Kovler Center for the Treatment of Survivors of Torture, The Marjorie 184

Kowals, Beth 228, 229

L

La Calle, Archbishop Saenz (San Salvador, El Salvador) 180

La Entrada de Copán, Honduras 239, 240, 241

La Merced (Parish in Chile) 35

La Mora, El Salvador 163, 184

LaPointu, Fr. Roger 25

Larouche (Daughters of Jesus, Canada), Sr. Lucy 54, 60, 251

Larson, Doug 14

Las Flores, Chalatenango, El Salvador 138, 139

Latin America iv–vi, 1–3, 5–7, 11, 12, 19, 20, 25, 29, 51, 58, 73, 82, 84, 87, 89, 91–100, 112, 130, 131, 188, 203, 239

Latin American Bishops' Conference, CELAM (Conferencia Episcopal de Latino América) 1, 7, 12, 92, 101

Latin American Bureau 1, 94

Latin American Church 1, 91, 93, 95, 98

La Tirana Shrine (near Iquique, Chile) 67

A Vine Transplanted – Proper Name Index

A Vine Transplanted – Proper Name Index

A Vine Transplanted – Proper Name Index

A Vine Transplanted – Proper Name Index

U. S. Church women - killed in El Salvador - Maryknoll Sisters Maura Clarke and Ita Ford, Ursuline Dorothy Kazel, and lay missionary Jean Donovan. 132, 167

U.S. Embassy 126, 228

U.S. Episcopal Committee for Latin America 1

V

Valentín 148

Vargas, Brigida Lozano (Franciscan Associate) vi

Vásquez, Mercedes 36, 81

Vasquez, Sasche, Julio Romualdo (Franciscan Associate) vi

Vatican embassy, Guatemala City, Guatemala 127

Vatican, Vatican II, and Post-Vatican II 1, 7, 12, 13, 23, 25, 26, 37, 38, 51, 91, 127, 180

Vergara, SJ (Jesuit), Fr. Ignacio 56

Vicariate of Solidarity (in the Archdiocese of Santiago) 69

Vicuña, Bishop Eladio (Chillán, Chile) 5

Vietnam 30, 96, 97, 101, 132

Vogl, Fr. Bob 31

W

Waldschmitt, OSF, Sr. Shirley 125, 209, 251

Washington, DC 181, 190

Waterloo, IA 43, 44, 81, 106, 133

Wellness center (in Suchitoto) 182, 184

Whetstone, OSF, Sr. Brenda v, 211–215, 217–219, 223–226, 230, 232–237, 239–241, 250

White Marches (Protests for better Health Care in El Salvador) 185

Wilhelm, OSU (Ursuline Sisters, Maple Mount, KY), Sr. Fran 127, 156, 250

Williams family from Webster City 18

Wilwerding, OSF, Sr. Maureen 11, 251

Wingert, OSF, Sr. Mona 210, 251

World Bank 185

W.R. Grace and Co. 96

X

Xavier Hospital 29, 55

Z

Zelaya, President Manuel (Mel) (Honduras) 215, 216

265

End Notes

Chile

1. Esquivel, Julia V. *Secrets of God's Reign/Algunos Secretos Del Reino:* Poems Bilingual Edition. English translation by Kathy Ogle, Cecilia M. Corcoran and Judith M. Noone. Published by EPICA Task Force, 2002, pp 69 and 71.

2. Casaroli, Msgr. Agostino, address to the Second U.S. National Congress for Religious, 1961.

3. The Apostolate in Latin America, an informational panel prepared by Sisters Matilda, Margaret Francis, Alfred, Narcissa, William, Paschal, and Antonia.

4. Sawyer, Mary. Interview of Sr. Amelia Thole, 2014.

5. Ibid.

6. Congregational annals written by Sisters Amelia, Albert and Shaun.

7. Sawyer, Mary, Interview Thole.

8. Annals.

9. Hodgson, Fr. Edwin, director of the Colegio Seminario, letter.

10. Lyons Crispo, Rosa, 2014 letter to Pat Farrell.

11. Neruda, Pablo. *Canto General.* Translated by Jack Schmitt. © 1991 by the Fundación Pablo Neruda and the Regents of the University of California. Published by the University of California Press. P. 148.

12. Quote attributed to Pablo Neruda. Original Spanish, Pueden aplastar algunas flores pero no pueden detener la primavera. English translation by Pat Farrell, OSF.

13. Illich, Ivan. The Seamy Side of Charity, *America,* January 21, 1967.

Central America: A Call to New Transplanting

14. Ezekiel 17: 22-23, Scripture quotation is from *The New International Version* (NIV) *Holy Bible, New International Version®*, NIV ® Copyright © 1973, 1978, 1984, 2011 by Biblica, Inc. ® Used by permission. All rights reserved worldwide.

15. Minutes of the 1984 General Chapter Proceedings.

A Vine Transplanted – End Notes

16. Bordes, SH, Sr. Laetitia, editor. *Our Hearts Were Broken, A Spirituality of Accompaniment*, Published by: Red Star Black Rose, 2000.

Guatemala

17. Esquivel, *Secrets of God's Reign*, p. 29. Placement.

18. Farrell, Sr. Pat, Interview of Sr. Darleen Chmielewski, 2014.

19. Chmielewski, Sr. Darleen. E-mail to Pat Farrell, 2014.

20. Posadas: a Christmas custom re-enacting Mary and Joseph searching for lodging before the birth of Jesus.

21. John 12: 24, Scripture quotation is from *New Revised Standard Version Bible*, copyright © 1989 National Council of the Churches of Christ in the United States of America. Used by permission. All rights reserved worldwide.

22. Ortiz, Sr. Dianna, with Patricia Davis, *The Blindfold's Eye, My Journey from Torture to Truth*, Orbis Books, Maryknoll, N.Y. 2007.

23. Farrell, Interview Chmielewski.

El Salvador

24. Romero, Archbishop Oscar, Homily, April 1, 1979, The Archbishop Romero Trust http://www.romerotrust.org.uk/.

25. Amos 9:14, Scripture quotation is taken from *The Holy Bible, New International Version* ®, NIV ® Copyright © 1973, 1978, 1984, 2011 by Biblica, Inc. ® Used by permission. All rights reserved worldwide.

26. Bordes, SH, Sr. Laetitia, *Our Hearts Were Broken, A Spirituality of Accompaniment*.

27. Ibid.

28. Ibid.

29. Farrell, Pat. Unpublished manuscript.

30. Donaghy, John. Unpublished manuscript.

31. Ibid.

32. Ibid.

33. Ibid.

A Vine Transplanted – End Notes

Mexico: In Partnership with the Archdiocese of Chicago

34.   Berte, Sr. Carol Ann. Diary: My Ministry in Mexico.

Sarah's Daughters: Transplanting the Franciscan Charism

35.   Area group: a geographically or intentionally based group of sisters
       that gathered regularly for personal support and dialogue about
       congregational affairs.

36.   Proceedings from the 2004 General Chapter of the Sisters of St. Francis,
       Dubuque, Iowa.

Honduras

37.   Meyerhofer, Sr. Nancy. Unpublished notes on her time in Honduras.